CW00643112

The Insiders' Guide to Independent Publishing

Independent Publishers Guild

Copyright © 2010 Independent Publishers Guild

First published in Great Britain in 2010 by
The Independent Publishers Guild
PO Box 12
Llain
Whitland
SA34 0WU
Tel: 01437 563335
Fax: 01437 562071
Email: info@ipg.uk.com
Web www.ipg.uk.com
Reprinted 2013
Reprinted 2014

A CIP record for this book is available from the British Library

ISBN 978-0-9566878-0-7

Edited by Tom Holman
Typeset by JS Typesetting Ltd
Project managed by Cambridge Publishing Management

Printed and bound in Great Britain by
Lightning Source UK Ltd
Chapter House
Pitfield
Kiln Farm
Milton Keynes
MK11 3LW

CONTENTS

INTRODUCTION

The Independent Publishers Guild is proud to present **The Insiders' Guide to Independent Publishing**. Written *by* publishers *for* publishers, we hope the book will help all companies to become even better at what they do.

One of the great advantages of belonging to the IPG is the chance to share in the vast experience and knowledge of our members. This book, compiled by some of our longest-serving and most-respected members and patrons, is the ultimate manifestation of that free and generous distribution of advice. We hope it will inspire new companies to start publishing professionally and profitably, and lead longstanding businesses to continued success. Three individuals merit special acknowledgement: former IPG Chairman, Will Atkinson, and IPG Patron, Kathryn Earle, for their invaluable contributions; and Tom Holman, whose editing and writing skills are superbly demonstrated.

The book is divided into 14 chapters, spanning everything from setting up a new publishing company to selling it. In between, it covers all the key disciplines of publishing—from editorial to printing to selling to marketing to distribution and much more besides.

The book can be read from cover to cover to provide a comprehensive grounding in publishing, or dipped into for help with specific subjects. Each chapter is crammed with practical tips for success in that field. Contact details for all the organizations mentioned in the main text can be found in the Resources section at the end of each chapter. Here you will also find places to get more help and suggestions for further reading on the subject. At the back of the book is a Directory of all the important publishing organizations you may need, as well as a handy Glossary that illuminates some of the industry's many baffling terms.

With all the challenges in the market, independent publishing is by no means easy. But as the burgeoning membership of the IPG proves, it is perfectly possible to survive and thrive, and have a lot of fun as you do so. We hope **The Insiders' Guide to Independent Publishing** will prove a valuable handbook to keep with you on your publishing journey.

Bridget Shine
IPG Chief Executive

IPG PATRONS

The IPG thanks the IPG Patrons for their support:

JOIN THE IPG

If you are not already a member, we warmly invite all new and existing independent publishers to join the Independent Publishers Guild. For more information about the IPG or to join, visit the website at www.ipg.uk.com, call 01437 563335, fax 01437 562071 or email info@ipg.uk.com

ABOUT THE CONTRIBUTORS

The IPG is grateful to all the following contributors to **The Insiders' Guide to Independent Publishing** for sharing their expertise and experience so freely.

Will Atkinson Sales and marketing director, Faber & Faber and former IPG board member

Richard Balkwill Managing director, Copytrain, and former IPG board member

Sophie Brewer Freelance rights consultant for Short Books, among others

Valerie Duff Rights director and associate publisher, Atlantic Books

Kathryn Earle Head of Visual Arts Publishing, Bloomsbury Publishing and IPG Patron

Joanna Ellis Former marketing director, Faber & Faber

Kate Griffin Former sales and marketing director, Profile Books

Chris Hamilton-Emery Director, Salt Publishing

Priscilla Hannaford Publisher, Brilliant Publications, and former IPG board member

Peter Kilborn Former executive director, Book Industry Communication

Sonny Leong Former managing director and chairman, Cavendish Publishing, and IPG Honorary President and Patron

Edward Milford Former executive chairman, Earthscan, IPG Patron and IPG development director

John Skelton Director, Acumen Publishing, Flame Tree Publishing and Salt Publishing; board member, Manchester University Press and The Policy Press; former managing director, Open University Press; IPG Patron

Jim Smith Former managing director, Bloomsbury Professional, IPG Patron and IPG board member

Lorna Summers Managing director, Turpin Distribution

David Taylor Senior Vice President, Content Acquisition International, Ingram Content Group and Group Managing Director, Lightning Source UK

John Walsh Managing director, BEBC Distribution

Brian Willan Former managing director, Willan Publishing and IPG Patron

Martin Woodhead Former managing director, Woodhead Publishing, and former IPG board member

Timothy Wright Chief executive, Edinburgh University Press, and former IPG board member

Tom Holman Editor

1 GETTING STARTED

CONTENTS

Research / Planning / Funding / Practicalities / Offices and facilities /
Support and advice / Partners / Qualities / Self-publishing / Resources

Starting an independent publishing company is not for the faint-hearted. Competition is intense. There are several thousand active publishers up and down the UK, between them publishing more than 100,000 books a year in every conceivable niche, each battling desperately for the attention of the public. The power of a handful of big publishing companies is increasing by the year, and overall the market for books is steady at best, increasing by only a fraction each year. Discounting is rife, cutting margins to the bone. In schools and higher education, the money available for buying books is squeezed ever more tightly. Here and in many other parts of publishing, the internet and digital technologies are eating into publishers' markets. Some respected commentators think the printed book is on its last legs.

That's the bad news. The good news is that, despite all the challenges, independent publishing in the UK is flourishing. The IPG welcomes many new members into its fold every year, of all shapes and sizes and publishing in a dazzlingly rich and diverse array of sectors. With hard work and clever publishing, new publishers can still reach readers through all the traditional channels, while grasping the web as an opportunity to make more money rather than as a threat. They are also invariably surprised and delighted by the levels of support that fellow publishers—even their rivals—are willing to offer them. Independent publishers enjoy one another's success, and this is where the IPG comes into its own. Linking the UK's network of independent publishing, we strive to help all small companies become the best they can be. Plus, of course, many new publishers grow out of professional societies, institutes or other bodies, and can draw on the support of their parent organizations.

So, if you are a new publisher starting out, don't underestimate the amount of work that lies ahead of you, but don't be daunted either. Strap yourself in for a rollercoaster of a journey, but enjoy the ride. Publishing is a wonderfully rewarding, stimulating and pleasurable industry, and, probably without exception, all IPG members who have set up their own companies enjoy their lives much more than they did when they were a cog in someone else's machine.

RESEARCH

Before you even think about starting a publishing business, research your market thoroughly. Many businesses fail not because of insufficient funding but because their product or service did not have a viable market. So work out as honestly as you can whether your company satisfies a need in the books business. Can you see who your customers will be? Although the IPG has some successful general publishers among its members, many more are specialists, sharply focused on their niches in the market. Can you, too, see a clear enough gap and demand? Ask yourself also how your company and books will be special or unique. Look closely at the competition you will face in the market. Are you confident you can do better? Is your idea a long-term one or a passing trend? Answer your own questions as honestly as you can.

Formal market research is tricky in publishing. But tell as many family and friends as you can about your idea—especially those with small businesses of their own—and gauge their reactions. Speak to as many publishers as will give you a hearing, and not just those in specialisms close to your own—companies in different fields will have advice too, and may be better placed to take a detached view of your idea. Attend IPG events, and introduce yourselves to other members. The IPG's Annual Conference in March offers a particularly good introduction to life in independent publishing and a useful chance to network.

It is important to soak up advice from booksellers too. Your nearest independent one is as good a place to start as any, and if you can find one with a particular responsibility or interest in your sort of publishing, ask them what they think about your business idea. Chat to agents, authors, librarians, printers, distributors and suppliers as well as publishers. Getting to know how they all fit together in the industry can take years, so start as soon as you can. Talk to anyone else you can think of connected with your potential market. Visit the London Book Fair, held each April. Read *The Bookseller* each week, either by subscribing or reading copies in a library or online, and keep an eye on BookBrunch and Book2Book, the online news and views services for publishing. Subscribe to any magazines or journals pertaining to your field of publishing, and join any relevant trade associations, societies and groups. Follow some of the publishing blogs on the web to get a feel for the day-to-day challenges of running your own business, and read some books about publishing and starting a business.

The customer is king, and it will be up to you to give him or her exactly what they want. So talk to as many of your potential customers as you can, and understand their needs from the very start; they will provide plenty of ideas for your business, and will give you an idea of whether there is a big enough market out there. Go online to research communities of people interested in your niche. Work out what makes them tick and what makes them spend. If you want to publish in the educational, academic or professional spheres, try to get to know the communities and organizations that might buy your books.

Scope the size of your different retail channels, segmenting the market and identifying the major players. Even if you can't produce your full books just yet, start to gather material that you can use to help sell them to these retailers. Advance Information (AI) sheets—which show everyone at a glance all the key bibliographic and content information they need about a book—jackets and samples can all be useful, and the sooner you get advance orders for books, the better. See the Sales and Marketing chapters for advice on producing this material—AI sheets in particular—and on courting customers.

PLANNING

Many publishing businesses start out as hobbies, some happily staying that way and others evolving into fully-fledged businesses. Some are begun by people who have picked up experience elsewhere in publishing and want to strike out on their own, while others are opened by people with plenty of experience of business and none of publishing. All are equally valid routes. But however you get started, the key to fulfilling your ambitions and making your publishing work as you want it to is exactly the same as it is in every sort of business— planning. Put down the building blocks of a sound business before you start to think too much about the books you hope will make you money. With very few exceptions, good businesses are good businesses from the start.

All serious new businesses need a business plan to help get them going, outlining their aims, strategies, markets and forecasts. Look at plenty of sample and template business plans before you start your own, and research your market thoroughly to help stimulate your thinking (see above). Then, consider who your business plan will be for. Might you need it to secure funding from banks, investors or grant providers? Some business plans will never be read by anyone except the person who wrote it—but they are no less essential for that, since they help to structure a new business, measure its success and avoid difficulties. Unless your publishing is going to be very small scale and ad hoc, every company should have one.

Business plans usually comprise the following:

An executive summary. A page or two overview of the whole business and a summary of the contents of the plan. Some busy readers will read only this, so make it snappy and professional.

The business offer. A succinct vision of what you are offering and who is going to buy it, plus details of your type of business and intended start date. Include a SWOT analysis, identifying strengths, weaknesses, opportunities and threats.

The sales and marketing plan. The who, how, where and why of your sales. Plus strategies for reaching buyers; the size, segments and details of your markets; their future; and some analysis of your competitors.

Your background. Details of your skills and experience, and potted biographies of anyone you will be working with.

Your operations. How you will work: your office, equipment, suppliers and partners—authors, printers, distributors and so on.

Financial planning. The numbers: detailed forecasts and budgets for at least the first three years. Include cash flow, sales and profit and loss projections and risk analysis, and use the numbers to work out the capital you will need. For more on this, see the Financial chapter.

Keep your business plan as succinct as you can. It is more likely to be read if you can keep it short and to the point. Write in plain English and cut out all jargon, which rings alarm bells in experienced business plan readers. Stick to the facts and avoid anything that sounds like speculation or assumption. Remember that readers may not understand the publishing world, so use simple terms when referring to the industry. Present your plan as professionally as you can, neatly bound on good paper. Produce a version that is ready to email. The business plan will be the first contact many people will have with your business, so it needs to create a very good impression.

Plans need not be rigid and will almost certainly change over time. Many publishers look back on their initial plans and find they bear no resemblance to how they ended up. But you should at least feel comfortable following it. Above all, it needs to be realistic. If you plan honestly and carefully, then your business has every chance of success. But if you look for short cuts or try to be overly ambitious in your targets, the chances are that you will be setting yourself up for failure. So budget what you think you will earn and achieve rather than what you hope for, and remember to factor into your cash flow the inevitable long delays in being paid. If anything, overestimate your costs and underestimate your sales.

Once you've compiled the first draft of your business plan, share it with people you trust to give you honest feedback. Ask any small-business people you know—preferably successful ones!—for their thoughts. Get advice from any local business support networks. Don't worry if people tear apart your business plan—it is better that they do so now than a bank or investor does so later. Take on board all feedback and fine-tune your plan. And don't file it away once your business is up and running. Instead, think of it as a living, working document, using it to monitor your performance and updating it whenever circumstances change.

FUNDING

The financial barriers to entry into publishing are low. For hundreds rather than thousands of pounds, anyone can produce and print a book and try to sell it. But to run a professional business that builds a list of books and is sustainable and profitable in the long term takes a lot more capital.

Most independent publishers are founded with money from their owners—perhaps using savings, an inheritance, a redundancy pay-off or the proceeds of a remortgage. Others raise capital from friends or family, in return for a share in the business; get support from corporate investors; or borrow from banks in the form of loans or overdrafts. Government support or local grants may be available. Many publishers use a combination of all the above.

However you fund your business, you will probably need at least a little money of your own. External investors like to see founders put up some capital as evidence of their commitment, and grants are likely to be on a 'matched' basis, meeting only part of the sum you need. If you don't yet have enough, don't give up the day job, and consider reducing your start-up costs or deferring your business while you save; you can still research and plan it in the meantime. Another way of subsidizing your new business might be to offer consultancy or freelance services in aspects of publishing you are already particularly good at—copy-editing, perhaps, or design.

New publishers often fail to realize what a cash hungry industry this is. Producing books soaks up money long before you start to see any come in, so it is essential to budget carefully for each of your books and to have either capital or another source of income in place to tide you over the first few years. Try to pay yourself a going rate in wages; many new publishers pay themselves a pittance while investing in the business, but your morale will suffer if you don't have enough money to live as you like. But at the same time, be sure you can cope with several years of financial uncertainty. Successful new publishers might typically expect to make a big loss in their first year; break even in their second; and turn a profit in their third, though it can often take longer and it may well be many years before you fully repay your early outgoings or borrowings.

Given that most businesses that fail do so in these very early years, rigorous budgeting is absolutely essential in the first few years. Don't bury your head in the sand when it comes to money. Instead, discipline yourself to account for every penny you spend and to draw up basic accounts at the end of every month. Successful small companies keep very tight reins on cash and stay rigorously on top of cash flow, doing all they can to ensure any money that is scheduled to go out of the business doesn't do so until enough money comes in. Forecasting cash flow regularly and accurately is one of the biggest steps you can take towards ensuring survival in the first few years.

If you don't have the necessary skills and focus, enlist the help of an accountant, or perhaps a mentor from another publisher or small business who is prepared to guide you through the money maze. The IPG's own mentoring scheme may be able to help you with this. The IPG also organizes day-long training courses on financial management for independent publishers, run by the excellent Publishing Training Centre in London. They are an excellent source of help for start-ups in particular. Whatever you do, don't shy away from money management.

For more on financial planning, funding, tax and the vital importance of cash flow, see the Financial chapter.

PRACTICALITIES

All new businesses have certain legal obligations to meet, including notifying various registers and government agencies. If you have one, your solicitor will be able to advise on what needs to be done when, and even do it for you. Business Link can also provide a useful checklist of practical things to be done by all start-ups.

First, choose a name for your company. This is fun but challenging. A name obviously has to create a good impression with your customers and, if you are publishing in a specific sector, it will help if it conveys what you do. In publishing, your name is your brand, among retailers and customers, in bookshops and on the web. If you need some inspiration for names, look at the IPG's online directory of members. Get tips from the National Business Register. Use Companies House to check that your intended company name is not already used by someone else, and check for registered trademarks at the Intellectual

Property Office. Also remember to check that the website domain for your company name is available too; Nominet can do this for you.

Next, you will need to decide which form of company you want to register yourself as. There are generally four options—sole trader, partnership, limited company or limited liability partnership—and each has pros and cons. Business Link has a good online tool to help you decide the right legal structure, and solicitors or business advisors will also be able to help. Bear in mind that the first two options, while simpler, leave you personally liable for business debts, while the second two give you protection. Small publishers are strongly advised to get this sort of protection, so that their personal assets are not at risk in the event of failure.

Limited companies must list themselves on the Registrar of Companies at Companies House, and all new businesses will need to register with HM Revenue and Customs. Contact each for the relevant forms and costs or ask your accountant or solicitor to register for you. Draw up your memorandum of association, outlining your company's name, address, objectives, liabilities and any share capital and shareholders; and your articles of association, stating the relationship between your company's directors and shareholders, the details of shares and the rights of shareholders. These can be done by your solicitor or yourself, perhaps based on templates available from a company formation agent or law stationer.

Sort out your company logo and stationery. You needn't spend too much on this, but a smart look helps to make your business look professional from the outset. Limited companies must also have a separate bank account, which can be set up once you are officially registered. As with everything to do with banks, shop around for the best terms, and look out in particular for charges and overdraft flexibility. Don't jump at the first account offered to you. Even in challenging economic times, banks should be competing for your business.

New publishers also need to register with the various agencies of Nielsen, in order to obtain ISBNs for their books and start supplying bibliographic data to customers. See the Bibliographic and IT chapter for much more about this.

OFFICES AND FACILITIES

Many independent publishers—perhaps the majority—start life in the homes of their founders. Basing yourself at home is certainly a good way of keeping down costs, though you need to check that your mortgage or tenancy and insurance agreements allow it and that you will be able to properly divide personal and work life. If you prefer to keep them separate, look in the local media for office facilities, and gather advice from as many sources as you can (see Resources for some ideas). Local councils and Yell.com are other good places to look. Some independent publishers occasionally offer new ones desk space in their office on fair terms if they happen to have the room, and this might enable you to share some publishing-specific facilities and soak up advice from more experienced publishers. Ask around in the IPG or seek advice on the forum if you are interested in sharing space. Wherever you get premises, check contracts carefully and have your solicitor scrutinize any agreements if you are unsure about them. Don't feel obliged to sign up to long leases if you don't want to, and sort out who is responsible for paying the utility bills. Register your new office with your local council for business rates, and don't forget insurance.

At their most basic, publishers need to equip themselves with nothing more than a decent computer, broadband connection, telephone and perhaps a fax machine. Apple Mac computers are widely used in publishing as well as PCs, and computers should have good design packages as well as word processing ones. Start learning as soon as you can about the systems you will need to meet industry standards on electronic trading, and incorporate IT spending in your business plan and financial forecasts. Take advantage of the huge amount of help provided by Book Industry Communication (BIC) and read the Bibliographic and IT chapter for more on this. Also register a website, even if it contains only basic contact details for the time being.

SUPPORT AND ADVICE

Get help with your business wherever you can. The IPG and its membership are the best first port of call for just about any question you have, so take full advantage of the website, forum, e-bulletin and other services. The IPG's mentoring service, pairing publishers with some of our more experienced members, has also been valuable to fledgling companies. And remember to take advantage of members' free access to the Croner Business Support Helpline, staffed by trained professionals and offering advice on numerous aspects of business law and practice.

The government's Business Link portal has masses of free, up-to-date information, including useful tools to guide you through the early months and a network of offices around the country providing one-to-one support. Wherever you are in the country, there should also be regional or local development agencies whose job it is to help you launch smoothly and operate successfully, and financial assistance might be available if you are in an area that has been identified for support; in England, start looking at the umbrella Regional Development Agencies' website. Many towns and cities have breakfast or lunch business clubs that can be a good source of support and potential partners. Use the networks of Enterprise Agencies and Chambers of Commerce for networking. And for training to sharpen up your business's competitiveness and profitability, get in touch with the Train to Gain project from the Learning and Skills Council.

Whether they seek it or not, all new businesses find themselves inundated with good-intentioned advice. Listen to all of it, but don't feel obliged to act on any of it. Much of what other publishers or small businesses tell you will be in the context of their own particular line of work, and no one knows your own company's requirements better than you. Take in what people tell you, but filter advice carefully and ultimately trust your instincts.

PARTNERS

All publishers will need stable, hardworking and reliable partners, so make finding them a priority. The quality of your partnerships may be the biggest factor in your success. Good small publishers realize that their size means they cannot do everything themselves, and that making partnerships work is essential.

In particular, think as soon as you can about who is going to print your books —assuming that print is your preferred medium—and who is going to distribute them. Other important partners include any external sales representation, both in the UK and overseas, and any help you might want with rights, marketing, publicity or editorial. Remember that cheapest is not automatically best when weighing up competitors for your business, and see the relevant chapters in this guide for advice about identifying good partners and maintaining good relationships.

Most small businesses will also want to have at least some contact with an accountant and lawyer. Ideally choose ones with some experience of the publishing industry, since it has quirks that not all will understand. As with banks, remember that these professionals will need your business even more than you need theirs, so negotiate good terms and don't settle for poor service. Accountants will often provide substantial free support and advice if they know they will get the contract to audit your accounts, and banks should be a good source of business advice as well as money; most will have piles of booklets and brochures available in branches and stacks of information online. Banks can often introduce you to useful people, so get to know your business manager and tap into their networks.

QUALITIES

What makes a good small publisher? The backgrounds of IPG members are incredibly rich and varied. With no professional qualification or experience required, publishing is an industry open to anyone. Perhaps the only firm conclusion is that anyone can do it if they put their mind to it.

Creative flair and a passion for the content you publish are obviously important. But so too are the sort of qualities essential to anyone running their own business—self-belief, commitment, drive and courage. Most good business people are also good salespeople, so start making yourself into one—this, after all, is the only thing that will actually make you any money. You are an entrepreneur and ought to feel like one. All businesses have ups and downs, so the ability to cope with pressure and deal calmly with both successes and failures is crucial. You will need support from your family and friends, and don't underestimate the personal sacrifices, exhaustion and isolation you will face. Good businesses reflect the personalities of the people who work in them, so don't change who you are to suit anyone else. Every book that is published is a gamble, so some kind of gambling instinct—whether safe or adventurous—is important.

Don't worry if you don't have any direct experience of either publishing or running a small business. Few independent publishers have both before they start, and none will have expertise in every sector. Instead, acknowledge the shortcomings in your experience or skills and fill in the gaps, either by outsourcing work or learning the ropes yourself. Train yourself as you go, and try to understand the basics of every discipline of publishing, even if you intend to outsource it in due course. Don't be afraid to ask questions, however naive they seem. Enthusiasm and energy can compensate for a lot, and a willingness to learn from others will help you to catch up.

SELF-PUBLISHING

Some people start their own publishing companies because they want a means by which to publish their own books. That might well be a valid enough reason, but anyone doing so needs to be doubly sure of their motivations for going into business. Consider very carefully if you are really able to make enough money from your book or books to cover your costs. Try to do so dispassionately, and seek the opinions of others you trust. If your books have been rejected by other publishers previously, ask yourself why, and consider whether there is really a big enough market for them. Making money is not the only motivation for publishing, of course, and seeing your book in print may be enough of a return. But do not enter publishing assuming that what you have written is good enough to make money. As it is with all publishers, the market will be the sole judge of that.

If you want to see your own book in print but do not want the risk of starting up a new company, there are a couple of options open to you. First, you could seek an established publisher for it; see the *Writers' and Artists' Yearbook* for tips on this, but accept that getting published can be difficult, and that publishers reject many more books than they take on. Consultancies like Writers Services offer help to authors wanting to sharpen up their work for publishers. Second, you could prepare your book for print yourself, using the tips gathered in this guide, and then ask a printer to produce a set number of copies for you. Print-on-demand specialists can be a good option, since they will produce small quantities for you and top up with more as required, and you will find the contact details of some in the Print and Production chapter. This is recommended for people who want to sell or donate copies of their book to a number of friends or family.

A third option is to publish your book with one of the so-called 'vanity' publishers, who will produce your book and sometimes sell or market it on your behalf in exchange for a fee. Tread extremely cautiously with these companies. Many are short-lived and leave behind them a string of disgruntled authors who have received little or nothing that they have paid for. Fees are often extravagant; the quality of service poor; and the percentage of people who sell enough copies of their book to recoup their outlay tiny. Without a proper publishing name or distributor behind it, you may well find it impossible to get bookshops to stock your book on any great scale. With one or two honourable exceptions, treat all offers and promises of sales with utmost caution. For sound advice on the perils of vanity publishing, see a free guide produced by the Society of Authors or an article in the *Writers' and Artists' Yearbook*.

RESOURCES
RESEARCH
IPG
Details of events at which to learn more about publishing, plus lots more useful resources including a searchable listing of all IPG members and contacts.
Web www.ipg.uk.com
Tel 01437 563335

Book2Book
Free-to-view website with industry news, links to other media and a daily e-bulletin.
Web www.booktrade.info

BookBrunch
Subscription-based website and daily bulletins to keep you in touch with publishing news.
Web www.bookbrunch.co.uk
Tel 020 7242 9972

The Bookseller
The weekly magazine for the book business, also available online.
Web www.thebookseller.com
Tel 020 7420 6000

London Book Fair
The UK's biggest annual gathering of the book business and a great place to learn more about all its facets.
Web www.londonbookfair.co.uk
Tel 020 8910 7910

PLANNING

BBC Business Plans
Useful, impartial guide to writing a plan.
Web www.bbc.co.uk/consumer/start_a_business/businessplan.shtml

Bplans
Hundreds of free sample business plans to learn from, plus tips for writing your own.
Web www.bplans.com

Business Link
Lots of advice on planning, plus sample and real-life business plans to read.
Web www.businesslink.gov.uk
Tel 0845 600 9006

Business Plan Services
Advice and links, plus consultancy help if you need it.
Web www.bizplans.co.uk
Tel 08450 574065

TRAINING

Financial Management for Independent Publishers
Highly recommended day-long course, organized by the IPG with the Publishing Training Centre and tailored to the needs of small independents.
Web www.train4publishing.co.uk/guideto/ipg/finindep
Tel 020 8874 2718

PRACTICALITIES

Companies House
The national centre for business registrations and information.
Web www.companieshouse.gov.uk
Tel 0870 3333 636

HM Revenue and Customs
Everything businesses need to know about tax. Regional offices also provide useful workshops for new businesses and employers.
Web www.hmrc.gov.uk
Tel 08456 070 143

Intellectual Property Office
Searchable database of trademarks.
Web www.ipo.gov.uk
Tel 08459 500 505

National Business Register
Sound online guide to choosing a company name.
Web www.start.biz/business_names

Nominet
The registrar for internet domain names in the UK.
Web www.nic.uk
Tel 01865 332211

OFFICES AND FACILITIES

Book Industry Communication (BIC)
Every publisher's best friend when it comes to equipping their systems for electronic trading and meeting industry standards.
Web www.bic.org.uk
Tel 020 7607 0021

Finding an office
Useful tips on securing premises.
Web www.smallbusiness.co.uk/channels/office-and-homeworking/finding-office-space

Tenancy advice
Tips on contracts from Communities and Local Government.
Web www.communities.gov.uk/citiesandregions/propertyissues/
businesstenanciesguidance
Tel 020 7944 4400

Yell.com
A good place to start looking for property agents near you.
Web www.yell.com

ACCOUNTANTS AND SOLICITORS

Institute of Chartered Accountants
Directory of accountants across the country.
Web www.icaew.co.uk
Tel 020 7920 8100

The Law Society
Directory of solicitors across the country.
Web www.lawsociety.org.uk/choosingandusing/findasolicitor.law
Tel 020 7242 1222

BUSINESS SUPPORT AND ADVICE

IPG
Website, forum, bulletin, events, mentoring and much more to help every new
publisher!
Web www.ipg.uk.com
Tel 01437 563335

British Banking Association
Tips on making the most of your business bank account.
Web www.bba.org.uk
Tel 020 7216 8800

British Library Business and IP Centre
Excellent resources to help start and grow businesses, with an emphasis on
protecting intellectual property. Visit in person or online.
Web www.bl.uk/bipc/index.html

Business Link
Government support, advice and resources for businesses of all sizes, with a network of local offices across the country.
Web www.businesslink.gov.uk
Tel 0845 600 9006

Chambers of Commerce
A countrywide network of businesses and support groups.
Web www.britishchambers.org.uk
Tel 020 7654 5800

Confederation of British Industry
Leading UK body for employers.
Web www.cbi.org.uk
Tel 020 7379 7400

Croner Business Support Helpline
IPG members get unlimited access to this invaluable helpline to answer your queries on countless aspects of business and law.
Tel 0844 561 8133, quoting the password supplied with your membership details

Department for Business, Innovation and Skills
Government department offering support for businesses.
Web www.bis.gov.uk
Tel 020 7215 5000

Federation of Small Businesses
UK-wide association with some information for start-ups.
Web www.fsb.org.uk
Tel 01253 336 000

Forum of Private Business
Has some useful resources for small- and medium-sized businesses.
Web www.fpb.co.uk
Tel 0845 130 1722

Institute of Directors
Membership association for directors with some useful advice and networking opportunities.
Web www.iod.co.uk
Tel 020 7839 1233

National Federation of Enterprise Agencies
Umbrella group for enterprise agencies supporting small businesses, and a good
first port of call for any help that might be available in your region.
Web www.nfea.com
Tel 01234 831623

Office of Fair Trading
Some advice on keeping your business within consumer and competition law.
Web www.oft.gov.uk
Tel 08454 040506

Regional Development Agencies
A network of eight English regions offering local advice and support to businesses.
Web www.englandsrdas.com
Tel 020 7222 8180

Small Business
Handy website of free advice and resources.
Web www.smallbusiness.co.uk

Small Business Journey
Useful help for small and medium enterprises, put together by the Small Business
Consortium.
Web www.smallbusinessjourney.com
Tel 020 7566 8650

Train to Gain
A free service from the Learning and Skills Council that offers training to help
businesses improve their competitiveness and profitability. The IPG sometimes
brokers courses especially for members on the scheme's behalf; look out for news
of forthcoming sessions.
Web www.traintogain.gov.uk
Tel 0845 600 9006

UK Trade & Investment
Government agency to help companies export overseas. Can help publishers set
up export links and identify opportunities for sales.
Web www.uktradeinvest.gov.uk
Tel 020 7215 8000

SELF-PUBLISHING

Society of Authors
Free guide to self-publishing and excellent advice on avoiding unscrupulous vanity publishers.
Web www.societyofauthors.org/publications/vanity_publishing

Writers' and Artists' Yearbook
The online version of the popular book—see below for the print version.
Web www.writersandartists.co.uk

Writers Services
One of the web-based consultancies offering advice to would-be writers.
Web www.writersservices.com

BOOKS

British Book Publishing as a Business Since the 1960s by Eric de Bellaigue (British Library Publishing, £19.95, 9780712348362)

From Pitch to Publication: Everything You Need to Know to Get Your Novel Published by Carole Blake (Pan, £6.99, 9780333714355)

A Guide to the UK Publishing Industry by Paul Richardson and Graham Taylor (Publishers Association, £9.99, 9780853863335)

A History of British Publishing by John Feather (Routledge, £21.99, 9780415302265)

How They Started: How 30 Good Ideas Became Great Businesses by David Lester (Crimson Publishing, £12.99, 9781854584007)

How to Write a Business Plan by Brian Finch (Kogan Page, £8.99, 9780749445539)

Inside Book Publishing by Giles Clark and Angus Phillips (fourth edition; Routledge, £19.99, 9780415441575)

The Insider's Guide to Getting Your Book Published by Rachael Stock (White Ladder Press, £9.99, 9780954821951)

The No-Nonsense Guide to Starting a Business (Business Link, free, available direct)

Publishing for Profit: Successful Bottom-line Management for Book Publishers by Thomas Woll and Philip Kogan (Kogan Page, £19.95, 9780749429409)

The Small Business Start-up Workbook by Cheryl Rickman (How To Books, £12.99, 9781845280383)

Spare Room Start Up: How to Start a Business from Home by Emma Jones (Harriman House, £12.99, 9781905641680)

Starting Your Own Business: The Good, the Bad and the Unexpected by David Lester (Crimson Publishing, £12.99, 9781854584014)

The White Ladder Diaries: The Pain and Pleasure of Launching a Business by Ros Jay (White Ladder Press, £9.99, 9780954821975)

Writers' and Artists' Yearbook (A&C Black, £14.99, 9781408102640; updated annually)

2 EDITORIAL

CONTENTS

Strategies and list building / Getting books 1—attracting authors and commissioning / Getting books 2—submissions and agents / Getting books 3—other ways / Assessing proposals / Contracts / Royalties and advances / Working with authors / Content, copy and project editing / Blurbs, AIs, prelims, marketing and design / Staff and skills / Outsourcing / Resources

Editorial is at the heart of publishing. Editors source and prepare the only thing that makes publishers any money, taking books from their conception all the way up to the point at which they are ready to be designed and printed. The copyrights they purchase can be used in a variety of ways besides manufacturing books, such as selling on rights. In short, editorial is the function from which others in publishing flow.

In larger publishing companies, editorial staff are usually split into several layers: commissioning or acquiring editors, who source titles and build lists; copy or desk editors, who work on manuscripts; and editorial assistants, who look after administration and offer general support. Above them all might be more posts such as editorial or publishing directors, responsible for big acquisitions and shaping the list. In more complex publishing that requires the pulling together of content from a variety of sources, the job may be more about project management than simple editing. But in smaller independent publishers, however, many of these roles are likely to overlap either in part or entirely, and editors will often be expected to handle all the work in getting books ready to print.

STRATEGIES AND LIST BUILDING

Whatever the size of your publishing company, it is essential to have a proper plan for the books you want to produce. Research the market you want to publish into very carefully, focusing on the gaps you are trying to fill. Get hold of any statistical information that is available in your field—university and student numbers following the subject about which you are publishing, for instance. Thoroughly analyse your competition and look at existing books in your field. Think about what they do particularly well, and consider what you could do better.

Also try to gauge public demand, by monitoring trends in your field and thinking about what might be popular a year or two from now. The knack is knowing precisely when the market will want your new publication. If you have travel books, for instance, which destinations are likely to be coming in or going out of fashion? In educational publishing, it is particularly important to track changes to the curriculum or qualifications so that your books are delivering relevant, essential content. If you can forecast correctly, you can prepare and publish a book just as interest is increasing, but act too late and you'll catch the trend on its downward spiral. Keep a close eye on your competitors' forward publishing plans so you can respond accordingly. Use book fairs to gauge what is hot and cold in publishing around the world and what your rivals are up to. Look out for reports on publishing trends from agencies like Book Marketing Ltd.

The number of books publishers put out in a year varies enormously from sector to sector and it is impossible to estimate how many books companies should aim to publish. Some editors will handle only a couple of big books in a year, while others will see 30 or 40 through to press. Budget carefully for how many books you can take on, from both a financial and a time point of view (see the Financial chapter for more on this). Tie your targets to your turnover projections in your business plan. Work out carefully when you want to publish each book, and bear in mind the cycles for your market. If it's a book that will appeal as a Christmas gift, for instance, September or October should be the target month; if it's a student textbook, you need to be in good time for the start of the academic year. Be wary of over-reaching yourself in your publishing; if you are rushed off your feet you won't be able to make every book the best it can be.

Try to think thematically about your publishing, drawing together your lists in clusters. For publishers working in small, defined niches, perhaps in specific academic or professional areas, it should be easy to discern the themes of your list, but if you have a wider scope then there are other ways of building identities for your lists. Consider drawing books together in a series, for instance—the 'For Dummies' collection is a good example of how this can be done effectively. Or consider creating separate imprints for your books—a fiction publisher might like to have separate crime or romance imprints rather than publishing everything under the same banner, for instance. Imprints can help both retailers and customers to understand and recognize your publishing brand. Strong brands are built on success but also consistency, so if you publish in a scattergun way, it is difficult for people to grasp what you are about. This is especially true in educational, academic and professional publishing as buyers here will begin to associate a publisher's name with particular areas and standards. Children's publishing, too, can be brand-led, since parents and teachers learn to associate imprint names with styles and qualities.

Focused publishing is vital, and so too is a critical mass of good content, built up over time. For this reason, try to think long-term. Successful publishers build solid backlists of books that will sell year in, year out. Selling large quantities of a book for a month or two is all well and good, but it is the steady sellers, reprinted every now and then and always stocked by retailers, that bring in the profits. Selling a thousand copies of a book each year for ten years is much better than selling five thousand in the first year and nothing afterwards. Every publisher in the world has books that sell above expectations and books that sell below, the one subsidizing the other. It is this that allows publishers to take risks.

If you are publishing in a specialist field it might be worth considering drawing up a panel of experts to help you, meeting a few times a year to discuss editorial strategies. In academia especially, there is a lot of goodwill towards independent publishers, and many people will be flattered to be invited to join a board of advisors. Educational and professional publishers will also benefit from the advice of a few people with experience as book buyers and readers in your field. As well as providing insights into what the market wants, they may well be able to identify new writers and ideas you hadn't considered before and could also help to assess the merits of individual book proposals. IPG members who have retired or sold their companies sometimes sit on other members' boards, providing invaluable expertise that can help new companies to find their feet. Publishing experience is not essential, however, and it may be just as useful for educational or children's publishers to have advisors with experience in schools or other learning environments. You may have to pay your advisory boards a small retainer or, at least, expenses.

GETTING BOOKS 1—ATTRACTING AUTHORS AND COMMISSIONING

Approaches to finding content will vary hugely according to the sector you are working in—but in most instances, good contacts are the key. This is very much a people-driven business, and personal relationships can often lead to successful publishing.

In many small publishers—and in academic, professional and STM sectors in particular—it is common to commission books from authors rather than waiting for them to come to you. Even if you haven't got an author for your publishing idea, it shouldn't be hard to find one. Get to know the leading figures in the fields in which you want to publish, and get yourself known in the right circles. Visit the key institutions, societies or companies in the fields you are publishing for, and gather as much feedback about your publishing and book ideas as you can. Conferences, fairs and other events are good places to identify authors and work out where the gaps in the market are. In educational publishing, build up a network of teachers on whom you can rely to tell you what the market needs. Remember that in schools and universities the academic background of your authors will be important, so make sure they have the right teaching or research experience to give them credibility.

Keep an eye on journals, magazines, websites or other publications related to your field and sign up to all the mailing lists going. In educational publishing, stay on top of government strategies and changes to the curriculum and make sure your publishing responds accordingly. Some publishers have been caught out by such changes, which can make some books obsolete overnight because they no longer meet the demands of the curriculum—but others look on changes as opportunities to publish new books to meet new needs. The IPG tracks important changes on members' behalf and sometimes arranges updates from and with the Department for Education and the Qualifications and Curriculum Development Agency, both of which are good sources of information. Sign up to the e-newsletters offered by both, and follow education news in the papers and specialist publications like the *Times Educational Supplement*.

Look on the web for people who can write in your field but have not yet been published; blogs are a good way to identify talent. After some research, the people who have the abilities and inclinations to write books for you should become apparent. If you are still looking to match your idea with a writer, try some of the member databases of author and illustrator associations like the Society of Authors.

GETTING BOOKS 2—SUBMISSIONS AND AGENTS

In other fields of publishing like adult and children's trade sectors, it is more common for books to come to publishers, pitched to you by authors or their agents. Inviting submissions can be a good way of building your list, but it can also bury you in a mountain of unwanted material—commonly and not very affectionately known as the slush pile. To stem the flow, draw up a submissions policy that closely reflects your editorial strategy and that you can post on your website and supply to interested authors.

Submission policies should outline as specifically as possible the sort of books you are interested in publishing and the form in which you want to receive submissions. Whether you want to see a synopsis, sample chapters or the full text of a book, state clearly what you want authors to provide. The looser you are in your requirements, the more you will be deluged by submissions that aren't relevant to your line of publishing and that you will spend all your working life trawling through. Most well-established publishers have submissions policies on their websites, so browse several and borrow elements of the ones that are most relevant to you to help produce your own. Also make sure that you are happy with your company's entry in the *Writers' and Artists' Yearbook*—this is where many prospective authors find publishers' contact details, so it needs to accurately reflect what you do and don't want from them.

In trade publishing in particular, some authors prefer to work through literary agents. These will represent authors when negotiating publishing contracts, in return for a commission of around 15% on all deals. Agents are more common at the bestselling end of the business, and the majority of small publishers will either never have cause to deal with them or else discourage authors' use of them since they add an extra layer to the supply chain. Agents tend to be more aggressive in their negotiations than authors—that's their job—but the rules for dealing with them are much the same (see Contracts, below). Some independent publishers have also found that increasing numbers of relatively well-known authors are being let go by much larger publishers because they have not achieved sales which would be more than acceptable to many independents. Again, agents will usually be responsible for 'selling' these authors to new publishers.

GETTING BOOKS 3—OTHER WAYS

Publishers might also pick up books from scouts, whose job it is to seek out talent in the UK or around the world and bring it to the attention of publishers in return for a fee. Their role is distinct from that of an agent in that they do not continue to represent the author throughout his or her career.

Another way of getting books is to acquire existing ones from other publishers around the world—perhaps by making contact with companies in the same sector as you, or by looking for suitable material at one of the major book fairs like London or Frankfurt. The costs of translating these books into English could be substantial, but grants are sometimes available to cover these; see the Rights and Copyright chapter for more about this. And if your book is on a subject that requires little specialist knowledge or can be drawn from existing material, you could consider producing it yourself without the need to pay an author. One final way is to get a book from a contract publisher or packager—see Outsourcing, below, for more on this.

ASSESSING PROPOSALS

Whichever way you obtain your books, make sure you have a robust strategy in place for deciding if they are worth publishing. Editors should be the primary filter, and in some popular fields of publishing, like adult fiction or children's books, their main job will be to reject 99% of all submissions. Independent readers or referees can be used to assess the merits of submissions and, if you have one, your board of advisers can provide feedback. Some specialist publishers like to build up banks of experts in their field who will provide an assessment of a book's merits in return for a fee. This peer review process is particularly important in academic and professional publishing, where the credibility of authors and content is crucial.

If you have more than one or two staff, consider holding acquisition meetings—perhaps once a week or month—where the pros and cons of books that you are considering publishing can be discussed freely. It is useful to collect as many opinions as you can before making a judgement on a proposal.

Unfortunately, good professional author proposals are much rarer than bad ones. What you should be looking for is evidence that an author has researched the market and has a clear vision of who will buy their book. It's not enough to say that 'everyone' will be interested in it, or to give broad categories of buyers like 'students'. Look instead for a close understanding of specific markets, plus an awareness of the competition that the book will face and a few ideas about how it might be marketed. Look particularly closely at the details an author provides about him or herself. Is he or she a recognized name in their field? Is there any evidence of a track record in publishing? How confident are you that the author will deliver what he or she promises?

Ask yourself if a proposed book fits the theme and tone of your existing list. Is it good enough to appeal to customers ahead of what is already on the market? Repeatedly and rigorously consider its sales potential, in both the short and long term. Will it sell for years or only a few months? How much of a risk is it? If you are in academic or professional publishing, the scale of the potential market should be readily apparent—there are only as many sales of a book about family law as there are family lawyers and legal libraries, for instance. In trade publishing, predicting sales is more of a gamble. But be ruthlessly realistic rather than optimistic about how you think it will fare, and complete detailed costing and revenue forecasting for each potential book (see Financial chapter for more on this). It can be difficult to reject a book you have a personal passion for, but have the guts to do so if it is likely to lose you money.

Think too about the possibility of selling rights. Is this a book that other publishers around the world might be interested in? If so, your chances of making money from it will be much improved. Also consider the marketing and publicity potential of any book you consider. Will you be able to secure reviews or other media coverage? Will bookshops be interested in promoting it? Could the author help to promote and sell it?

Assessing a book need not mean giving a straightforward yes or no to the author or agent. Some publishers provide feedback on proposals and ask authors to improve them before considering them again. Even if you reject a book outright, it is a courtesy to send the author a letter telling them so. Many authors value any personal feedback you can provide, though constraints on your time might mean a standard rejection letter is all that is possible. Remember that if an author is interested in being published by you then they are probably a potential fan and evangelist for your list, so it is worth giving appropriate time to them.

CONTRACTS

Once you are confident that a book is right for you and can make you money, it's time to agree terms and contracts—also called agreements.

There are endless versions of author contracts and they can vary from sector to sector, but most are variations on a broad template—sometimes called a boilerplate. Unless your publishing is very varied, establish a contract model of your own that can be adapted for all purposes. The essential handbook for all contracts is *Clark's Publishing Agreements*, edited by Lynette Owen and available to IPG members at a discount. This contains everything you will ever need to know on every sort of publishing agreement. Other publishers will have their own standard contracts, of course, and you might beg or borrow versions on which to base your own from fellow IPG members. Experienced authors may also bring their own contracts with them if they have been published elsewhere already, or ask their agents to do so.

Standard contracts should include details of the book's proposed title, approximate length in words and delivery date, plus an outline of the agreed advance, royalties and payment schedule (see below for more on this). By signing a contract, authors licence their copyright to you and give you permission to publish their work as you like. They also agree to warranties, usually guaranteeing that their work is not plagiarized or libellous.

Contracts should stipulate very carefully which rights the publisher has to a book and which are kept by the author. In most cases with independents, the UK publisher will sign world rights in a book, giving it the opportunity to sell subsidiary or sub rights both domestically and overseas, and to license content in other ways, both in print and electronically. All contracts should stipulate the splits of each sort of rights income between author and publisher. For more on all this, see the Rights and Copyright chapter.

For all these reasons, getting your first boilerplate contract right is crucial. It might seem boring, but agreeing tight definitions of rights terms and covering the legalese is essential if you are to protect your interests should any issues arise in the future with, for instance, copyright, rights deals or libel actions. Ask a contracts advisor or legal specialist if you are unsure on any clause or need a contract tightened up in some way, and make sure that whoever you use has publishing experience, since a general lawyer will not have sufficient knowledge of the industry. Authors too will sometimes have their contracts vetted—by their agents if they have one, or by the Society of Authors if they are a member—and you may have to negotiate some clauses.

ROYALTIES AND ADVANCES

Publishers usually pay authors for their work in two ways: a fixed fee or royalties. Fixed fees are a good way of managing your costs and can be a profitable way of publishing since you will not have to pay anything more in royalties, but authors and agents can be wary of them since they offer no share in the success of a book. They also tie up publishers' cash up front, and authors might feel they have no incentive to deliver a really good book if they are not going to receive any further payment.

Royalties offer authors more of a motivation to write and sell. Proportions that publishers pay vary, but they are typically between 5% and 15%, based on either the publisher's list price or the net sales. So, on a £10 book that a publisher sells to a retailer at 50% discount, a 10% royalty based on list price would pay the author £1 per sale. The same royalty based on net sales would pay only 50 pence. Some publishers also like to include escalators that mean they pay lower royalties on high discount sales. So, on that same £10 book, a sale to a retailer made at 60% discount might qualify the author for a reduced royalty of 8% of net sales—32 pence. This obviously helps to maintain margins, but authors and agents may well not appreciate your reasons for lower rates. Escalators can also go up, perhaps giving an author an improved royalty when sales reach a set target. Contracts sometimes include a clause holding back a certain amount of royalties as a provision against future returns of unsold copies of a book.

Whatever your rates, royalty payments are generally calculated once or twice a year, and paid two to four months after the end of the period they cover. Calculating and paying royalties can be a fiddly and time-consuming process, and some publishers prefer to outsource the job to an accountant or—if they offer the service—their distributor. Software packages are also available to help you calculate royalties; see the Financial chapter for details of providers. If you have a small number of books for which to calculate royalties, it should be easy enough to devise a spreadsheet to do the sums for you.

Royalties may be offset by an advance—a sum of money paid to an author ahead of any royalties, and fully deductible against them. Advances are usually paid in three equal instalments: on agreeing contracts; on delivering the manuscript; and on publication. Advances can prove your commitment to a book to an author and will help to pay for his or her time to write it. Staggering payments is a good way of keeping authors motivated to deliver and publish on time. But they also tie up money without a guaranteed return, and there will always be a risk that a book will not 'sell out' its advance—in other words, never earn enough in royalties to pay back that initial outlay. For this reason, many independent publishers prefer not to offer advances at all, instead concentrating purely on royalties. Other publishers keep advances as low as possible, limiting them to a few thousand pounds per contract. As a rule, advances should generally never exceed more than 50% of the royalties forecast from a book in its first year on sale.

The balance between advances and royalties will vary from sector to sector and your perception of risk. But unless you are a trade publisher facing a lot of competition to secure an author's services, there should be no need to pay big advances at all. Try to think what you can give authors instead, emphasizing the potential value of royalties (while remaining realistic in your projections), or offering extras like more free copies of the book for an author. If a rival publisher is offering a bigger advance, try to show authors why yours will be a better home for their book. Authors often value enthusiasm and professional publishing plans above an advance, and this gives small publishers a head start over some of their larger rivals if there is a battle to sign an author. Some, especially in academic and professional sectors, might not need to be paid at all, the prestige of being published being more important compensation than money. If they are required at all, advances here are usually lower than in trade publishing.

WORKING WITH AUTHORS

Once a book has been commissioned, the relationship between an editor and author is crucial. It is a special bond and trust built up over years, but it should quickly become clear if a relationship isn't going to work.

Start by making it very clear what you and your author can expect from one another. Outline the tasks they are obliged to do and the tasks you expect to be left to you. Some authors will be happy to deliver a book and be done with it, but others—especially first timers—might expect to be involved in processes like cover design and marketing. A little time spent agreeing on who does what and when can save lots of aggravation later on. As a rule, involve authors on a need-to-know basis—keep them informed on important things like their books' covers, but be wary of getting them involved in too much detail.

The most common source of tension between authors and publishers is deadlines. Be crystal clear about when you expect authors to deliver their work and whether you will receive it in stages or in full. Explain the importance of all deadlines and how any delays will impact on publication schedules. Be sensitive to their timescales, especially—as is often the case in educational, academic and professional publishing in particular—if they are writing alongside another career. But equally, don't be afraid to check on progress. Regular friendly calls to check all is well can be appreciated by authors without feeling that they are being nagged. Experienced publishers know that it can be next to impossible to dictate schedules to authors, so factor in delays when you agree delivery dates.

Also be clear about how you want to receive material—invariably these days by email or disk. With very rare exceptions, any author who insists on delivering a typed or handwritten manuscript that has to be rekeyed is probably best avoided. Produce some standard guidelines to help all your authors, including things like how you would like material to be formatted; the ways in which you would like things like tables and graphs presented; and what file formats you would like to receive images and graphics in. The presentation of text is fairly straightforward in trade publishing, but in areas like educational, academic or professional there may well be more complex material to prepare. It will save a lot of time if authors can at least indicate where they have sourced things like photographs from, since securing permissions can be time-consuming. Ideally, make it a contractual obligation for the author to clear permissions on any third-party material that is used. Controlling delivery in this way will save a lot of time later on and reduce the need to re-work and re-format material.

Right from the start of a relationship, it is essential to manage authors' expectations. Be honest, open and accessible at all times, and remember that publishing is in many ways a service profession. Make it clear to authors what they can and cannot expect from working with you, especially financially. Don't suggest to them that their book might sell 50,000 copies when you know full well that it will only sell 500. Authors in academic and professional publishing should be more realistic about the scope of their sales than trade authors, who may not be aware of the challenges in the market. Share your marketing plans, and ask for authors' input into these and any publicity plans you have in mind.

Personal contact counts for a lot among authors, some of whom find writing a lonely and daunting profession. Your honesty towards them will almost always be repaid in goodwill. And most authors will prove great to work with—hardworking, efficient and engaged. Inevitably, a small minority will be difficult, complaining about the way their work has been edited, published or sold. Be sensitive to their concerns, but don't forget, either, that it is you rather than they that will be taking the risk on a book. Unless they are essential to your business, the best advice for dealing with troublesome authors is to drop them as soon as possible. Demand to be published far outstrips the number of opportunities to be published, so unless you are involved in a very specific niche you should always be able to find someone else to write your books.

CONTENT, COPY AND PROJECT EDITING

Editing a book properly is about much more than tidying up spelling, grammar and punctuation before sending it to the printers. It usually starts with scheduling, outlining a timetable for the dates by which a manuscript is to be received; copy-edited; designed; typeset; proofread; and sent to press. Editors need to be good project managers, ensuring that all jobs get done on time.

Preparing a book usually starts with structural editing, looking at its whole arrangement and construction and ensuring it is correct before beginning the fine-tuning. This involves checking everything is ordered correctly and that illustrations, graphics, tables and other supplementary material are all in the right place. Sections might have to be moved or broken up, and substantial parts may require reordering or rewriting.

Editing of the actual text—copy-editing or desk editing—is undertaken either in house or, increasingly, by a freelance specialist (see Outsourcing, below). Either way, it should be done with a very fine toothcomb to ensure that all mistakes are eliminated. Copy-editing is increasingly done on a computer screen with specialist tools designed for the purpose, though many editors find that it is still a job best done with pen and paper—and you should certainly never rely on a computer spell or grammar checker to tidy up text. Look out for inconsistencies and factual errors, and ensure that a book is in keeping with the rest of your output, especially if it is part of a series or range. If you are just starting out, developing a house style should be high on your agenda, since it sets the tone for all of your output and gives you something to work from at both the copy-editing and proofreading stages. It doesn't have to be extensive—a couple of pages of guidelines over style and presentation relevant to your sort of books will do—and you can borrow from some of the many guides already available. The most important thing with a style guide is to stick to it at all times.

While working through a text, editors also need to make sure it has a commercial edge, correctly serving and appealing to the target market. They should check closely for copyright and legal issues, ensuring that all material taken from external sources is properly sourced, acknowledged and perhaps paid for (see the Rights and Copyright chapter for more on permissions). Be sensitive to your market, and make sure that no material is likely to be inappropriate or offensive. If anything seems particularly contentious, have it read by a libel lawyer.

Once the editor has settled on the final manuscript, it goes to the author for approval before being passed to the production department for design and layout. If an editor has the technical know-how, he or she might also structure and code the final manuscript with XML tagging so that it is ready to be published in various electronic formats as well as print, though this is more usually a job that is outsourced later. For more on these stages, see the Print and Production and E-publishing chapters.

As the main link with the author of the book, editors are responsible for ensuring that both sides are happy with the finished product. Good ones will understand their authors' aims in writing a book, dealing sensitively but rigorously with any issues or queries that arise and explaining any major changes that need to be made. Some authors resist any interference at all with their carefully wrought prose, but others will be delighted to have their ideas turned into logical text. The best editors strike the right balance between rewriting and restraint, editing the text appropriately without imposing their own voice on the book.

Of course, not all books are simply continuous text requiring rigorous but straightforward editing. Some, especially in academic, professional and educational sectors, incorporate material from several authors, or require illustrations, photographs, diagrams and extracts from other publications. Some publications may have extra elements like websites, CD-Roms, workbooks or teachers' guides. In these cases, the editor does much more than copy-edit. He or she will be the hub of the publishing project, co-ordinating authors and freelancers so that the elements of the publication are pulled together accurately, on time and to budget. This is project editing, and in some large companies the whole process is overseen by a production editor or an editorial services controller.

BLURBS, AIS, PRELIMS, MARKETING AND DESIGN

Beyond editing the main text of a book, editors have a few other jobs to get done. One that needs to be completed as early in the publishing process as possible—sometimes even before a book has been delivered—is to put together a blurb and an Advance Information (AI) sheet—sometimes called a Title Information (TI) sheet—for it.

A book's blurb is a short, snappy synopsis of its contents, to be printed either on its back cover or the flaps of the dust jacket. Writing a good one is quite a skill, and since it will be a major influence on people's decisions about whether or not to purchase, it is vital to get it right. Blurbs should show a browser at a glance what the book is about and why it is worth buying. They should be short—100 to 150 words is usually enough—and cover all the questions that you think a customer might have about a book. Include a brief endorsement or positive review if you have one. A blurb will probably also feature on the book's AI sheet, which shows everyone at a glance all the information they need about a book and which should be written at least six months in advance of publication. See the Marketing chapter for more on AIs.

Other jobs to be done early on in the editing process include assigning a book an International Standard Book Number (ISBN) and Cataloguing-in-Publication (CIP) details (see the Bibliographic and IT chapter); and putting together its prelims. Sometimes called front matter, this is the 'furniture' of a book that appears before the text proper. It usually includes a right-facing title page, followed overleaf by a copyright page outlining your company's name and address; a copyright ownership notice and standard 'All rights reserved' text; the ISBN, CIP details and edition number; and where it has been printed. This page of a book varies little, and picking up any published book will show you the standard to follow. Prelims following the copyright page might include a book's dedication, contents, preface, foreword and acknowledgements if there are any.

At the back of the book, end matter might include appendices, an index and bibliography, which also need to be thoroughly copy-edited. Indexes are compiled late on in the process, since all pages need to be firmly in place before they are cross-referenced. Contracts often put the responsibility for compiling an index on authors, who either do it themselves or pay to have it done professionally. The Society of Indexers is a good source of freelancers. If you are using one, typesetters may also offer an indexing service.

Editors will also need to brief whoever is designing the book, whether they are in-house or freelance. Designers should be given a very clear idea of what a book is about and who it is for so that they can devise a suitable look. Feed through any ideas you or the author may have for the cover design, typefaces and feel of the book. Editors should also be starting to think as soon as they can about the job of selling, marketing and publicizing the book so that it gets every chance of success. Good ones will be a book's champion within a company, convincing colleagues it will sell and suggesting ways how. See the Print and Production, Sales, Marketing and Publicity chapters for more on all of this.

STAFF AND SKILLS

Editorial staff tend to be regarded as the highest profile in publishing, and they are certainly pivotal in any company's output—even if they do not always have as much impact on its success as, say, their colleagues in sales. They often need to be jacks of all trades, with at least some of the skills required in other disciplines. Commissioning editors need to understand the basics of rights, marketing, publicity and sales, since all these things influence a decision to take on a book in the first place. A strong commercial nous—knowing whether a book is likely to sell and why—is important, as is the need to stay on top of publishing and consumer trends. Perhaps surprisingly for a creative profession, strong numeracy is essential, as editors will need to calculate the likely sales, costs and profitability of any book they take on. They need to be outward facing, confident in networking and enthusiastic enough about their publishing to be able to sweep others along with them.

Prerequisites for copy-editors are good communication skills, excellent command of language and a close eye for detail. Sound judgement and the ability to juggle jobs and hit deadlines are useful. Since more and more editing is being done digitally, so too is computer literacy. A keen interest in people, places and current affairs can be handy, as is the ability to cajole and sympathize with authors. Skills of diplomacy and negotiation are constantly called upon. Editors will often be contacted by designers, typesetters, indexers, publicists, sales and marketing people and others—many of them freelancers—and should have an interest in what these people do and need, if not necessarily an in-depth understanding.

For editors involved in specialist publishing—niche trade subjects as well as academic, scientific and professional sectors—knowledge relevant to that specialism is obviously crucial. So too is an understanding of the key players in those markets—both authors and readers—and a good contact book can be worth a great deal. Most publishers insist on degree qualifications as a minimum, though in some instances subject knowledge might be considered more important. Educational publishers often like to use teachers who know their material inside out, rather than an editor who knows lots about publishing but little about the subject.

In some ways, finding good editors is the hardest job of all in staff recruitment. If you get an outstanding one, do all you can to keep him or her. Recruiting for editorial jobs will bring you more applicants than for any other in publishing, but many will be speculative and non-specialist. When considering who to hire, it might be useful to see candidates in action. Present them with a page or so of unedited text, and ask them to get it ready for publication and then comment on it. You will soon be able to assess their eye for detail and judge if they can develop a book beyond simply correcting typos.

OUTSOURCING

Editorial functions are common ones to outsource. With more and more publishers preferring to use freelancers rather than employ extra staff, it is now possible to get external help with every facet of the editorial process, with copy-editing and proofreading among the most popular jobs to contract out.

It is even possible to get a book made for you without ever having to source an author, copy-edit anything or design any pages. Book packagers or contract publishers will do as many or as few of the publishing jobs as you like, from basic copy-editing to delivering ready-made books to your desk. Whether or not this is technically publishing is open to question—though it is still up to the client to market, publicize and sell the finished book, of course.

If you outsource, it is crucial to brief very carefully to ensure you get what you want. If you are contracting out copy-editing, for instance, specify the depth of editing you want and the exact tasks to be performed, and supply details of house style and the series format if relevant. Agree deadlines and fees upfront. If you are outsourcing more than a simple job, try to get several quotes for the work; ask for endorsements or examples of previous jobs; and get to know the people who will be doing it. Test any potential editors with a piece of work before you take them on; this is standard practice and all editors should be happy to prove their competence in a trial.

The Society for Editors and Proofreaders (SfEP) has guidelines for basic rates of freelance pay, as does the National Union of Journalists. By all means try to negotiate better rates, but be wary of freelancers working for rates well below others, since you generally get what you pay for. Much editorial outsourcing is now done to cheap, developing markets like India, where high standards of English language teaching make for a plentiful supply of labour.

Wherever you outsource, tread carefully, research all freelancers and companies, and test them before you hire them. Ask around in the IPG for recommendations, and use book fairs as a way of meeting outsourcing specialists. The SfEP is a very good source of copy-editors, proofreaders and other editorial support, with a directory of hundreds of members available for work that is searchable by specialism.

RESOURCES
TRADE ASSOCIATIONS AND SOCIETIES
Society for Editors and Proofreaders
A good place to learn more about the editorial process, with masses of advice for members. Also offers training and accreditation.
Web www.sfep.org.uk
Tel 020 8785 5617

Electric Editors
Online forum for editors, proofreaders, writers and publishers, with lots of resources to help with editing processes and style.
Web www.electriceditors.net

SOURCES OF AUTHORS

Association of Illustrators
Represents illustrators in all forms and a very good one-stop shop if you need some help illustrating a project. You can search artists and inspect portfolios online.
Web www.theaoi.com
Tel 020 7613 4328

Children's Illustrators
Online database of children's illustrators for publishers and agents, with portfolios of work to choose from.
Web www.childrensillustrators.com
Tel 0845 094 6407

Freelance Directory
Database of writers and editors from the National Union of Journalists.
Web www.freelancedirectory.org

Institute of Translation and Interpreting
An excellent source of book translators should you need one.
Web www.iti.org.uk
Tel 01908 325250

JacketFlap
Useful site for finding children's authors and illustrators.
Web www.jacketflap.com

National Union of Journalists
The book branch of the NUJ holds a database of freelancers and guidelines for pay.
Web www.nujbook.org

Society of Authors
The leading association for UK writers, with a searchable directory of members.
Web www.societyofauthors.org
Tel 020 7373 6642

Society of Children's Book Writers and Illustrators
UK branch of the worldwide association, providing advice to unpublished as
well as published authors.
Web www.britishcbwi.org

UK Children's Books
Databases of children's authors and illustrators—a useful resource if you want to
find someone to work on a particular book idea.
Web www.ukchildrensbooks.co.uk

AGENTS

Association of Authors' Agents
A good place to find out more about how literary agents work. Also has a code of
practice and a directory of members.
Web www.agentsassoc.co.uk

STYLE

Economist Style Guide
Renowned guide to house style for the weekly magazine, used as a template by
many publishers.
Web www.economist.com/research/styleguide

Plain English Campaign
Runs an editing service and has downloadable guides to help make all written
text crystal clear.
Web www.plainenglishcampaign.com
Tel 01663 744409

Times Style and Usage Guide
Another highly respected style guide. Like the *Economist*'s, also available in book
form.
Web www.timesonline.co.uk/tol/tools_and_services/specials/style_guide/

Write Better English
Online forum with the aim of raising standards of written English.
Web www.write-better-english.com

INDEXING

Society of Indexers
Professional body for indexing, with a list of freelancers and some useful resources.
Web www.indexers.org.uk
Tel 0114 244 9561

OUTSOURCING HELP

Freelance database
Directory of freelance members of the Society for Editors and Proofreaders available to hire.
Web www.sfep.org.uk/pub/dir/directory.asp
Tel 020 8785 5617

Book Production Consultants
Web www.bpccam.co.uk
Tel 01223 352790

Cambridge Publishing Management
Web www.cambridgepm.co.uk
Tel 01954 214000

Etica Press
Web www.eticapress.com
Tel 01684 565739

Keyline Consultancy
Web www.keyline-consultancy.co.uk
Tel 01636 822201

Publishing Services
Web www.publishing-services.co.uk
Tel 020 8222 6800

Sunrise Setting
Web www.sunrise-setting.co.uk
Tel 01803 322635

EDUCATIONAL DEVELOPMENTS

Department for Education
The government department for educational publishers to follow for details of curriculum changes and schools' requirements.
Web www.education.gov.uk
Tel 0870 000 2288

Qualifications and Curriculum Development Agency
The agency responsible for schools' curriculum and exam development. It provides useful updates for publishers serving the schools market.
Web www.qcda.gov.uk
Tel 0300 303 3010

Times Educational Supplement
An excellent source of news about schools and curriculum changes affecting publishers.
Web www.tes.co.uk
Tel 01858 438805

BOOKS

Book Commissioning and Acquisition by Gill Davies (Routledge, £18.99, 9780415317894)

Butcher's Copy-editing: The Cambridge Handbook for Editors, Copy-editors and Proofreaders by Judith Butcher, Caroline Drake and Maureen Leach (Cambridge University Press, £45, 9780521847131)

Clark's Publishing Agreements: A Book of Precedents (seventh edition) edited by Lynette Owen (Tottel Publishing, £85, 9781845927851). A discount on this book is available to IPG members buying direct from Tottel; see www.ipg.uk.com for details.

Copy-Editing by Barbara Horn (Horn Editorial Books, £45, 9780955340413)

Copyediting and Proofreading for Dummies by Suzanne Dilad (Wiley, £13.99, 9780470121719)

Editorial Project Management by Barbara Horn (Horn Editorial Books, £20, 9780955340403)

The Effective Editor's Handbook by Barbara Horn (PIRA International, £9.99, 9781858021867)

The Oxford Dictionary for Writers and Editors edited by Robert Ritter et al. (Oxford University Press, £12.99, 9780198610403)

The Oxford Style Manual (Oxford University Press, £25, 9780198605641)

Publishing Law by Hugh Jones (Routledge, £29.95, 9780415384278)

Usage and Abusage: A Guide to Good English by Eric Partridge (Penguin, £10.99, 9780140514421)

Writers' and Artists' Yearbook (A&C Black, £14.99, 9781408102640; updated annually)

3 PRINT AND PRODUCTION

CONTENTS

Production workflows / Designing a book / Sourcing extra material /
Cover design / Typesetting / Proofreading / Finding a printer / Paper /
Setting print runs / Print-on-demand / Digital production / Staff and skills /
Outsourcing / Resources

The production of a book is where a publisher really adds value to its content. No matter how well written or useful a book is, it will struggle to sell unless it is nicely designed, attractively presented and professionally printed. Standards of design and production have never been higher, and even the smallest of publishers needs to make their books as smart and appealing as possible. Books have only a matter of seconds to make a good impression on their prospective buyers, and each one needs to stand out from the crowd. Good independent publishers have the freedom and creativity to make this instant impact, giving their books every chance of success from the moment they reach bookshops' shelves.

PRODUCTION WORKFLOWS

As with most things in publishing, it is important to have proper workflows in production. Produce tight plans for what needs to be done to a book and when, and make sure you stick to them. Work backwards from the time you need to get finished books into your distributor's warehouse or ready for your own dispatch, usually a few weeks before the publication date; and forwards from the time you need to start working on the raw typescript, anything from four to twelve months earlier, depending on the amount of input required. In between, set down the points at which the book will be designed, typeset, proofread and printed, and allocate responsibility for each job, whether in or out of house.

Take the focus away from producing a book and on to engineering the workflow, and you will find that books are completed much more efficiently. Document your workflows and make sure everyone knows what happens when.

Try to keep the number of steps in the workflow to a minimum, and streamline unnecessary procedures. Documenting workflows reduces the chances of any nasty surprises or delays in the production process and strips out any duplication of jobs. If you can, identify someone in your business to set and analyse workflows. It might initially cost you time and money to do, but you will benefit in the long run from a much smoother operation.

It is also essential to bear in mind how the production function, department or person slots into the rest of the business. What do sales, marketing and publicity people need to know or obtain from a book while it is being produced? When do they need it? If you are to successfully sell your book in to shops you will need at least some basic information like the cover, format and look of the book well in advance of the printing of it. Make sure that parts of the production workflow like cover design run in parallel to other parts of your business.

At every stage of the production process, it is essential to manage, save and label your files diligently. Devise a system for storing your electronic files securely and logically, so that you can track back to them at any time. Some publishers have horror stories about sending an uncorrected version of a book to print and having to pulp the entire print run. Archiving and updating files properly will avoid any such calamities.

DESIGNING A BOOK

Good design starts with good preparation. Whether it is being done in or out of house, a sound, detailed brief—sometimes called a spec or specification—will make sure that the book gets the right look. This is something about which all sides of the business—author, editor, sales, marketing, publicity—should have a say. Each should outline what they expect the book to look like, based on its content and its intended audience. The spec will also cover the book's print and production budget, based on your overall costings for the book (see the Financial chapter for more on this).

Design will be influenced most of all by the format of book you choose. This needs to be done very carefully, as the wrong format can scupper a book's fortunes. Formats can vary widely, but very common ones are the A format and B format paperbacks, measuring 178 mm by 110 mm and 198 mm by 129 mm, and sometimes called mass market paperbacks and trade paperbacks, respectively. Hardback formats are less rigid, but popular ones include the royal octavo and demy octavo, measuring 234 mm by 156 mm and 216 mm by 138 mm respectively. If you are in doubt about which format to use, look at which ones your competitors are using. There's no obligation for you to mimic them, of course, but your books might well need to fit in with a certain look. A debut novel published in A4 hardback would look very odd in the marketplace, for instance, as would a school textbook in mass market paperback format. When weighing up formats, consider how the printing process will affect them—paper and production costs are generally lower for standard size books than they are for unusual formats.

Specs also need to consider page layout. Specify the following: typeface (which may need to be bought); font size (usually based on the length you want the book to be and how tight you want the text to be set); text layout, whether justified or unjustified; headers and footers, usually incorporating the book or chapter name and page number respectively; and the style of any tables, graphs, panels and captions you will use. A well laid out page is neatly organized and easy on the eye, helping the reader through it as effortlessly as possible. Consistency is vital, so make sure things like tables and quotations are presented in exactly the same way every time. When setting the extent of your books, remember too that they are printed not page by page but in spreads of 8, 16, 32 or 48 pages. As a result, most books have a total page length that is a multiple of one of these.

Because many small publishers don't have the design skills to produce a professional book, it is very common to outsource this job, probably to a local designer within easy reach. Some IPG members offer design services for fellow publishers, and printers can sometimes help with design and getting a book ready for press. If you want to save money, students at nearby universities or art colleges might help out at reduced rates or even for free in return for a reference. But the best way of keeping costs down, of course, is to do the job yourself. Design software is becoming more and more user-friendly, and either of the two leading publishing packages, Adobe InDesign or Quark XPress, are recommended, if not exactly cheap. Set aside plenty of time to get to know the software, and ask around in the IPG if you have any difficulties with it; plenty of members are experienced in using both. If you want to get serious about design, there are plenty of books available to teach you the finer details of the art.

Whether or not you choose to outsource will probably depend on the type of books you are publishing—highly illustrated, full colour reference books would certainly benefit from a professional design, for instance, whereas a 200-page black and white novel could probably be laid out in-house. The process is also easier if you can work to a standard design, fitting your books into pre-set templates. This is particularly easy if your books are part of a series, but even if they are quite different, establishing a basic template to work from will save a lot of time and money. In publishing workflows, it pays to standardize as much as possible. At the risk of homogenizing publishing, as with the format it is worth getting your books looking roughly like your competitors' versions. For most subjects there is a fairly standard look and feel to books, and both customers and booksellers will expect new titles to embrace that template.

Designing a book is a lot easier if you get your raw material in the most suitable format in the first place. So impress on your author the need to get his or her material as ready for layout as possible, and draw up some tight guidelines about the style in which you would like things presented. See the Editorial chapter for more tips on working with authors to save you time in design and production.

SOURCING EXTRA MATERIAL

Even if you can master design yourself, there are likely to be some things that you will have to outsource as you prepare a book. An army of illustrators, artists, photographers, cartographers and others are available to help; see Resources for some contact details. Brief freelancers like these on jobs as far ahead as you can, and factor plenty of time into the design process for delays in the supply and revision of material.

Non-fiction publishers will probably need to source photography in particular from third parties. This can be done via a specialist picture researcher, who can work to a brief of what is required. If all the material is on a single subject—photos of food for a cookery book, for instance—you could commission a photographer to set up a photoshoot. If you want to track down existing material for your own use, reference libraries, museums, picture agencies and professional societies can all be helpful. For specialist academic or professional subjects, university libraries or staff might be a good place to start. You will usually have to pay reproduction or licence fees, request permission and give proper acknowledgement in your book, but you should be able to find value by shopping around. If you are using a picture researcher, brief him or her carefully on the money you have to spend.

Once illustrations have been sourced, they have to be got ready for print. You can do this yourself, scanning and saving files in a format approved by the printer (usually jpegs or tiffs); or get a specialist reproduction (repro) house to do it all for you.

COVER DESIGN

The layout of a book's pages is very important, but its cover design is crucial. The front and back has to show the browser at a glance what the book is about, and in many cases they present the only opportunity to convince a reader to buy. They will also be a major factor in a retailer's decision to stock and promote the book. Covers must be different enough to stand out from the competition, but familiar enough to show at a glance what it is about. Aim to make your books look like the others it is competing against in the market—only better. Simple and striking is the rule. Avoid closely detailed covers that need deciphering and that do not reproduce well in miniature—as thumbnails on internet retailer websites or in your catalogues, for instance.

Unless you have a talent for design and a very good understanding of your market, and even if you are doing the rest of a book's layout yourself, consider hiring a freelance designer to produce your cover. He or she will be able to come up with good ideas, tweak them until you are happy, and source any photographs or illustrations that are needed. Provide freelancers with a clear brief and agree the status of rights to the design; you need to be sure that you can use it again in the future without having to seek permission every time.

A book's cover is required by various people—including bibliographic agencies and retailers—well in advance of publication. Cover design can change, of course, but try to settle on a look as far ahead of publication as possible; ideally at least six months. As with layout, make sure the people who will sell the book are happy with the cover design, and run it past your authors, for whom covers can mean a great deal. Don't forget that covers need to incorporate standard material like an ISBN, bar code and, usually, price. Take a look at other books to see the typical presentation, and see the Bibliographic and IT chapter for more on ISBNs and bar codes.

TYPESETTING

The art of typesetting—preparing the text and other content of a book's pages for printing—has been turned into more of a science by computer software and automation. Some think it is dying out altogether as a distinct part of the publishing process. Many small publishers are quite happy to typeset their books themselves, using software packages to organize the flow of their books from page to page, while others leave the job to their freelance designers. In some cases, with the right experience and software, authors may be able to do the typesetting job themselves.

Plenty of dedicated typesetters do remain, however, and they are worth considering for jobs where a high quality of text layout is important, or if the job is particularly fiddly—as in scientific texts with lots of formulae, symbols, notations and so on. Some typesetters also now specialize in setting up books for delivery on electronic platforms (see below). The Society for Editors and Proofreaders is a good source of qualified typesetting experts in the UK, but cheaper labour costs mean that many more are now found in developing countries like India. Book fairs are a good place to meet these offshore specialists.

PROOFREADING

Once a book's material has been designed and typeset, it is proofread. This is a job usually done by both the author and publisher, though sometimes by one of them only. It is a convenient and relatively inexpensive job for publishers to outsource to a freelance proofreader, who can bring professional experience and a fresh pair of eyes to the job. The Society for Editors and Proofreaders is an excellent place to find one, and most experienced IPG members will be able to recommend good people. The SfEP recommends hourly rates of around £20 for proofreaders, though this is at the high end of the scale for most publishers, and most will work through roughly ten pages of standard text an hour. Flat or page rates may also be available.

Proofreading involves checking a book very carefully for spelling and typing errors and making sure that authors, editors, designers and typesetters have completed their jobs properly. Proofreaders should make sure that the text, style and design is consistent throughout and adheres to any style guide that is being used. They should also highlight anything that is not clear or correct in the text and check material against previous versions if necessary. Proofreaders mark the text with notes, marks and symbols, the standard guide for which is produced by the British Standards Institution and available to buy from its website. Some publishers prefer to develop their own set of proofreading marks for use on all their products to ensure consistency in style.

There are likely to be a number of proofreading stages. This is not the time to edit the text again or make substantial changes, but it is an opportunity to ensure that there are no errors or out-of-date information. By the time final proofs are issued (sometimes known as sign-off proofs), the production process is quite advanced and even minor changes may have a substantial impact if they affect pagination or layout. It's important, therefore, to make only necessary changes.

Authors should be given very clear guidelines about proofreading in order to reduce the workload for you. If they are not familiar with them, provide a guide to proofreading symbols and style. Indicate very clearly when you want to receive completed proofs back. Make sure everyone knows what stage a book is at in the proofing process at all times.

Proofreading in the past involved sending bulky packages of pages backwards and forwards in the post, but it can now usually be done by email or over the web. Many publishers now email their authors a proof version of their book, while some have FTP (File Transfer Protocol) websites where they can post proofs for authors to pick up. Authors can then either mark up the proofs electronically—special software is available to enable this, Adobe being the most popular source—or print out the pages before emailing a list of corrections for the publisher to make. Since email communications are much quicker, cheaper and more reliable than the post, proofing like this saves time and money.

Proofreading is an iterative process, requiring as much work as necessary to ensure that everyone is happy with the final product, but that doesn't mean that you shouldn't set a deadline for production and stick to it. Once the final proof copy has been signed off by author and publisher, return it to your typesetter or designer for correction or do so yourself before gathering it together in a master file or cluster of files. Your printer will indicate the file type best suited to their requirements, but it is usually a PDF (Portable Document Format), something that is easily produced from desktop and design packages. Files can be supplied by email, FTP or disk.

FINDING A PRINTER

Choosing a printer will be influenced by the type of books you are producing. Some printers specialize in full colour illustrated books, for instance, while others focus on low cost black and white paperbacks. The largest will take on almost any type of project. Depending on how many titles you have to print, you can get quotes from printers on either a job-by-job basis or—if you have a lot of books on your forward publishing list—a longer term contract of a year or more. Most publishers use no more than two or three printers, and many use just one.

Whatever your print requirements, it is worth tendering for a shortlist of printers to choose from. Start by drawing up a technical specification for your book or books, outlining format, size and length, the quality of paper and finish you are seeking and the print run you require. Supply it to a selection of printers—or complete the online quotation forms offered by many—and draw up a table to compare prices and services and assess which is the best. Unless you are printing very few copies, always try to use a recognized book specialist rather than a general printer; most people will instantly be able to see the difference in quality between the two.

Remember that price is not the only thing to consider when weighing up options. Ask as many fellow IPG members and publishing colleagues as you can for recommendations—a straw poll of a dozen or so companies will soon give you an idea of printers' reputations. If you want to find a printer close to you, use the online directory of British Printing Industries Federation members, searchable by location.

Ask printers for samples of books they have printed so you can see if their production quality is up to scratch. Check turnaround times and try to assess their ability to meet your deadlines. Look closely at price estimates for breakdowns and hidden extras; the price per unit that is quoted is not always as simple as it looks. Visit printers if you can, since this gives you a good idea of capabilities and the people you will be working with, and an excellent sense for whether or not your two companies will be a good fit. Even if your knowledge of printing is limited, you should also be able to tell from your visit whether a company's machinery is in good order and up to date in technological terms.

An important consideration for all publishers lately has been whether to print in the UK or abroad. The UK has plenty of advantages: quality is, generally, excellent; delivery times can be rapid because finished books do not have far to travel; you will be able to stay in close contact with the company providing your books; and you will be supporting other UK businesses. But printing overseas has its plus points too, the most important of which is price. Italian, Spanish and Eastern European printers provide very competitive quotes on illustrated colour books in particular, while companies in India, China and elsewhere in Asia are excellent value for an increasing variety of books. Low costs in these and other territories have hit British printing hard, sending a large number of printers to the wall in the last decade. Again, recommendations from fellow IPG members are the best way to find good, reliable overseas printers, and book fairs are excellent places to meet them in person.

Printing overseas, while cheap, can be time-consuming, since books will have to be shipped or trucked back to Britain then forwarded on. Some publishers use Asian or Eastern European printers if they have plenty of time, but British ones if they need books in a hurry. Much will depend on the turnaround times you are working to. Educational publishers, for instance, often have to respond quickly to curriculum changes, and would face long and damaging delays if they printed overseas. The cheap prices quoted by overseas printers can soon escalate once transportation and storage costs are added in, and you can save distribution costs if you print locally. If you are printing small quantities, it may even be worth printing very close by and picking up the books in a car or van yourself. Fluctuating currency rates will also affect deals, and a weak pound can make cheap overseas deals look less attractive.

Environmental concerns might influence your decision about where to print. Shipping books halfway across the world undoubtedly adds to publishers' carbon footprints, and the environmental credentials of many printers in Asia in particular are not as strong as their British counterparts. For more about green issues in printing, see the Publishing and the Environment chapter.

Wherever you decide to print, don't be afraid to haggle on price. Although the number of British printers has fallen substantially, it is still a competitive industry where supply outstrips demand. And remember too that payment terms can be just as important as price—if not more so. Negotiating longer payment terms frees up cash in your business, and you should aim for a cash neutral situation such that payment for sales comes into your account before you pay your printer. If you have to pay your printer within 30 days but don't get paid for sales by your distributor until 90 days, for instance, then you have a clear shortfall that could cause cash flow problems. Try to negotiate generous payment terms to make best use of your cash.

An annual review of prices and services will help to keep your suppliers on their toes. Frequent reviews are also essential because printing technology is changing so fast, and you need to be certain that your printer is meeting your requirements. If you're not happy with the way your work is being handled, tell your supplier and ask them to improve their service and/or lower their prices. If they can't, look elsewhere.

PAPER

Large publishers buy the paper on which to print their books from a paper mill, merchant or wholesaler, using their size to negotiate good deals. If you want to do the same, the National Association of Paper Merchants is a good place to start. The majority of smaller independents, though, will find it easier to get their paper direct from whichever printer they are using. Printers will be able to suggest and source suitable papers for each job, and will have choices to suit all books and budgets. Paper is more expensive this way, but unless you are buying in large quantities it is rarely cost or time effective to source paper yourself.

Whichever way you get it, it pays to learn a little about the choices of paper on offer. Things to think about include weight, measured in grams per square metre (GSM); and bulk or thickness, measured in microns. Short books can be made to feel longer by using paper that is high in bulk and weight, while long ones feel shorter if they use less bulky paper. Paper that is high in bulk and weight generally feels more luxurious, but don't forget to consider how the thickness and weight of a book will affect its dimensions and, as a result, your costs. Big, heavy books can cost a lot more to distribute and post, paring away at your margins. Chunky, outsize books might also be tricky for retailers to shelve.

If it is important to you, consider also the shade of your paper, which can be cream rather than white. You will have to specify if you want it coated or finished or not, and you may also want to know its opacity—the extent to which you can see through a paper and, hence, see the print on the reverse of a page. Your choice will also depend on how you want a book bound, whether sewn or glued—this is something that will usually be done by your printer, though it is possible to get your books bound elsewhere if you want a particular, specialist finish to them. With all paper matters, ask your printer for guidance if you're not sure what qualities are important for your book. They can also advise on, and usually source, extras like marker ribbons, inserts, slip cases and cover stickers.

As with most things in printing, paper sourcing is the subject of much debate when it comes to environmental consequences. If you are concerned about where the pulp for your books has come from and the consequences for the world's forests, you might choose to print on paper that is either fully recycled or certified by the Forest Stewardship Council. There is also a cross-publishing scheme called PREPS that allows members to check the environmental credentials of various papers before you use them. See the Publishing and the Environment chapter for more.

SETTING PRINT RUNS

Selecting a printer will also be influenced by your print run. Getting this right is crucial. Being left with too many copies of a book brings unnecessary costs, but having too few means lost sales. Research your market as carefully as you can and be realistic in your estimates about sales. Too many print runs are set on what a publisher hopes to sell rather than expects to sell. Publishers should generally aim to keep enough copies of a book in stock to last about a year—less if you are publishing in popular trade sectors, and more if you're publishing in very specialist niches. Don't forget to factor into your print runs six copies for legal deposit (see Bibliographic and IT chapter for more on this); copies for your author (most contracts stipulate ten free ones, with more available to buy at a discount); and any copies you want to send out for marketing or publicity purposes.

Forecasting print runs is done in different ways. For publishers large enough to have sales reps, gathering feedback from booksellers about the potential of a book can be very useful. Paying for access to sales data from Nielsen BookScan will give you an accurate record of previous sales for an author or for similar books. But even if you have a wealth of data and research, predicting sales and setting print runs is at best an imprecise science and at worst guesswork.

As a rule, the greater the number of books you print the cheaper the price per unit becomes. But be careful not to be lured into printing too many books, and remember that you can always return for reprints, which need to be judged equally carefully and ordered far enough in advance to ensure you don't run out of stock. Reprinting may incur you further set-up costs, but paying a little extra for short runs that you can sell is better than being left with a large pile of unsold books. Because they have prepared your book for printing once already, printers can turn round additional print runs quicker than the first. For more on forecasting, see the Sales chapter.

PRINT-ON-DEMAND

Publishers' strategies have long followed the pattern of printing and then selling, but this model has always carried risks. One is that a publisher will print too many books, tying up cash in stock and perhaps being left with piles of unsold copies; another is that not enough books will be printed, leaving it unable to satisfy demand. The first is unsatisfactory for publishers; the second is frustrating for booksellers and authors.

But the traditional model started to change from the mid-1990s, when digital printing technology opened up another way of doing things—printing *after* sales are secured. This has evolved into print on demand (POD), whereby publishers can produce books in whatever quantities they need to satisfy the market on a short-term basis.

It is a method of printing that has grown in popularity fast, and its advantages can be substantial. POD cuts the waste of books, which is good for cashflow and the environment. It slashes returns, since unwanted books are not printed in the first place. And it means that books can, in theory, be kept in print forever, their content stored digitally and then brought to life as and when required. This is very good for backlist titles that might otherwise go out of print, or for previously discontinued books that can now be revived, and it removes the need for tricky decisions around whether to reprint a book or send it out of print.

The quality of POD books has improved drastically, to the point that most people would not now be able to tell the difference from a copy printed with the offset method. Speed has accelerated too, and a well-oiled supply chain of printers, distributors and wholesalers means orders can be printed and supplied in a timeframe that is comparable to traditional printing and distribution.

POD take-up has been particularly high among small independents, who can get their books into print at a far lower cost than previously. It also reduces risk, since big upfront print orders are no longer required, and this can help publishers to test the waters in new or niche markets before making bigger commitments to them. Publishers are now starting to emerge that will only ever employ POD.

For much the same reasons, POD has become very popular with self-published authors too. For both, its use has grown amid the rise in ebook sales, which has meant that fewer print titles are now needed in many sectors of publishing. POD is an excellent way to maintain the momentum of print sales in this changing landscape.

Printers in the POD space have been led by the Ingram group of companies, which first launched a digital printing service in 1997 called Lightning Print. This has evolved into Lightning Source, which now prints around two million books a month from a list of some 11 million titles, with an average order of about 1.8 copies. Other printers have followed Ingram into the market, both in the UK and around the world; see the Resources section at the end of the chapter for details. A notable new arrival has been Amazon, which uses its own POD service to keep many of its titles constantly available.

Choosing a POD supplier should be done with care. Alongside price, print quality and speed of supply are the main things to bear in mind, and publishers need to be sure that suppliers have the digital printing, IT and distribution infrastructures to provide a consistent service. There is a distinction to be made between companies that offer ultra-short print runs and those who can genuinely provide a single-order, single-print service. Publishers should also think about POD from a contractual point of view, since a recent trend has been for authors to reclaim rights on neglected books and publish themselves. Consider how your authors' contracts allocate rights and define out of print, because POD has made this once common term virtually obsolete.

DIGITAL PRODUCTION

Whereas production departments would once only turn words and pictures into bound books, now they have to prepare content for any number of electronic platforms too.

The best way to do this is to use the XML (eXtensible Mark-up Language) format to tag material. This is one of the most user-friendly of the various mark-up formats, and is designed to help structure all the various information in a document. Once tagged with XML, content can flow very neatly and easily into a huge number of electronic platforms like web-based e-books or hand-held readers. So, if your material is in XML, you will find it much easier to convert it into formats that you can sell, and take advantage of any new digital channels that might emerge, as well as allowing them to be produced in any format of print book too. Put simply, XML future-proofs your content.

If you do not start to use XML now, it is likely that you will have to do so at some point in the future, leaving you with a long list of books to convert and a larger bill than if you start doing it now. It needn't be a daunting job, and publishers can either learn how to work in XML themselves or get one of a growing number of specialists to mark up books for them. More and more designers and typesetters in the UK are offering an XML service and—as with these jobs—it is becoming a popular one to outsource. The world's XML hub is India, where the combination of English language and IT skills has produced a deep pool of specialists. Many exhibit at book fairs, which are a useful opportunity to get to know them. If you want to control the flow of your content across a lot of different platforms, it might also be worth investing in a Content Management System (CMS). See the E-publishing chapter for more on XML and digital delivery.

STAFF AND SKILLS

For a publisher large enough to be able to afford separate staff resources for design and production, it's important to get the right mix of skills. These people can make the difference between a professionally produced, desirable book and a rushed, error-strewn job.

Most book designers start their careers with a professional qualification. They need a mix of technical expertise and commercial nous, combining a knowledge of typography and software packages with a sound awareness of what motivates and influences book buyers. Designers need to work well to briefs, interpreting the requirements of colleagues and customers alike. Pestered by editors, authors, printers and many others, they need to juggle projects and do their best to keep everyone happy, even if that's usually impossible. Good freelance contacts and the ability to manage them effectively are useful.

Proofreaders need a forensic eye for detail, very good knowledge of English and sound judgement. Good communication skills are useful, as the job may require tact in raising queries with authors and editors. Depending on your subject matter, specialist skills may also be required—a detailed scientific academic text will demand close understanding of the subject, for instance. A highly organized, clear mind is the hallmark of a good proofreader.

If you are a large enough company to have someone dedicated to managing production, look for professional qualifications and an in-depth knowledge of printing, buying and logistics. Strong project management and numeracy skills are vital, and the ability to negotiate with suppliers and freelancers to get the best possible deal is very useful. Like designers, they are caught in the middle of editors and printers, and will face pressure and demands from both.

Publishers with more than a few books should get their design and production staff to follow—and perhaps devise in the first place—a house style that sets out guidelines for the style, format and look you want your books to have. See the Editorial chapter for more on this.

OUTSOURCING

Design and production jobs are some of the most common to be outsourced in publishing. Many small publishers rely on freelancers and agencies for every stage of the publishing process from copy-editing onwards, and while you will obviously have to pay for it, there is a vast pool of talent out there to draw from. Outsourcing gives you access to first-rate professionals, many with long track records in publishing, that you would not be able to employ on a full-time basis.

As with most outsourcing jobs, getting and following personal recommend-ations is the key to success. Ask around in the IPG for suggestions. Reputations about freelancers spread quickly, whether good or bad, and you will soon start to recognize names. Also search the IPG's online membership database, since some of our service members associates specialize in design and production services. If you want help with a specific service, you might also consider asking IPG members for tips via the e-bulletin or forum. Industry societies like the Society for Editors and Proofreaders can also be a good place to find freelancers. Before you hire any freelancer, inspect CVs and samples of work closely, test anyone whose abilities you are unsure about, and produce a clear, tight, written brief for them to work from, outlining the jobs to be done and the agreed rates of pay.

Whether or not you outsource will depend on how flexible you want your business to be. Some publishers prefer to keep everything in-house, but even if you think you have a heavy publishing programme, be wary of taking on too many production staff as you will have to continue paying them even when things are quiet. But be equally wary of outsourcing too much and making your business too reliant on the expertise of other people. As with printers and all your suppliers, keep a close eye on the work being done for you out of house and review your pool of freelancers on a regular basis to make sure you are getting the best people and the best value.

RESOURCES
DESIGN SOFTWARE
Adobe
Now overtaking Quark as publishing's market-leading package. Produces InDesign, Photoshop, Acrobat and an all-in Creative Suite package.
Web www.adobe.com
Tel 020 8606 1100

Quark
Produces XPress and other publishing-specific products.
Web www.quark.com
Tel 0800 1787 8275

PROOFREADING
National Union of Journalists
Database of freelancers and guidelines for pay.
Web www.nujbook.org/freelance

Society for Editors and Proofreaders
Downloadable advice on proofreading standards and techniques.
Web www.sfep.org.uk
Tel 020 8785 5617

Standard proofreading marks and symbols
The British Standards Institution looks after the standard (number BS 5261-2:2005).
Web www.standardsuk.com
Tel 0845 367 0242
See the Resources section of the Editorial chapter for links to some online style guides for use in proofreading.

UK BOOK PRINTERS

Select Printer
Directory of members of the British Printing Industries Federation, searchable by specialism and location—a good starting point for finding a printer.
Web www.selectprinter.com

Berforts
Web www.berforts.co.uk
Tel 01424 722733

Butler, Tanner & Dennis
Web www.butlertanneranddennis.com
Tel 01373 451500

Clays
Web www.clays.co.uk
Tel 01986 893211

CPI Group (Cox & Wyman, Mackays, Antony Rowe)
Web www.cpi-group.net
Tel 0118 953 0500 (Cox & Wyman); 01634 864381 (Mackays); 01249 659705 (Antony Rowe)

Cromwell Press
Web www.cromwellpress.co.uk
Tel 01225 711400

Hobbs
Web www.hobbs.uk.com
Tel 023 8066 4800

Lightning Source
Web www.lightningsource.co.uk
Tel 0845 121 4567

MPG Books (Biddles)
Web www.mpg-books.co.uk
Tel 01208 73266

MRT
Web www.mrtbooks.co.uk
Tel 01761 241761

Print on Demand Worldwide
Web www.printondemand-worldwide.com
Tel 01733 237867

RDW Digital
Web www.rdwdigital.co.uk
Tel 01484 534323

PAPER

Forest Stewardship Council
Runs certification schemes to indicate if a type of paper has been properly and sustainably sourced.
Web www.fsc-uk.org
Tel 01686 413916

National Association of Paper Merchants
A good place to find a supplier for the paper you need to print your books.
Web www.napm.org.uk
Tel 0115 841 2129

Prelims
Online umbrella group for publishers wanting to find ways of making their manufacture processes more ethical and environmentally friendly.
Web www.prelims.org

PREPS
A co-operative database to help publishers assess the environmental credentials of various choices of paper.
Web www.preps-uk.com
Tel 020 7812 7130

Programme for the Endorsement of Forestry Certification
Cross-Europe scheme to promote ethically sourced paper.
Web www.pefc.org
Tel 00 41 22 799 45 40

PRINTING ASSOCIATIONS AND NEWS
British Association for Print and Communication
Trade association for graphic arts, print and communication.
Web www.bapc.co.uk
Tel 020 8736 5862

British Printing Industries Federation
Main body for UK printers and a good source of information about printing in general.
Web www.britishprint.com
Tel 020 7405 4085

Print Week
Trade press covering news and views in the printing industry.
www.print-week.com
Tel 020 8267 4397

FREELANCE HELP
IPG
Associate members can provide help with many design, production and printing jobs.
Web www.ipg.uk.com
Tel 01437 563335

Association of Illustrators
Useful for help with cover design in particular.
Web www.theaoi.com
Tel 020 7613 4328

Association of Photographers
Database of UK photographers available for hire, searchable by specialism and location, with folios of work available to view.
Web www.the-aop.org
Tel 020 7739 6669

British Association of Picture Libraries and Agencies
Excellent starting point for finding suppliers of images for your books.
Web www.bapla.org.uk
Tel 020 7713 1780

Chartered Society of Designers
Searchable directory of accredited UK designers in various specialisms.
Web www.csd.org.uk
Tel 020 7357 8088

Children's Illustrators
Online database of children's illustrators with portfolios of work.
Web www.childrensillustrators.com
Tel 0845 094 6407

Picture Research Association
Trade body for picture editors and researchers, with a register of freelance members available for work and some useful advice about obtaining pictures for use in books.
Web www.picture-research.org.uk
Tel 020 7739 8544

Publishing Training Centre
Database of accredited freelancers in various disciplines.
Web www.train4publishing.co.uk
Tel 020 8874 2718

Society of Cartographers
A good place to start if you need help with maps for your books.
Web www.soc.org.uk

Society for Editors and Proofreaders
An ideal starting point if you're looking for freelance help, with a database of accredited members indexed by subject, skills and location.
Web www.sfep.org.uk
Tel 020 8785 5617

PRIZES

British Book Design and Production Awards
Prizes to encourage high standards of design and production.
Web www.britishbookawards.org
Tel 020 7915 8338

BOOKS

The All New Print Production Handbook by David Bann (Rotovision, £20, 9782940361380)

Book Design by Andrew Haslam (Laurence King, £24.95, 9781856694735)

Bookmaking: Editing, Design, Production by Marshal Lee (Norton, £32, 9780393730180)

Book Typography: A Designer's Manual by Michael Mitchell and Susan Wightman (Libanus Press, £35, 9780948021664)

A Designer's Guide to Adobe InDesign and XML by James Maivaid with Cathy Palmer (Adobe, £31.99, 9780321503558)

Guardian Dictionary of Publishing and Printing (A&C Black, £9.99, 9780713675894)

New Book Design by Roger Fawcett-Tang (Laurence King, £25, 9781856693660)

On Book Design by Richard Hendel (Yale University Press, £25, 9780300075700)

The Oxford Style Manual (Oxford University Press, £25, 9780198605641)

The Picture Researcher's Handbook by Hilary Evans (PIRA International, £65, 9781858023403)

Print-on-Demand Book Publishing by Morris Rosenthal (Foner Books, £9.95 9780972380133)

Teach Yourself XML in 24 Hours by Michael Morrison (SAMS, £22.50, 9780672327971)

Type and Typography by Phil Baines et al. (Laurence King, £22.50, 9781856694377)

Writers' and Artists' Yearbook (A&C Black, £14.99, 9781408102640; updated annually)

XML in Easy Steps by Mike McGrath (Computer Step, £10.99, 9781840783377)

4 SALES

CONTENTS

Sales strategies and forecasts / Terms and negotiations / Returns / Pricing / Chain bookshops / Independent bookshops / Wholesalers / Internet retailers / Supermarkets / Sales and marketing promotions / Special and direct sales / Remainder sales / Academic and schools sales / Library sales / Sales representation / Export sales / Staff, skills and help / Resources

Selling books is tough—perhaps tougher than ever. In the trade, fierce competition means that publishers have to fight for every inch of space they can get in retailers—and if they do get their books on the shelves, high discounts and the possibility of returns present barriers to profitability. In academic and educational sectors, meanwhile, pressures on buyers' budgets forces publishers to scrap for every sale. Whether selling books in to retailers and institutions or out again to readers and students, publishers have to work hard for their money. But despite the mounting challenges, there are still plenty of sales avenues for publishers to pursue and plenty of buyers interested in your content. Whether you decide to sell books yourself or get someone else to do it for you, investing time, energy and money in sales should pay off on the bottom line.

SALES STRATEGIES AND FORECASTS

Selling books starts well before they are published. As early as you can, work out where a book is likely to sell and who to, and project if it is going to earn enough to exceed your costs. If it's not, you probably shouldn't be commissioning it in the first place, unless you are happy to lose money on it. See the Editorial chapter for much more on acquisition strategies.

Forecasting sales is something that every publisher finds a challenge and a gamble. Doing it well requires a blend of experience and intuition, and it is something that everyone gets wrong at one time or another. To improve your forecasts, try to break them down as much as possible. Split your potential market up into segments and try to estimate sales through each. In academic, professional or educational publishing, the scale of possible sales should be easier to calculate, but in the trade, where potential is more difficult to gauge, it might help to split the market into chains, independents, the internet and specialists.

Be realistic, and don't assume that every channel will be interested in your books. Try to predict the pattern of your sales too—is this a topical book that will sell for a few months and disappear, or one that will sell on for years? Sketch a graph of your predicted demand. Involve as many people as you can in forecasting; acquiring editors in particular should have a good idea of how a book will sell. Once the budget is set, it should then be owned and monitored by whoever in the business is in charge of sales. Remember that commissioning a book is like investing in a market—something that is done with no cast-iron guarantee of a return but that should be based on reasoning rather than emotion.

Sales estimates, together with firm advance orders, sometimes called sub or subscription orders, can help you set print runs for your books. But they will not take into account late orders or the effects of any marketing and publicity campaign ahead of publication, which can increase orders at the last minute. So publishers must print enough copies to satisfy unexpected demand, but not so many as to be left with piles of unsold stock. It is a difficult balance to strike, but as a rule, it's probably best to forecast cautiously and print too few books than too many; that way you won't be disappointed by low sales and you won't have money tied up in wasted stock. Some of the worries in forecasting sales have been eased by the advent of print-on-demand, which allows publishers to respond very quickly to demand and to print small quantities for small orders. For more on this and setting print runs, see the Print and Production chapter.

Some publishers use forecasting software to help predict demand, though most general packages on the market will not be able to factor in the fluctuations in demand that are peculiar to publishing. Some also use data from Nielsen BookScan, the agency monitoring book sales at point of sale from retailers across the UK. This can, for instance, show you sales figures and patterns for an author's previous books, or books on a similar subject to your own—but remember that past performance is not always a reliable indicator of future performance. The data can be too expensive for many small publishers, though limited slices of data are available for smaller budgets and the IPG occasionally negotiates special deals. And its coverage is also far from comprehensive in some non-traditional areas of book sales like direct mail, making it a far less effective tool for specialist publishers.

When forecasting, remember the difference between budgets—an honest assessment of what you expect a book to give you—and targets—which can help you to set priorities for your sales strategies. Remember also the distinction between volume and value, and base forecasts on the money you'll make rather than the number of copies you'll sell.

TERMS AND NEGOTIATIONS

All publishers have to open accounts and negotiate terms of trade with the people who will sell their books. These typically offer the retailer a discount on the recommended retail price (RRP) of your book. The level of this will depend on both the type of book and the seller you are dealing with. Publishers of very specialist professional or academic information with little competition, for instance, might give sellers as little as 10 to 20% discount, while textbooks might approach 30 to 40%. General books with plenty of competition might sell to high street independent booksellers at a similar or slightly higher rate, and to chains or supermarkets at 50 to 60% or more. These larger retailers do sometimes accept that smaller publishers cannot afford the high discounts offered by the publishing heavyweights, and may be prepared to settle around 45% as a base for discount. Terms of payment are usually between 30 and 60 days. Extra margin of 10 to 15% must be allowed for sales to wholesalers, since they will have to take their slice of revenue.

Retailers' discount usually increases in line with their power and influence on the market. Independent booksellers buying single copies of a book from wholesalers will, for instance, command a lower discount than a chain or supermarket buying thousands of copies direct. As with all sales negotiations, your book will only be worth what someone is prepared to pay for it, but that does not mean you will not be able to haggle over terms. At some point, all publishers will face pressure to agree to terms they think are too steep, and whether you walk away from an unsatisfactory deal will depend on how important that sales channel is to you. Whether you offer preferential terms to your key customers or try to give the same flat rate to everyone, regardless of size or importance, is another decision you will have to take.

Sales operations may also have to consider whether to take part in retailers' promotional campaigns like three-for-two offers or 'Book of the Week' deals, though these will usually be at the invitation of retailers. See below for more on the pros and cons of these promotions.

RETURNS

Deals between publishers and retailers or wholesalers are either firm sale, whereby the buyer pays up front (or, rather, usually on terms of 30 to 60 days) and carries all responsibility for selling the books on; or sale or return, whereby the buyer can return any books that have not sold. Because firm sale is risky for booksellers and invariably requires a greater discount from publishers, sale or return is still very much the norm in the trade at least. One popular form of it is consignment or see-safe sales, whereby retailers are able to return books within a specified period, with payment for any copies sold due at the end of that period.

As a result, returns can be a major blight. In trade publishing it is not unusual to have one in four books—or more—returned to publishers unsold, though in academic, educational and STM publishing the proportion is much lower because those buying the books to sell on can be more precise about demand. Returns are in exchange for credit, to be used to purchase other books, and booksellers usually bear the cost of returning the book to the publisher or distributor. Returned books are then recycled—either by selling them again elsewhere or by pulping them. Another option is to give them away, perhaps to a local charity or a global one like Book Aid International.

High returns can play havoc with publishers' cash flow, especially if they appear without warning several months after they have been sent out, or if royalties on them have already been paid on the assumption that the books have been sold. For this reason, publishers often hold back a certain amount of royalties as a provision against future returns.

Returns can be reduced if publishers and retailers work more closely to forecast sales more accurately. Persuading retailers to take smaller quantities of books than they'd like might seem counter-intuitive, but it may be in publishers' best interests in the long term. There are some signs that environmental concerns about the waste produced by returns is pushing some publishers and retailers towards more firm sale deals. Another weapon against returns is print-on-demand, which allows books to be printed in small quantities as demand requires.

Returns are also the subject of much work by Book Industry Communications (BIC). Its Industry Returns Initiative (IRI) means participating publishers, distributors and retailers must request, confirm and credit returns electronically, and stipulates that they cannot be authorized until three months after publication; or after 15 months since the last supply of the book. Those who sign up to the initiative also agree to adhere to other industry standard rules, and it has made returns less burdensome to administer, even if it hasn't fully solved the problem of them for publishers. Also worth investigating is the Batch Returns system, which helps retailers to use the IRI. For most small publishers, the challenges of working with the schemes will be met by distributors—just one reason to get one.

PRICING

Publishers used to set their RRPs in a very straightforward way—by working out the cost per unit of producing and printing a book, and adding on a set margin they wished to work to. Old rules of thumb in the trade went that the price you sell to your retail customers should be anything between three and five times your cost, and the price on the book seven to ten times your cost—though publishing varies so much that it is difficult to set targets.

Prices also have to take into account the demands and sensitivities of the market. Think about the perceived value of your book and your brand among the people you hope will buy it. Are they likely to be very sensitive to price, or does your book have enough that is appealing or unique to mean that people will not mind too much what they pay? High-quality books for a very specialist audience can often command high prices, but generic fiction will have to be priced quite low, for instance. Look, too, at the book's competition in the market. It is not always essential to undercut your rivals, but you will have to pitch in roughly the same range. Look for the common price points in your particular sector and format—mass market paperback novels, for instance, are usually priced at £5.99, £6.99 or £7.99. Stepping outside common brackets like these can make your book look odd and out of touch to both retailers and customers.

Pricing in academic and professional publishing, meanwhile, tends to be more to the market. This is because print runs tend to be much shorter and higher margins need to be made per title to cover overheads. This market can generally bear a higher price than the trade, though again publishers must be mindful of the price points of similar books in the market. When setting prices, also consider whether it is an individual who will buy the book or his or her organization; the latter is likely to bear a higher price point than the former. Educational publishing falls somewhere between academic and trade when it comes to pricing: this market is competitive and budget-conscious enough to make price a consideration, but not so fierce that buyers are not prepared to pay extra for quality or distinctiveness.

In the trade, at least, publishers also have to price their books with discounts in mind. You might not like the idea of your book being cut in price by chain bookshops or supermarkets, but it is a fact of publishing life if you want to sell in big numbers. This is particularly applicable to glossy hardbacks and in the Christmas season, when cuts of up to half are common on books in the £15 to £25 range.

Used tactically, price discounting can sometimes work to your advantage. Working with one or more major retailers to offer a big cut for, say, a week can be a good stimulus to sales and propel a book further up the sales rankings. That, in turn, will be noticed by other retailers, and might prompt more people to stock the book.

CHAIN BOOKSHOPS

For most consumer publishers—and some educational or specialist ones too—the most important sales outlets will be the big book chains: WH Smith, Waterstone's and Blackwell. Small publishers sometimes complain that they suffer prejudice from these chains compared to their larger rivals, and worry that range is contracting as firms focus on a smaller and smaller number of sure-fire hits. But for independents with the right books and powers of persuasion, chains can still be excellent partners, accessible to even the smallest publisher. Support from one of the big chains can be the thing that kick starts a new company or lifts an existing one to new heights.

Chains now do the bulk of their buying centrally, scaling out stock across individual branches. So it is head offices rather than stores that you need to persuade to stock your books. How you supply them will depend on your size. If chains consider you will be a fairly frequent customer and can get your books easily enough from a recognized distributor then they may choose to set up a regular account with you. Otherwise they might wish, for the time being at least, to acquire your books from a wholesaler; Waterstone's, for instance, sources books from many small publishers from Gardners. That doesn't have to mean that you have a lower chance of getting your books stocked—just that you might have to work a bit harder at it. See below for more on working with wholesalers.

If you want to approach the chains direct, start by identifying their key buying personnel. Some, like Waterstone's, have a buyer dedicated to working with small or new publishers who will become your first port of call. The IPG often has up-to-date details of these contacts and chains' teams of buyers on the website, or you can usually find help tracking down the right person via the forum. Websites, telephone numbers and addresses for the key chains can be found in the Resources section.

Next, work out what information buyers want and when. Patterns change, but they generally need to be approached four to eight months before publication of a book and, as a rule, the earlier you can make an approach the better. The more you adhere to chains' buying cycles, the more you are likely to sell.

Buyers for the chains are invariably busy and pressurized, dealing with demanding targets and dozens of publishers a day. Try to put yourself in their shoes and work out exactly what they might want from you and how they would like to deal with you. The best way to make yourself popular is to be as easy, friendly, professional and quick to deal with as possible. Don't give buyers long spiels about your books; they won't have time to listen to them and it's simply not enough to argue that your book is great—everyone thinks that. Don't be aggrieved if you get a negative response or no response at all, but plan how you can turn it into a positive one in the future.

For example, provide buyers with all the things they need to weigh up the value of your books. If you're contacting them for the first time, enclose a friendly letter introducing your company. If you have the skills and time to do so, try to make an impact with a slickly produced little file or dossier outlining your aims and specialisms, tailored to each buyer you write to. And try to make the approaches yourself. Contact from people calling themselves managing directors or publishers—or whatever job title you care to give yourself!—always carries more gravitas than calls from junior staff, however good their sales skills.

Send chains your catalogues as soon as they are ready, and Advance Information (AI) sheets for every new book you want them to stock (see the Marketing chapter for tips on producing good ones). Outline details of any publishing, marketing or publicity plans you have. Try to convey as simply as you can the content and appeal of your book, and provide the answer to every buyers' top question: who will buy it? Every publisher should be able to sell any book in a sentence. Use counterpoints and comparisons, borrowing previously published and popular authors or books to give a feel for its appeal. Lines like 'J K Rowling meets Jeffrey Archer' may sound corny but they do provide a buyer with a picture of how a book might appeal. Use references to other media like TV series or films too. Enclose a proof or final copy of your books if you can—it is difficult to argue that a book is the best ever written on its subject if you can't offer a copy to prove it—and at least a cover if you can't. Some publishers send out promotional gifts or gimmicks to tie in with the book and make it stand out from the crowd, though these often go straight into the bin. Provide all the contact details a buyer will need for you and your distributor or wholesaler so that they can order easily. Good salespeople think carefully about how to pitch every book and the hooks to hang it on. Work on these two things and you'll stand a good chance of success.

Many publishers like to follow up mailings with an email or a phone call, but plan what you want to say and say it briefly. It can count for a great deal if you are courteous and cheerful; buyers spend much of their days wrangling over terms with hard-nosed salespeople, and often find it a pleasant change to talk to enthusiastic, friendly independents. Passion and belief in your books will make a difference. Aim to be the best contact of their day.

If you can't get any sales or interest from chains' head office, an alternative is to visit the branches of chains one by one. Although individual branches don't now have great control over core stock, they do retain some autonomy over ordering so that their stock reflects local tastes and demands. So if you have a book about Manchester, for instance, branches of the chains in that city will have the power to take orders if they think the book will do well for them, even if their head office doesn't think it's worth taking it on centrally. Calling on shops can be quite straightforward in instances like this where a book has local appeal—but it is obviously hard work if you want to visit chains nationwide. If you're doing so, most of the above tips about approaching buyers apply. If you're finding it impossible but want that local contact, consider hiring a sales agent; see below for more on this.

The IPG offers members lots of help to get to know key chain booksellers and buyers. 'Meet the Buyers' evenings and 'Speed Dating' style sessions at the London Book Fair are excellent ways to talk to many of the trade's top buyers under one roof, and the Annual Conference provides a chance to talk to many of them in a relaxed and friendly environment. Keep an eye on the website and bulletin for details of forthcoming events.

INDEPENDENT BOOKSHOPS

The booksellers that many independent publishers naturally feel the closest affinity to are independents. If you know ones where you think your book might sell well, it may do no harm to approach them direct, and you may well find you get a fairer hearing here than in the chains.

Like the chains, many independents will find it easier to get your books from wholesalers than direct from you. If you want to get into the network of independent bookshops use the Booksellers Association's online or print directories of members to search for targets. The BA also runs various events aimed at independents, sometimes in conjunction with the IPG, that might be worth attending. Internet searches should also turn up any independent shops specializing in your line of publishing.

Independents are particularly supportive of local publishers and local-interest books. Ask them what you could do to help boost their sales, suggesting things like events, signed copies, posters or dumpbins (see Marketing and Publicity chapters for more). If you want to sell in person, good presentation skills and a flexible, friendly approach are key. Do your homework, and try to establish independent booksellers' particular tastes and interests. Phone in advance to book a time to call in, avoiding busy times like weekends or lunchtimes. Come prepared with all the sales materials you would send to the chains (see above). Be upbeat about your books, but honest and realistic too. Ambitious claims about a book's potential will be treated with deep scepticism by experienced booksellers and can lead to mistrust.

A good new tool for reaching independent bookshops in particular is Batch Connect, a service run by the Booksellers Association with Nielsen Book to connect publishers with retailers. Publishers who register with the service can use it to offer shops special discounts or other incentives on particular books, whether new or backlist. It is also a good way of offering authors—who can themselves register—for tours, signings or other events. Publishers pay to use the service.

WHOLESALERS

Book wholesalers act as intermediaries between publishers and booksellers. They are particularly useful for small publishers, providing them with a means of supplying books to retailers who otherwise do not do enough business with them to have a direct account. They don't actually sell books for you but in effect act as booksellers' external storerooms, able to deliver any one of more than half a million books to them at short notice—often the next day. They also service a large number of websites on behalf of independent bookshops in particular. The leading trade wholesalers in the UK, responsible for well over half the market, are Bertrams | THE and Gardners.

Publishers sell their books direct to wholesalers on much the same basis as they do to booksellers. Just as it is up to you to convince the chains to stock your book, so it is your job to persuade the wholesalers that their customers might want it, so use the same techniques (see above). In particular, wholesalers like to see catalogues and sample copies. After seeing your books, wholesalers will decide whether to stock them—buying orders from you on consignment and keeping them in their warehouse—or simply list them—meaning they will come back to you if any of their customers requests them. Even if they don't decide to stock one or any of your books straightaway, they may do so later if they find that bookshops are asking them for it, and both lists and stocks are constantly under review.

Wholesalers will want to set a 10 to 15% margin between the price they pay for books and the price they sell them at, so they typically require discounts from publishers of around 50 to 60%. You can also pay extra for marketing activities like space in their monthly buyers' guides or special promotions, which can be a good way of making your books more visible to their customers. If they are particularly keen on them, wholesalers might sometimes also pitch your books to the chains or independents at one of their regular meetings.

INTERNET RETAILERS

Online retailers provide the perfectly level playing field for small publishers. In theory, at least, all books are available on an even footing, giving independents' titles just as good a chance of being sold as large conglomerates' books. For the vast majority of independents in all sectors, the rise of web booksellers like Amazon has been very good news.

The shortest cut to improving sales through online retailers is by supplying accurate and timely bibliographic data. Having the right title, author, ISBN and other details for all of your books will make customers' searches more likely to turn into sales. Setting up direct feeds to provide internet retailers with extra materials like covers, synopsis and contents via bibliographic agencies like Nielsen BookData will increase the chances of browsers exploring it further. See the Bibliographic and IT chapter for more on this.

You can also encourage internet customers to browse your books by signing up to Amazon's Search Inside The Book programme. This allows customers to look at more of your content for free—as they would in a bookshop—and may increase sales if it proves to them that your book has what they need. Browsing in this way is particularly useful for buyers of specialist, educational, academic or professional content, who need to be sure that a book contains the specific information they require before they buy it. Look out on its site for Amazon's other marketing opportunities, like the facility to post short clips of your authors talking about their books.

Working with Amazon presents no issues around core stock as with the chains, and returns are likely to be much lower as it measures its buying very carefully against demand. But if you deal direct you may face some tough negotiations over terms, reflecting Amazon's increasing power in the market. It also offers participation in special promotions that will increase your books' visibility—as with chains, at a cost. Keep an eye on Amazon's site for promotional opportunities like its Small Publisher of the Month feature, brokered by the IPG.

Small publishers might also consider signing up to Amazon's Advantage scheme, whereby you can sell direct to customers on the Amazon platform. Amazon handles dispatch, pays you for sales at the end of each month, and will ask you to supply more copies of books according to demand. In return, you give Amazon a generous, variable discount and a small annual fee. It is a good way of using Amazon's power and reach, though the costs are obviously high. A large number of IPG members are involved with the Advantage scheme.

Although Amazon is by far the biggest online books retailer in the UK, don't forget others. Play.com is a general entertainment retailer and like Amazon has a marketplace for sellers (PlayTrade). The Book Depository is a fast-growing books specialist, sourcing books from a combination of distributors, wholesalers and publishers. It is very supportive of independents and welcomes contact; get in touch in particular about its Publisher of the Week promotion. Inpress is a very good internet bookseller specializing in books from small presses, supported by Arts Council England and offering better margins than most retailers; contact it for details about promotions and marketing initiatives. Chains and supermarkets all have their own internet retail operations while more and more independent booksellers are selling online, usually powered by wholesalers. Look out for online stores specializing in your subject too; a quick Google search should turn up anyone you ought to be dealing with.

Sales can also now be generated from Google, and search engine optimization here and elsewhere can make a big difference to internet sales. Think of the keywords associated with your book and aim to get links to a place where people can buy your book at the top of the search results. You can improve your chances with Google AdWords, though if your book is specialized that shouldn't be necessary. While Google's BookSearch programme might also be a way of generating online sales. See the E-publishing chapter for more about this, and about the importance of metadata in making your content visible to potential buyers.

SUPERMARKETS

Sales to supermarkets will only be a possibility for a handful of consumer publishers. They will be high volume and low profit, providing you with a large quantity of orders but invariably at a high discount that is on a par with promotional discounts offered to the book chains. A big order from one of the key supermarkets can almost single-handedly propel a book into the bestseller lists, but it will entail low margins and might lead to high returns or cannibalization of sales elsewhere.

Supermarkets receive their books either direct from publishers or from large wholesale intermediaries and merchandisers, who make selections and monitor stock levels on their behalf. As with chain booksellers, identify the buying contact for any supermarkets you want to approach, but be sure you can provide the high discount and high volume they will want. The four major supermarkets for books in the UK are Tesco, Asda, Sainsbury's and Morrisons. Waitrose is another big player.

SALES AND MARKETING PROMOTIONS

Chain bookshops—as well as supermarkets and wholesalers—may invite publishers to join with them in running special promotions. These include things like three-for-two offers, seasonal promotions, front-of-store tables, 'Book of the Week' deals or window display space, and it comes as a shock to many new publishers that participation here has to be paid for by a flat fee and extra discount, often stretching up to 60%. Retailers' head offices can supply their rate cards for their promotions, and there is usually little room for negotiation. Chains' promotions are a good way of getting prime space in their stores, and some trade publishers say they provide a good return on investment. But taking part in retailer promotions can be a Faustian pact, offering the chance of high volume but at high cost and high risk. Any books that go unsold will come back to you as returns.

Most small publishers instead direct the bulk of their marketing budgets to the consumer rather than retailer. But if you are spending money to market a book to readers, don't be shy of saying so; booksellers may be inclined to order more copies if you can prove that it will be widely promoted and advertised. Mention your promotional spend for any book on its AI sheet.

Because chains buy centrally and co-ordinate marketing from head office, that is where you will usually have to go to discuss marketing plans. The exception to the rule of dealing with head office is when you have books of local interest, of which individual branches of chains can be very supportive. If you approach them direct, think about marketing from the bookseller's point of view. Why is it in their interests to support this book? What can you offer them? Try to think of angles for the book that will appeal, and suggest promotions that are practical and easy for them to arrange.

SPECIAL AND DIRECT SALES

Special sales—usually defined as sales made through channels that aren't considered traditional for books—can be very valuable. By adding to your print runs through these sales, you'll be bringing down the unit cost of your printing, too. Think about where your books might appeal beyond the usual high street channels—Marks & Spencer might be good for cookery books, for instance, or National Trust shops ideal for heritage or countryside books—and make an approach direct or via their supplying wholesaler. Newsagents, convenience stores, service stations, garden and DIY centres are all other possibilities. Special sales are, by their nature, difficult to predict so it's best to look upon these as bonus sales rather than to budget for them.

If you are a specialist, don't forget shops with products along your lines, even if they don't have a history of selling books. Publishers with books about well-being or exercise, for instance, might approach health food shops, while children's publishers could consider toyshops or learning and play centres. Access to these individual stores is usually on a direct basis, but sometimes involves dealing with a wholesaler.

It is increasingly common for specialists to bypass the high street altogether and sell direct to consumers, either online, via mail order or in person. Any sales direct from your website need to be managed carefully, either by yourself or, for a fee, by your distributor or a wholesaler. However you do it, you will need to be able to provide excellent customer service or risk damaging your brand and reputation. Be careful too that your sales do not start to compromise sales through other channels, or you will upset your retail customers.

Several firms specialize in selling books direct to customers. The Book People is Britain's leading such firm, taking books to people's homes and workplaces via independent agents, mail order, websites and events. The good news is that they tend to buy books in large quantities and on firm sale; the bad news is that they will have to be at very high discount. Like remainder sales (see below), they can be a good way to shift large quantities of unsold or returned stock several months after publication. Direct sales through book clubs are another possibility for many general consumer publishers, though these will again be at high discount and are usually conducted as rights deals (see the Rights and Copyright chapter for more).

REMAINDER SALES

If you have got your forecasts and print runs wrong and are left with piles of unsold or returned stock, it may be possible to sell it to remainder or discount booksellers or their intermediary dealers. This will have to be done at a very large discount—10% of RRP is a reasonable minimum—but it at least recoups some of your costs and helps to clear your stock on firm sale. Remainder dealers can also sell stock domestically or overseas for you. The London and Frankfurt Book Fairs are good places to meet them, as are specialist remainder fairs run by CIANA.

Be warned that bargain and remainder bookselling is one of the most volatile sectors of the market, with chains coming and going at a high rate. Publishers have had their fingers burned by retailers going bust before paying for stock, and those chains that are left are threatened by the very cheap prices now on offer elsewhere. Publishers also need to be careful that they do not chase remainder sales too early and cannibalize more profitable sales elsewhere.

ACADEMIC AND SCHOOLS SALES

Academic publishers may well find branches of chains on campuses—Blackwell and John Smith & Son among them—more receptive to visits and personal contact than their trade counterparts. The key slot for selling into campus booksellers is the few months before the start of the academic year in September, when students pick up the books they require for their courses.

As well as bookshops, academic and educational publishers will also sell to institutions like universities, colleges and schools. Budgets here are tight and, by some measures, declining, but institutions can still be valuable markets.

Buyers in primary schools are often headteachers or their deputies, while in secondary schools budgets often devolve to heads of departments. Librarians may also have separate money for purchases. In higher education, sales tend to be spread more widely, to end-user students via academic staff as well as to institutions' libraries. Discounts in educational and academic publishing are less of an issue than in trade publishing, though deals may occasionally have to be negotiated on large orders.

Presented with the UK's wide network of schools, all but the largest of educational publishers will find it prohibitively expensive to visit schools to present their lists and books face to face, and often choose to use a specialist rep force instead. It is common for forces to charge per visit, and some may offer trials for a limited time or with a set number of reps. Be very clear on the services you are paying your reps for, and research potential partners carefully. See below for more tips on working with reps. Small publishers without networks of reps will find it difficult to cover many schools, but could at least try local ones, ringing in advance to book appointments. Visits can also give publishers valuable inside information about schools' budgets, interests and gaps in the market that need to be filled.

Another way of selling to schools is via direct mailings. Schools are inundated with mailshots, so you will have to work hard to make yours stand out from the crowd. Be as specific as you can in your targeting so that your mail reaches the right person at a school direct; if it doesn't do so straightaway, it will likely be lost or binned. Set out clearly and concisely what your books offer, and try to present them as a solution to teachers' needs or problems. Make them topical if you can: if there has been a recent change to the curriculum that makes your books more relevant, for instance, flag that up on your mailshot. Always ask yourself what it is that schools want from their books or e-content, and try to meet that demand. Many teachers will want to see a copy of a book before they adopt it for use, so consider sending out inspection copies or make it clear on your mailing that they are available on demand. See the Marketing chapter for more tips on successful direct marketing and obtaining mailing lists.

Schools may also buy through educational suppliers, who offer the convenience of a one-stop shop. These companies and their catalogues can be an excellent way for small publishers to reach a wide audience, though you will have to negotiate a discount for them. There is no harm in approaching some of the main suppliers to ask if they might stock your books; the British Educational Suppliers Association is a good place to find contact details. If you publish into a specific subject or specialism, see if there is an educational supplier working in your niche. Schools may also get their books via local authority agencies, though since more budgets were devolved direct to schools, these have fallen in importance.

Schools' purchasing patterns vary enormously and sales can be spread throughout the calendar. Common peaks are just after budgets come through in April and May; at and just after the start of the new school year in September; and at the start of the calendar year when residual budgets need to be used up.

Academic sales meanwhile tend to be most concentrated before the start of the academic year in early autumn. These sales can also be chased directly, by sending flyers, catalogues or promotional materials to individuals with the responsibility of choosing books for particular courses. Here, it is quite common to send inspection copies so that people can see a whole book for themselves before choosing to adopt it. Academic sales are also chased by specialist reps calling on campuses, and in addition can go through booksellers; specialist scientific, technical, medical or legal distributors, wholesalers and book clubs; conference or exhibition organizers; or training companies who use the books as part of their courses.

Academic and educational sales can also be achieved at exhibitions and conferences, though these are increasingly more of a marketing and publicity tool. Big events include The Education Show and, for e-content providers, BETT. It is also worth looking out for smaller exhibitions: local authorities, teacher associations and universities all have gatherings, sometimes dedicated to a particular subject or age group, and these can be good places to meet key buyers if not to sell to them on the spot. Remember, too, that some schools buy their books through a local bookshop, so it may be worth talking to them if you are targeting a particular area of the country.

LIBRARY SALES

Public, academic and school libraries are generally small but useful customers for publishers, but crucial for some academic, professional and STM publishers. A trend in public libraries is towards buying consortia—groups of library authorities pooling their buying together in order to get economies of scale and better deals—and this has increased the pressure on suppliers for better discounts. Another change is the growing popularity of electronic material over print, and some academic libraries are, like their public counterparts, teaming up to buy digital books and other material in consortia. One constant is libraries' budgets for buying material, which are always tight.

Libraries may occasionally buy direct from publishers, but they usually source their books from specialist public, academic or school library suppliers. This model gives libraries the advantage of dealing with a single supplier that gets their stock ready for their shelves. Like wholesalers, library suppliers run marketing promotions with publishers and often also export books to libraries around the world. There has been much consolidation in the library supply sector over the last few years, with far fewer companies than there once were.

In academic publishing, an important sub-market for library sales is journals, which historically have been one of the most profitable parts of the industry. These sell on a subscription basis to libraries and are a global business dominated by powerful STM publishing houses. Direct mailings, exhibitions, conferences and subscription agents are all sources of sales for journals, and some publishers offer libraries bundled deals on a range of journals. The sales model in this sector of publishing may be changing thanks to pressure for an 'open access' policy whereby end-users are able to read the content for free and authors or institutions pay to be included instead. Here more than anywhere else in publishing, sales have migrated from print to digital content, though in many cases print has not been abandoned altogether. See the E-publishing chapter for more on this.

SALES REPRESENTATION

Publishers large enough to have their own sales forces usually divide them by territory or by type of customer. But many small publishers without the time, resources or skills to sell their books themselves prefer to outsource the job.

If your list of books is a complementary fit—but not overlapping—with that of a larger publisher, one option could be to outsource your sales to that company. Many medium- or large-sized firms already represent smaller ones, and others might be open to the idea. Publishers can also sell their books via the sales force of their distributor if they have one. Both these options might suit niche publishers working in specialized, clearly defined markets, especially if your partner already has good relationships with your key customers. Ask around in the IPG for suggestions and talk to publishers working in the same field as you.

Another option is to work with freelance sales reps on a commission basis. Agents can save you a lot of legwork and admin and can get your books in places you might not have considered, but even the very best ones will be a bit removed from your own publishing—and the standard commission rate of 10% can take a big chunk out of your turnover. Outsourcing like this also removes from your control the bit of the business that makes you money.

Taking on freelance sales representation is a big decision, so spend time getting it right. Research your options—see the Resources section for some suggested freelance individuals and companies—and ask around in the IPG for recommendations, perhaps via the forum or e-bulletin. Look for those specializing in your area—repping educational books is very different from selling trade ones, for instance, so you need to find someone who knows your market intimately. Reputable reps will be happy to let you talk to some of their existing clients, and you should be wary of anyone who steers you away from this.

Meeting the people—reps on the ground as well as the director of the company—is essential. Contacts are everything in sales, so ask potential representatives about their access to your retail customers. Do they get to visit chains' head offices regularly? Which buyers do they meet? How many individual stores do they call on? Have they got the whole country adequately covered? If they are selling educational materials, what is the extent of their contact with schools? Ask too about the other publishers they represent and where you will fit on their list. If yours is the last publisher of dozens to be pitched in a sales meeting, you might not get much of a look in.

Once you have found a partner you can work with, agree your contract carefully. Don't tie yourself in to very long deals, and consider a trial period so they can prove their worth. Agree targets you want your agents to meet, and consider bonus schemes to reward exceptional performance. Keep a close eye on performance and get regular feedback from your sales partner so you can understand which of your books are selling well and which need more attention. You will have to be realistic in what you ask your sales partner to produce for you, but aim to get reports on orders and returns as frequently and regularly as you can.

Sales reps will need regular input from you, too. Set aside time to update them on your publishing plans and new releases so they have a proper understanding of your plans and targets, and aim to have at least two conferences or meetings a year dedicated to this. Even the best sales rep will struggle to sell a book they know very little about and care for even less. They also need to have timely supply of all your publishing and promotional materials like catalogues, AIs and posters.

EXPORT SALES

Sales to overseas markets can be an excellent addition to turnover for small publishers. Overall, export sales count for around a third of UK publishers' totals and, in sectors like English Language Teaching and some academic fields, much more. Some export sales, achieved by international booksellers or wholesalers or one of the increasing number of global internet retailers, will not require any extra effort. But any you want to achieve by going direct to local markets will require some hard work and research.

Publishers' export sales can be organized on either a closed market basis, where publishers grant exclusive distribution rights to one particular local agent; or an open market basis, whereby publishers deal with multiple agents and routes to market. That local agent might be a distributor, wholesaler or large publisher, who will usually take on the jobs of selling and promoting your books as part of the deal. For most small publishers, appointing a single agent like this in each territory makes life much easier than trying to crack the market open yourself, though you will have to rely on your agent to achieve success. Local agents can also chase bad debts much more successfully than you can from afar.

To get started in export sales, identify first of all which markets you have the rights to sell into, and then try to work out which would be interested in your books. The biggest export market for the UK by some distance is the US, followed by Ireland, Germany, Australia and the Netherlands. France, Spain, Japan, South Africa and Italy complete the top ten, and Canada and India can also be very important. But each publisher will have its own priorities. Once you have established yours, try to find the right local agent, perhaps by asking around in the IPG for recommendations, looking on other publishers' websites to find names of their agents, or by meeting possible candidates at book fairs like London or Frankfurt. See the Distribution chapter for more on working with overseas distributors.

Communication with your overseas sales agents is just as important as it is with your UK ones. Get to know them, visiting if you can and meeting at book fairs if you can't. Make sure they have everything they need to sell your books, like catalogues, AIs and promotional materials if they aren't producing their own local ones. Make sure they understand your publishing programme and are fully briefed on all the books they are selling. Get regular feedback on their progress, and if they are struggling to sell, try to find out why.

If you have an eye on a particular market for exports, a visit there can pay for itself many times over. Do your homework before you go, identifying possible channels for sales and arranging appointments to see as many people as you can. Look out for any book fairs or other events that might help you see contacts under one roof. And keep an eye on the IPG's e-bulletins and website for news of trade missions to particular territories or regions, organized by various bodies like the British Council or UK Trade & Investment and sometimes offering financial support for small- or medium-sized businesses to join. Research the issue of piracy too—this is a big problem in some developing markets and can decimate your sales despite efforts to protect your copyright.

You might also consider setting up a local office in especially strong markets. Many independents have done this particularly successfully in the US, the top priority export market for most. The office doesn't have to be grand; a shared desk will be enough to give you an address and demonstrate your commitment to the market. More important than location is to hire people who know your target market intimately and who are self-reliant enough to work to their own strategies and goals. If you have a very good export market, it may also be worth considering a partnership there with a local publisher so you can work together on projects and share resources.

If you think your books will appeal in the US in particular, it may also be worth approaching the major retailers or wholesalers—Borders, Barnes & Noble, Ingram and Baker & Taylor—direct. Remember Amazon.com too. If you are selling direct to customers about whom you have cause to worry about payment, invoice on a pro forma basis—whereby payment is received before goods are dispatched. Don't forget to include carriage costs in all quotes for any overseas orders.

Educational publishers who want to sell into overseas schools should consider working with UK-based suppliers. These can include your books on their catalogues and mailings, and consolidate orders on your behalf. Look at the membership of the British Educational Suppliers Association for the contact details of companies to work with. Major schools conferences and exhibitions can also be very good places to meet overseas customers and collect orders.

Government support is sometimes available for small companies wanting to increase their overseas business. Another way of doing business overseas is to sell rights to your books rather than selling them direct; see the Rights and Copyright chapter for more advice about doing this.

STAFF, SKILLS AND HELP

Qualifications are less important in sales than in many other publishing disciplines, and experience and personal skills usually count for more. The specifics of publishing can always be taught, but the basics of selling often can't. Negotiation skills are all important when it comes to selling a book into bookshops, and a good memory is useful, since salespeople will have to remember lots of books and lots of details about them. A passion for books and the ability to pass it on are invaluable when it comes to persuading retailers to agree deals.

Good contacts and a sound reputation among booksellers are hugely valuable, since much will rely on personal relationships and trust. Bags of energy and a clean driving licence will be essential if a salesperson is expected to tour round retailers. If you are selling into educational institutions, a knowledge of how they work and good contacts are both important. Export sales staff obviously need good local knowledge including sensitivity to local commercial and cultural ways of doing things, plus fluency in the languages of your key markets.

Given the competitive nature of the industry, publishers are remarkably free with their advice to one another. Use the IPG to soak up tips and stories from other publishers, and try to talk in particular to companies selling in similar or adjacent fields. While publishers never share the terms and numbers of deals and shouldn't be asked for them, you may be surprised at how much other help they offer if you ask. IPG events are ideal for this, and members can post questions or pleas for advice on the forum. Beyond the IPG, book fairs are good places to pick up useful intelligence about sales, and *The Bookseller* magazine can keep you informed about commercial developments that you need to be aware of.

RESOURCES

FORECASTING

Nielsen BookScan
The agency responsible for measuring book sales in the UK.
Web www.nielsenbookscan.co.uk
Tel 01483 712222

RETURNS

Batch Returns
The Booksellers Association's system to make₁ returns and other transactions more automated and painless.
Web www.batch.co.uk
Tel 020 7802 0847

Industry Returns Initiative
BIC's project to reduce the costs and numbers of returns.
Web www.bic.org.uk
Tel 020 7607 0021
Chain booksellers

Blackwell
Web www.blackwell.co.uk
Tel 01865 333000
Write to Beaver House, Hythe Bridge Street, Oxford OX1 2ET

British Bookshops
Web www.britishbookshops.co.uk
Tel 01273 507999
Write to Unit 6, Crowhurst Road, Brighton, East Sussex BN1 8AF

John Smith
Web www.johnsmith.co.uk
Tel 01273 877035
Write to Ash House, Headlands Business Park, Salisbury Road, Ringwood, Hampshire BN24 3PB

Waterstone's
Web www.waterstones.com
Tel 020 8742 3800
Write to Capital Court, Capital Interchange Way, Brentford, Middlesex TW8 0EX

WH Smith
Web www.whsmith.co.uk
Tel 01793 616161
Write to Greenbridge Road, Swindon, Wiltshire SN3 3RX

INDEPENDENT BOOKSELLERS

Batch Connect
Electronic service linking publishers with booksellers, and a good way of promoting your books to independents in particular.
Web www.batchconnect.com

Booksellers Association
The Booksellers Association has a searchable database of more than 4,000 bookshops in the UK—a useful starting place for planning sales and marketing. A print directory is also available.
Web www.booksellers.org.uk/bookshop_dir

SUPERMARKETS

Asda
Web www.asda.co.uk
Tel 0113 243 5435
Write to Asda House, Great Wilson Street, Southbank, Leeds, West Yorkshire LS11 5AD

Morrisons
Web www.morrisons.co.uk
Tel 08456 115000
Write to Hilmore House, Gain Lane, Bradford, West Yorkshire BD3 7DL

Sainsbury's
Web www.sainsburys.co.uk
Tel 0800 636262
Write to 33 Holborn, London EC1N 2HT

Tesco
Web www.tesco.com
Tel 01992 632222
Write to Tesco House, Delamere Road, Cheshunt, Hertfordshire EN8 9SL

Waitrose
Web www.waitrose.co.uk
Tel 01344 424680
Write to Southern Industrial Area, Bracknell, Berkshire RG12 8YA

INTERNET RETAILERS

Amazon.co.uk
Web www.amazon.co.uk
Tel 020 8636 9200
Write to Patriot Court, 1–9 The Grove, Slough, Berkshire SL1 1QP

The Book Depository
Web www.bookdepository.co.uk
Tel 01452 307905
Write to Goodridge Business Park, Goodridge Avenue, Gloucester GL2 5EA

Inpress
Web www.inpressbooks.co.uk
Tel 020 8832 7464
Write to Office 66, The Collingwood Building, 38 Collingwood, Newcastle upon Tyne NE1 1JF

Play.com
Web www.play.com
Tel 0845 800 1020
Write to PO Box 179, Third Floor, 40 Esplanade, St Helier, Jersey JE4 9RJ
Wholesalers

WHOLESALERS

Bertrams | THE
Web www.bertrams.com
Tel 0871 803 6600
Write to 1 Broadland Business Park, Norwich, Norfolk NR7 0WF

Gardners
Web www.gardners.com
Tel 01323 521777
Write to 1 Whittle Drive, Eastbourne, East Sussex BN23 6QH

The Booksellers Association's database of general and specialist wholesalers.
Web www.booksellers.org.uk

DIRECT SALES

Book Club Associates (BCA)
Web www.bca.co.uk
Tel 0844 499 0000
Write to Greater London House, Hampstead Road, London NW1 7TZ

The Book People
Web www.thebookpeople.co.uk
Tel 01483 861144
Write to Catteshall Manor, Catteshall Lane, Godalming, Surrey GU7 1UU

Direct Selling Association
Tips on selling direct.
Web www.dsa.org.uk
Tel 020 7497 1234

REMAINDER SALES

CIANA
Runs fairs specializing in remainder sales.
Web www.ciana.co.uk
Tel 020 8682 1969

REMAINDER DEALERS

The Booksellers Association's database of UK remainder dealers and booksellers.
Web www.booksellers.org.uk

LIBRARY SUPPLIERS

Askews
Web www.askews.co.uk
Tel 01772 555947
Write to 218–222 North Road, Preston, Lancashire PR1 1SY

Bertram Library Services
Web www.bertramlibraryservices.com
Tel 0871 803 6900
Write to Elmfield Road, Morley, Leeds, West Yorkshire LS27 0NN

Blackwell
Web www.blackwell.co.uk
Tel 01865 333000
Write to Beaver House, Hythe Bridge Street, Oxford OX1 2ET

Coutts Library Services
Web www.couttsinfo.com
Tel 01425 471160
Write to Avon House, Headlands Business Park, Ringwood, Hampshire
BH24 3PB

Dawson
Web www.dawsonbooks.co.uk
Tel 01933 417500
Write to Foxhills House, Brindley Close, Rushden, Northamptonshire
NN10 6DB

Holt Jackson
Web www.holtjackson.co.uk
Tel 01253 737464
Write to Preston Road, Lytham, Lancashire FY8 5AX

Peters
Web www.peters-books.co.uk
Tel 0121 666 6646
Write to 120 Bromsgrove Street, Birmingham B5 6RJ

SCHOOLS

British Educational Suppliers Association
Trade group for companies selling into schools, and a good place to find out more about suppliers to work with.
Web www.besa.org.uk
Tel 020 7537 4997

SALES REPRESENTATIVES

Bounce! Sales and Marketing
Web www.bouncemarketing.co.uk
Tel 020 7745 2370

Broomfield Books
Web www.broomfieldbooks.co.uk
Tel 01342 313237

Chris Lloyd Sales and Marketing
Web www.chrislloydsales.co.uk
Tel 01202 649930

Compass DSA
Web www.compass-dsa.co.uk
Tel 01628 559500

Portfolio Books
Web www.portfoliobooks.com
Tel 020 8326 5620

Publishers Group UK
Web www.pguk.co.uk
Tel 020 8804 0400

Quantum Publishing Solutions
Web www.quantumpsl.com
Tel 0141 884 1398

Signature Books
Web www.signaturebooks.co.uk
Tel 01904 633633

SSM Educational Representatives
Web www.ssmeducationalrepresentatives.co.uk
Tel 01462 423942

Vertigo Communications
Web www.vertigocommunications.co.uk
Tel 020 7100 2523

EXPORT SALES

British Chambers of Commerce
Some useful advice about getting started in exports.
Web www.britishchambers.org.uk/6798219245540598384/export.html
Tel 020 7654 5800

British Council
Promoter of UK culture around the world, and occasional partner of the IPG and other publishing organizations on overseas missions.
Web www.britishcouncil.org
Tel 0161 957 7755

Business Link
A useful portal for export advice from various sources.
Web www.businesslink.gov.uk

Export Credits Guarantee Department
Official export credit agency, protecting companies from non-payment.
Web www.ecgd.gov.uk
Tel 020 7512 7000

Global Publishing Information Reports
Detailed profiles of several dozen book markets around the world, available to access by IPG members and subscribers as well as for individual purchase.
Web www.publishers.org.uk
Tel 020 7691 9191

Publishing Exports Group
A sub-group of the Creative Exports Group that looks at ways to increase publishers' overseas trading, run by government departments including the DCMS and UKTI.
Web www.culture.gov.uk/what_we_do/creative_industries/3266.aspx#ceg
Tel 020 7211 6448

SITPRO
Government agency helping UK companies to trade internationally.
Web www.sitpro.org.uk
Tel 020 7215 8150

UK Trade & Investment
Government advice for companies wanting to start exporting, plus support for more experienced sellers and details of funding opportunities.
Web www.uktradeinvest.gov.uk
Tel 020 7215 8000

5 MARKETING

CONTENTS

Publishers' marketing is concentrated on two fronts: the people who will sell their books to customers and these end-users themselves. Put simply, marketing in this industry is all about getting your books in front of people and persuading them to buy. It is the engine that drives sales.

With so many routes to readers and opportunities to connect with them both physically and virtually, there have never been as many avenues for marketing books. For independent publishers, this presents both a great opportunity and a headache. Small companies do not have the budgets to buy the massive marketing or promotional campaigns of their larger rivals, but they do have the agility to be much more adventurous and creative in their marketing and, often, more successful. And with a bit of imagination, much of it can be achieved at very low cost or for free.

MARKETING PLANS AND BUDGETS

Planning really pays off in marketing. Begin the process as early as you can, and get into the habit of thinking up ideas for marketing books right from the moment you commission them. Authors and editors alike should have one or two marketing plans even before the book is written. If they struggle to come up with any, there's a good chance the book won't sell.

Try to draw up marketing plans for each book, setting targets for what needs to be done when. They needn't be too detailed or rigid—and you will need to be flexible enough to pursue opportunities as they arise—but setting down your ideas on paper helps to distil your ambitions for a book and focus on timescales. It can also be instructive to look back on marketing plans some time after publication to see how much has been achieved; what went right; and what went wrong that can be fixed in the future.

It is a well-worn buzz phrase, but the marketing mix or the four Ps of marketing—product, price, place and promotion—are worth bearing in mind as you plan. Begin by defining, as precisely as you can, your target audience, and think about all the different ways you might reach them. Make your targets specific, breaking them down into primary and secondary categories if need be. 'Men of all ages' doesn't cut it, so think deeper: think about buyers' lifestyles, tastes and habits. Do a SWOT analysis—Strengths, Weaknesses, Opportunities and Threats—so you can identify your book's strong marketing points as well as its competition in the marketplace. Try to boil down your marketing strategy to a single sentence—your angle when pitching it to anyone who might be interested in stocking or buying it.

Marketing plans are very useful in shaping budgets, which also need to be set as early as possible. These are usually calculated as a proportion of expected sales for each book, rather than by spreading money evenly between your total number of books. Publishers have to accept that some books will sell many more copies than others, and that while some titles will need a big marketing push, others will have to rely on other stimulants to sell. The vast majority of books receive no marketing budget at all, though that shouldn't stop you from trying to plan what you can get for free. And it would be a mistake to have no money set aside for marketing a select number of books or your company as a whole. Since it is difficult to measure what it achieves, it can be tempting to cut marketing budgets, especially when times are tough, but this is usually a false economy. Don't throw good money after bad, but don't be afraid to spend more in challenging market conditions either.

An overall marketing plan for your whole company can be useful too. Think of your key marketing objectives for the year and distil them into a top ten, inviting input from everyone in the company. At the end of the year, see how far you got towards reaching them. See below for more on marketing your company.

MATERIALS: AIS AND CATALOGUES

Good marketing needs good materials. And for the majority of publishers, the basis of all marketing activity for each book is a professional Advance Information (AI) sheet for each of their books, supplied to booksellers, sales forces, wholesalers, reviewers, bibliographic agencies and many others. AIs incorporate details of a book's title, author, format, extent, dimensions, ISBN, price, publication date, rights holder and any rights available, contact details, a short blurb outlining its contents, appeal and key selling points, another one about its author and details of any promotional activity you have planned. Include the book's cover, even if it is a dummy one, and perhaps an author photo. It is particularly crucial to include all the bibliographic data that anyone might need to sell your book, so check you comply with the guidelines suggested by BIC. See the Bibliographic and IT chapter for more about this. Also remember that metadata is becoming more and more important as a way for users to identify and discover your content; again, see the Bibliographic and IT chapter for more about this.

Good AIs are concise and neatly presented, ideally one page in length and certainly no more than two. Their job is to sell. AIs should show at a glance why it is a good book, but more importantly tell busy booksellers how it is going to sell and who to. Be as enthusiastic about the book as you can while keeping on the right side of honesty, and single out its unique selling points. If it is entering a sector of the market that is already crowded with books, you will need to convince people that it stands out.

Take a look at other publishers' AI sheets to see how they are typically presented, and draw up a template of your own on which to base future ones. Writing material for AIs is quite a skilled task, and it often falls to a book's editor since he or she will know the contents and the author best. Alternatively, you may wish to hire a professional copywriter if you can spare the money—or ask a talented friend or even the author of the book to do it. Draw up an AI as early as you can after you have acquired a book, even if it contains only some of the standard information and you haven't yet settled on things like a cover design. You can update it as more information becomes available, making sure that it gives retailers the fullest possible information about a book at the times when they need it. Prepare a PDF version for distribution via email and the web.

The catalogue is another important marketing tool, and any publisher with more than a handful of books should consider one. Catalogues instantly create a professional impression and are very useful to distribute to everyone you work with and those who you are interested in working with. They are the perfect calling card.

There are no hard and fast rules for catalogues, and they vary enormously. As with AIs, browse some competitors' versions—they are often available for download from their websites—to gather ideas. The aim is to present your company and books to the people who might buy them in as interesting and accessible a way as possible. Catalogues are usually sent to all parts of the supply chain—booksellers, libraries, wholesalers, sales reps, distributors, etc.—as well as direct to individual buyers, the media and, in education, to schools, colleges and universities. Publishers with busy schedules often publish two catalogues a year—usually for spring and summer, then autumn and winter—though smaller firms make do with one. Time them to suit your selling cycles, and consider producing different versions for different audiences. Trade-oriented catalogues are not really suited to general readers, for instance.

Catalogues should contain much the same information as your AI sheets, which can be used as a basis. You should also be able to draw information from your database if you keep one, and software is available to automate this process for you and populate your catalogues without the need to rekey anything. If you have many different subjects, group books by theme or consider a smaller catalogue for each topic. You will have to decide how to divide up your catalogue space, either giving equal prominence to all your books or, more commonly, allocating greater room to your key titles. Most publishers list their available backlist books at the back of the catalogue too. Make the catalogue lively— graphics, photos and bright colours all help—but ensure all the key bibliographic information is clearly presented so that your customers can order easily. If you have a distributor or sales representatives, include their contact details so customers know where to order from. List any rights and overseas sales agents if you want to mail the catalogue abroad.

As with AIs, prepare an electronic version of your catalogue and place it prominently on your website for download. A simple PDF is usually enough, but you might consider using websites like Yudu.com to smartly format and host your digital catalogue before sending the link to your contacts. Some publishers have abandoned their print catalogues altogether, directing people instead to electronic versions online. This can certainly save on print and postage costs, but you will have to be led by the demands of your customers.

As well as AIs and catalogues, some publishers, especially in general trade pub-lishing, like to produce point-of-sale marketing materials to help market a book. Posters, dumpbins, copy holders or customer giveaways like badges or bookmarks can all be useful ways of catching people's attention, and international customers particularly appreciate these. But chain bookshops in particular are deluged with them and there is no guarantee that anything will be used unless you pay for the space they take. Independent booksellers, many of whom do not receive much promotional support from publishers, may be more open to using materials. Try to gauge demand for any materials you plan before you order them, or you risk having them cluttering up the office unused.

Perhaps the most important marketing material of all is your bibliographic data, which should be neatly ordered and stored in an accessible place; scrup-ulously checked for accuracy; updated fastidiously; and supplied to retailers, wholesalers and whoever else needs it in a timely fashion, usually via Nielsen BookData. Even if you can't get your books stocked by the large chains, pro-viding good data means they can be ordered at a stroke from any retailer taking a feed from bibliographic databases, including all the internet-based ones. See the Bibliographic and IT chapter for much more about this.

MARKET RESEARCH

Publishing isn't renowned for its use of market research, possibly because it has such a diverse and ever-changing range of products that it is difficult to measure the potential and impact of individual books. But it can be a good way of understanding your target audience and spotting new gaps in the market.

Book Marketing Ltd is the industry's leading research agency, offering market reports and data and conducting ad hoc research commissions. Even if you can't afford to commission your own research, its annual 'Books and the Consumer' report and conference provide a very useful round-up of retail and consumer trends. Other research companies such as Mintel also have plenty of market intelligence, though they are not publishing specialists. Book sales data from Nielsen BookScan can be a good source of marketing inspiration, and many publishers use it to look at authors' track records or the performance of rivals' books as well as their own. The data does not come cheap, but the IPG sometimes has special deals for members.

Specialist, non-consumer publishers will find it easier to conduct market research. Educational publishers, for instance, could send questionnaires to teachers of subjects they are publishing for, or hold small focus groups to find out what the market needs and wants. Online forums and communities also present ready-made discussion groups for niche publishers; a publisher of books about gardening, for instance, could quickly find forums dedicated to the subject with members who might be prepared to answer some questions.

MARKETING TO RETAILERS

Marketing usually starts with the people who will be selling your books before moving on to the people who will be buying them. The first aim is to persuade booksellers and other retailers that your book is worth stocking and is going to sell.

Larger publishers may hold events for buyers to meet their authors or tell them more about particular books, though these usually require big budgets. If you want to market your book to the trade via advertising, you could try *The Bookseller*. Full page or cover ads here are not cheap, but there are sometimes good deals to be had on supplements like its Independent Publishers Catalogue. Some booksellers say they do take note of advertising in *The Bookseller*, but others argue that money spent here would be better used on advertising direct to book buyers. Best of all is to get exposure for free via editorial coverage in the magazine, either by suggesting news stories around your books well ahead of publication or trying to get space in one of its product features. The magazine runs various category previews and booksellers' selections, and has print and online versions of its schedules. Get to know what *The Bookseller*'s previewers want and when, so that you stand the best possible chance of inclusion. Pitch for space as often as you can; there's never any harm in trying.

Another good way of promoting your books to shops and flagging up special marketing offers or discounts in particular is the Batch Connect website from the Booksellers Association. For more on this and other tips for selling through booksellers, see the Sales chapter.

MARKETING TO LIBRARIES

For some publishers, libraries—public, academic, school, professional or other-wise—will be an important source of sales and a well-established marketing channel. But even if you don't normally sell your books to them, don't forget libraries in the marketing mix. They can be excellent venues for staging pro-motions and events, and they have enviable access to a ready-made audience of readers.

Short of budgets and forgotten by many publishers, libraries are often very amenable to marketing approaches, especially if you are prepared to help organize and promote events. They are particularly keen on local-interest readings or talks, and children's authors also go down well. Posters and other marketing materials may be welcomed, but remember that you will probably have to make special arrangements if you want to sell your books in libraries as well as promote them. The Reading Agency keeps a database of libraries that are willing and able to host events.

ADVERTISING

Perhaps because it has such a high turnover of products to promote, publishing has not tended to advertise very heavily by comparison with many other industries. The high cost of it is usually difficult to justify in sales terms, partly because it is so difficult to measure the return on investment. If money is tight, approach advertising with caution. In academic and educational publishing in particular, the effect of advertising is particularly dubious, and money is probably better spent on other forms of marketing.

Any advertising that is bought needs to be well researched and focused. Draw up a list of possible outlets for your books, and check circulation figures of any magazines, journals and newspapers carefully. Ring round for rate cards and quotes on advertising, and always haggle on price. Many newspapers and magazines are increasingly desperate for advertising and will always be able to improve their initial quotes. Another trick is to check for last-minute deals on advertising—if magazines need to fill space urgently they will often sell it very cheaply.

For specialist publishers, advertising can be relatively straightforward. Analyse the publications aimed at your readership—email-based newsletters and websites as well as print magazines, journals or papers—and get to know both their editorial and advertising staff. Niche publications can help you reach an already receptive audience, so advertising spend is usually much more likely to produce a return on investment here.

You might like to think too about radio, outdoor or transport advertising, especially in London, though these sorts of campaigns usually only start to produce a return if the spend is high, so reserve them for a small number of books by relatively well-known authors rather than spreading budgets thinly across a whole list. Some publishers use advertising agencies or buyers to help secure good deals, but these are usually for very large clients only. If you use them, brief them closely about what you want and keep an eye on budgets. Try to track sales before, during and after any advertising campaign to measure its effectiveness. Note any particular spike in sales, but remember that they might coincide with something other than your advertising.

DIRECT MARKETING

Direct marketing is common in sectors of publishing like academic, professional, educational, STM and specialist niches. Here, it should be relatively easy to identify and target the people who might be interested in your books, either by gathering together your own contacts or by purchasing a mailing list from a third party. Plenty of firms specialize in this or you could try working with associations, societies, conferences or even other publishers to share or buy lists. If you're buying in a list, make sure you know what you're paying for, as different tiers of information will often be available. In educational publishing, for instance, it may be possible to buy complete lists of schools or deeper information like individual teacher contacts or departmental heads with responsibility for budgets. There are rogue as well as reputable list providers, so ask fellow publishers for recommendations.

Ask your authors for their contacts too. Over time, publishers should try to build their own mailing lists, kept up to date with details of each contact's interests and purchases, so that they can be targeted with the right information and offers. Specialist databases are available to help manage lists like this, but often an Access file or Excel spreadsheet will do just as well. Also remember to stay within the law—which can be complicated in direct marketing—particularly when you are using lists or data from other organizations. The Information Commissioner's Office is a useful first port of call when assessing legal issues around data protection and privacy.

Make your direct mailings concise but eye-catching. The bulk of direct mail goes straight in the bin, and you don't have much time to persuade someone to read on. Make it as easy as possible for people to buy your books after reading your mailing, presenting simple options and prominent contact details where they can get more help. Direct mailshots commonly include a covering letter, catalogue and flyers for books of particular interest. Much direct marketing is still done by post, and you can get competitive rates from outsourcing specialists around the world if you are not inclined to stuff envelopes yourself, though an increasing amount is also now done via email (see below). Measure the effectiveness of all direct marketing campaigns to decide if you are doing it in the right way and targeting the right people. Good conversion to sales rates are difficult to estimate: some aim for 5 to 10% of all contacts mailed, though for others 1 or 2% is respectable.

When marketing textbooks directly to academics, it is common to offer a copy for inspection as most will not endorse a book based on marketing information alone. Journals publishers usually market their products direct to librarians and researchers to try to secure subscriptions.

WORD OF MOUTH

The holy grail in marketing is word of mouth—the process whereby people recommend your book to others. Research has shown that in trade publishing at least this is by some distance the most important prompt to purchase among shoppers—and as a bonus it's completely free. Unfortunately, it's also the most elusive to capture and the most difficult to measure. Even experienced marketing people find it difficult to produce concrete theories for how word of mouth spreads, and it is something that is resistant to even the most thorough marketing strategy. In fact, sometimes the more you try to achieve it, the more immune the market appears to be to it.

Clearly, word of mouth can't start if you don't get your book in front of enough people in the first place, so media coverage and prominent display in bookshops are often triggers. Celebrity endorsements can help, but for word of mouth to get going, books require more than just a few purchases—they need to have a special quality or an interesting side story, plus access to a network of people to spread interest in it. In specialist publishing, this can often be best achieved online (see below). And in fiction, at least, one of the best networks is the vast number of reading groups across the UK. Publishers are increasingly trying to appeal to these by producing extra print or online material to facilitate and support discussion around their book. Accessing the groups can be difficult, but public libraries can be a good place to start, and The Reading Agency holds a database of many of the library-based groups in the UK. In educational and academic publishing, meanwhile, word of mouth starts with teachers and lecturers—the people who will endorse your books to their students and trigger sales.

MARKETING YOUR COMPANY

Although the majority of consumers do not buy books because of who publishes them, there are sectors of the market in which the publishing brand has an impact. Teachers and academics are sometimes influenced by the identity of a book's publisher, for instance, and reference genres are at least partly brand driven. If you are publishing into a small niche—with books about a specialist hobby, for instance—the name of your company or imprint will soon become well known. Your brand will also be important when it comes to selling your books overseas, either through rights or in exports. If you can establish a reputation for high quality, good service and reliability, overseas publishers and booksellers will begin to recognize your name and be more receptive to approaches.

Given all this, it is worth spending some of your marketing time and budget making sure that your publishing brand is clearly defined. Think about the strengths of your company and the things that make it stand out. Work out where you need to be making your name better known—at fairs, conferences and events relevant to your books, for instance. Many events will let you take a stand or other promotional space, usually in return for a fee, or you might consider sponsoring a particular seminar, speech or social occasion. Anything that gets your name more widely known in the community into which you are selling is beneficial.

E-MARKETING

Marketing via email and the internet is still in its infancy compared to many forms. Most publishers are still figuring out their way through the maze of new channels, so if you can harness the web effectively you will be ahead of the game. You may also find that e-marketing provides the cheapest and most effective way of reaching your readers and of building communities around your books.

Online marketing works best for publishers specializing in particular subjects or niches that have defined audiences. In these cases, it should be quite easy to identify and reach prospective buyers of your book online. If you have a book about a hobby like card-making, for instance, search online for relevant websites, discussion forums, newsgroups and so on. Any good search engine will turn up lots of sites, but don't forget to explore links to others that aren't logged by the engines. Use Google Alerts to keep up to date via email with developments in your sector, and sign up particularly to alerts that feature your company and its keywords so you know who is talking about you.

Email marketing campaigns are excellent ways of getting your books in front of the right people. Right from your first sale, try to build up a database of people who are interested in your books, and ask everyone who contacts you for their email addresses. As with direct postal marketing material, keep your email shots concise and readable, and as eye-catching as you can without using graphics or fonts that clog up people's email servers. Avoid attachments, which take up both memory and time to download. Avoid words like 'Free' or 'Offer' in the header as these will lead filters to consign the email to junk. Test each mailing on friends or colleagues before sending it to everyone. Avoid emailing too frequently, or your impact will be diluted; many publishers find that once a month is about right. And remember that much the same legal issues apply as with direct marketing (see above). Emails can also incorporate e-book widgets—digital files holding a book's cover and sample pages with a link to a place to buy it. These are a great way of advertising a book, allowing people to click through for more information, and can easily be hosted on websites too. Specialist software is available to help you write email newsletters.

For further inspiration, look around at what other publishers are doing with their email newsletters. And try to measure the success of each email campaign—in terms of sales or feedback—so you can work out what you are doing right and wrong. If you are using it, software will track the rates at which your emails have been opened and clicked on, giving you an idea of your penetration. If you have not been as successful as you would have liked, it's a good opportunity to experiment. Try changing the day or time at which you send your emails; alter the title of the message to something more compelling; or re-jig the order of the main text. Continue tracking penetration rates to see what brings the best results.

Publishers' websites are often the first opportunity to market your books. All but the tiniest new publisher should have at least a basic website, acting as a showcase for your titles and brand, and even if you don't immediately include facilities for people to buy, consider providing links to Amazon or another retailer so that they can purchase if they choose. Web building packages make it very easy to build a site yourself, and this will be much cheaper than hiring someone to do it for you. Learn the basics of search engine optimization, and think about the search terms that people will use to find you. If you publish books about crafts, for instance, you should aim for your website to turn up in searches for things like cards, sewing, knitting and so on. If you are operating in a niche, your site could quickly become the first port of call for many people interested in that niche.

Once you have found people, you need to work hard to keep them coming back. Frequent emails and discussion forums can do this, while RSS (Really Simple Syndication) feeds will alert people to updates to your sites. It can be useful to offer some free content, even if it's just a sample page or two, made available as a PDF. This can be particularly helpful in educational or academic publishing, where buyers like to be convinced of the value of a book before they buy.

Another way of getting people returning is to host a blog, something that can be done very easily and cheaply with basic blogging software. Blogs can spread interest in your books, even if you can't afford a full-blown site yet, and they can be used to discuss forthcoming books or just day-to-day publishing life (see the Directory for some popular publishing blogs to give you ideas). Downloadable podcasts—short interviews with your authors about their new books, perhaps—are another nice extra for visitors. Whatever you host online, try to keep it reasonably fresh, since badly out of date websites drive people away, never to return. Update little and often.

If you have the technical know-how and the time, you could also set up dedicated websites for individual books, with extra resources like author inter-views, interactive games or updates of the book's material. In some sectors of publishing, like travel or academic textbooks, add-ons like the latter are now fairly standard rather than optional.

Other people's blogs are useful for marketing too. Try to find anyone blogging about your book's subject, and contact them via email or their blog comments. Ask if they'd like to review your book on their blog, suggest an online interview with the author, or offer a few copies for a competition prize. The most popular blogs reach thousands of readers, and a recommendation there can count for a lot. Social networking sites like MySpace and Facebook can be good marketing channels too, free to use and an excellent way of building communities. If your authors use them, get them to promote their books directly to their contacts, or set up a fan or group page on their behalf. Book networking site Library Thing is another way into the online community, and publishers can build a buzz here by sending out review copies to members. A useful site for learning more about marketing books via social networking media is Publishing Talk.

As with email campaigns, try to track the success of your website marketing. Get some analytics software—Google Analytics is recommended—and use it to track traffic, to assess the success of any campaigns, and to better understand how, why and when people are visiting your websites.

E-marketing is a very fast-moving area of publishing. To stay in touch with the latest techniques and issues, keep a close eye on what other publishers are doing and attend the IPG's Digital Quarterly Meetings, which round up the latest news and views in e-marketing.

STAFF, SKILLS AND OUTSOURCING

Marketing is a popular career, so you should not find it too hard to recruit people to do the job for you. Publishing requires very different skills and techniques to other industries, but a fresh perspective can be very useful and marketing professionals have some of the most varied backgrounds of all publishing personnel. In small publishers, it is more usual for marketing responsibilities to be shared around several members of staff in other departments, overlapping with sales and publicity in particular. But try not to think of sales and marketing as skills that can be bundled together—they are actually very different.

Marketing people need to be both creative and organized. They should be good project managers as they will be juggling lots of campaigns. A passion for books is obviously useful, as is a good book of contacts in the industry. An outward-facing nature and the confidence to negotiate, haggle and cajole are always handy when it comes to working with retailers, but perhaps most useful of all is an ability to second-guess the people you are trying to sell to and understand what makes them tick. It is a numerate discipline, so an ease with budgets and calculations is important.

There are plenty of consultancies and freelancers who can help with marketing, and given its importance some publishers like to outsource it, at least in their early days, to help get their company better known. Many freelancers have long track records in publishing and will bring a wealth of expertise to your projects—though they will often bring it at a fairly hefty price. Ask around in the IPG for recommended freelancers, and check the service membership for specialists. If you use them, sales agencies and distributors often offer marketing services in addition to their core activities, though you need to be sure that they can provide everything that you want. Be wary of outsourcing marketing completely, and keep at least half an eye on anything that is being done on your behalf. If you can, trial people before you hire them.

RESOURCES
MARKETING ASSOCIATIONS, FORUMS AND NEWS
Book Marketing Society
Group for marketing professionals with regular events and resources. It is a particularly useful source of news about new and ongoing initiatives and promotions across publishing.
Web www.bookmarketingsociety.co.uk
Tel 0870 870 2345

Chartered Institute of Marketing
Professional body for marketing staff.
Web www.cim.co.uk
Tel 01628 427500

Marketing Week
Trade press for the marketing industry. Some useful ideas from other industries and a place to advertise if you need marketing staff.
Web www.marketingweek.co.uk
Tel 020 7970 6300

Springwise
A great forum for picking up new marketing ideas from other industries around the world, with a weekly newsletter.
Web www.springwise.com
Tel 00 31 20 638 38 68

MARKETING MATERIALS
BIC BASIC
Industry standards for bibliographic data in the supply chain, to which all publishers and their marketing materials should adhere. BIC has downloadable guides to help you comply.
Web www.bic.org.uk/17/BIC-Basic
Tel 020 7607 0021

Nielsen BookData
The UK's bibliographic services agency and the source for your bibliographic data.
Web www.nielsenbookdata.co.uk
Tel 0870 777 8710

Yudu
Website to help you publish and host online marketing materials like catalogues.
Web www.yudu.com

MARKET RESEARCH

Book Marketing Limited
The leading provider of book-specific research, with ongoing and one-off surveys into sales and reading habits.
Web www.bookmarketing.co.uk
Tel 020 7440 8930

Mintel
Various intelligence on the book market, though it's not a publishing specialist. Much of their work is quite expensive, but you can usually access something for free.
Web www.mintel.com
Tel 020 7606 4533

Nielsen BookScan
Detailed sales data that can be used to inform marketing strategies. Check for special deals negotiated by the IPG.
Web www.nielsenbookscan.co.uk
Tel 01483 712 222

MARKETING TO RETAILERS

Batch Connect
Electronic service linking publishers with booksellers, and a good way of promoting your books to independents in particular.
Web www.batchconnect.com

The Bookseller
Contact the advertising team for help with buying space, and build contacts on the editorial side for free coverage. A calendar outlining features, previews and supplements for the year ahead is available to download.
Web www.thebookseller.com
Tel 020 7420 6000
See the Resources section of the Sales chapter for full contact details of chain booksellers, plus databases for finding independent booksellers and wholesalers.

MARKETING TO LIBRARIES

Libraries and reading groups databases
Searchable directories of both libraries willing to host events and library-linked reading groups across the UK, maintained by The Reading Agency.
Web www.readinggroups.peoplesnetwork.gov.uk

Public libraries database
Directory of all libraries in the UK. A useful starting point if you want to arrange events or promotions.
Web www.peoplesnetwork.gov.uk

The Reading Agency
Co-ordinates the Reading Partners scheme linking publishers and libraries, and has lots of good advice for working with libraries and those looking for partners.
Web www.readingagency.org.uk
Tel 0871 750 1207

DIRECT MARKETING

Business Link
Free, government-endorsed advice about privacy and data protection issues.
Web www.businesslink.gov.uk/bdotg/action/layer?topicId=1074448560

Direct Marketing Association
Trade body for those doing direct marketing, with some useful hints and tips.
Web www.dma.org.uk
Tel 020 7323 4426

Information Commissioner's Office
Useful advice about data protection and publishers' legal obligations in direct marketing.
Web www.ico.gov.uk
Tel 08456 30 60 60 (Helpline)

E-MARKETING

Facebook
Social networking site.
Web www.facebook.com

Google Alerts
Good, free way of keeping informed about news relating to your company and publishing.
Web www.google.com/alerts

Google Analytics
Applications to measure your website traffic.
Web www.google.com/analytics

Google Search
The number one search engine on the web. Get to know how it works and how you can get to the top of it.
Web www.google.co.uk

Library Thing
Book-based social networking site.
Web www.librarything.com

MySpace
Social networking site.
Web www.myspace.com

Publishing Talk
Useful forum for learning more about online marketing.
Web www.publishingtalk.eu

CONSULTANTS AND FREELANCERS

Andrea Reece Marketing
Tel 020 8889 1292

Cameron Publicity and Marketing
Web www.cameronpm.co.uk
Tel 07903 951957

Dara O'Hare
Tel 01373 474617

Eurospan
Web www.eurospangroup.com
Tel 020 7845 0804

FMcM Associates
Web www.fmcm.co.uk
Tel 020 7405 7422

Frontline Global Marketing Services
Web www.frontlinegms.com
Tel 01327 359298

Gotch Solutions
Tel 020 7733 0882

Inpress
Web www.inpressbooks.co.uk
Tel 020 8832 7464

Julie McNair
Tel 020 7704 2995

Marketability
Publishing consultancy offering training and an informative free e-newsletter about book marketing.
Web www.marketability.info
Tel 020 8977 2741

Oxford Creative Marketing
Web www.oxfordcreative.com
Tel 01865 861669

The Oxford Publicity Partnership
Web www.oppuk.co.uk
Tel 01327 357770

Publishing Services
Web www.publishing-services.co.uk
Tel 020 8222 6800

Tou-Can
Web www.tou-can.co.uk

Vertigo Communications
Web www.vertigocommunications.co.uk
Tel 020 7100 2523
See the Resources section of the Sales and Publicity chapters for details of freelance sales agents and publicists who may also offer marketing services.

BOOKS

85 Inspiring Ways to Market Your Small Business by Jackie Jarvis (How To Books, £10.99, 9781845281670)

Commonsense Direct and Digital Marketing by Drayton Bird (Kogan Page, £24.95, 9780749447601)

Directory of Booksellers Association Members (Booksellers Association, £37, 9780955223372)

Email Marketing by the Numbers by Chris Baggott and Ali Sales (John Wiley, £15.99, 9780470122457)

Get Into Bed with Google: Top Ranking Search Optimization Techniques by Jon Smith (Infinite Ideas, £8.99, 9781905940493)

Get to the Top on Google: Tips and Techniques to Get Your Site to the Top of the Search Engine Rankings and Stay There by David Viney (Nicholas Brealey, £14.99, 9781857885026)

How to Market Books: The Essential Guide to Maximizing Profit and Exploiting All Channels to Market by Alison Baverstock (Kogan Page, £25, 9780749450205)

Judging a Book by its Cover: Fans, Publishers, Designers and the Marketing of Fiction edited by Nicole Matthews and Nikianne Moody (Ashgate, £50, 9780754657316)

Marketing in Publishing by Robin Birn and Patrick Forsyth (Routledge, £21.99, 9780415151344)

Marketing to the Social Web: How Digital Customer Communities Build Your Business by Larry Weber (John Wiley, £15.99, 9780470124178)

The New Rules of Marketing and PR: How to Use News Releases, Blogs, Podcasting, Viral Marketing and Online Media to Reach Buyers Directly by David Meerman Scott (John Wiley, £9.99, 9780470379288)

6 PUBLICITY

CONTENTS

Strategies and budgets / Dealing with the media / Press releases /
Reviews / TV and radio / Other media coverage / Authors and publicity /
Book signings, events and launch parties / Festivals / Prizes /
Staff, skills and outsourcing / Resources

Publicity is often regarded as one of the most glamorous parts of publishing. And when it comes to hosting glitzy launch parties, organizing TV appearances and staging book signings with queues around the block, it can be. But the reality of the job for most independent publishers is rather different, demanding hard graft and lots of cajoling for every inch of media exposure that is gained.

For companies with limited resources though, it can be a great way of growing book sales and getting the business better known. Marketing promotions with chains and big advertising campaigns can cost a fortune, but beyond the time and energy needed, good publicity can generally be achieved for free. With a bit of creative thinking and planning, it's something that all publishers, however small, can do.

STRATEGIES AND BUDGETS

Start thinking about publicity from the moment you have an idea for a book or the manuscript for it is delivered. From the first time you read it, try to put yourselves in the shoes of people working in the print, TV and broadcast media, and consider what aspects of it they might be interested in. Ask everyone who is involved in a book for their publicity ideas; editors in particular should have a good feel for what is newsworthy or topical about it. What you are looking for are angles on the book that you can use to persuade the media to publicize it on your behalf.

Nearer publication, each book should have a publicity plan, outlining the kind of coverage you hope to achieve, where you want to secure it, and a diary of what is happening when. Timing is crucial in publicity, and you want coverage to build gradually until it peaks around the time of publication. So plan carefully when to start your campaign, when to send out books for review and so on.

Publicity plans should be regularly updated so that all staff can tell at a glance where a book has been reviewed or featured and how it has been promoted. After the publicity is at an end, review the success or otherwise of the campaign and try to assess its impact on sales. This will show you which media channels and publicity techniques are successful and which are a waste of time. Learn where to look for the 'big wins' in publicity, and put your resources there in the future. A couple of minutes' coverage on the BBC Radio 4 *Today* programme will reach more people than long newspaper reviews in all the national newspapers put together, for instance.

Beyond the people costs, budgets in publicity are usually low to non-existent, but you may need to set aside some money for the distribution of review copies and perhaps some costs for events. Most publishers concentrate their publicity budgets on the books that are most likely to become their bestsellers. In an ideal world, budgets would be evenly spread around a publisher's list, but most companies have to accept that some titles and authors will be more media-friendly and saleable than others.

DEALING WITH THE MEDIA

Securing publicity with newspapers, magazines, TV and radio requires confidence, chutzpah and a thick skin. Most media people claim to be very busy and inundated with material to cover, so you will need to be courteous and efficient in all your dealings. You will not always get that back in return, but try to stay patient and calm.

Personal relationships are very valuable in the media, and people you contact may well be more inclined to cover something if they know and trust you. So get to know as many of them as you can, starting by drawing up a list of key contacts and building them up over time into a database. If you are publishing in a specialist field with a small, specialist media, this should be quite straightforward, but it will involve a bit more internet and telephone research if your subjects are more general. Try some of the print and online directories listed in the Resources section, and use the Publishers Publicity Circle's website and events to keep yourself up to date. If you can't find a suitable contact for a particular media outlet, ring its reception and ask for one. Media contacts come and go at a high rate, so try to keep your database up to date with changes.

Get to know what kind of information different media outlets want, and the way in which they like to receive it. Learn their deadlines and, hence, the best time to contact them. If your local paper goes to press on a Thursday, for instance, try to supply material for that week's issue by the preceding Monday, and avoid disturbing them on Thursday mornings, when staff will be flat out. Some media have long lead times while others may be very short—a glossy magazine might need material three months ahead of publication, while a daily TV show might only book guests a day or two in advance. As a rule, make contact as soon as you can. It is generally never too early to make an approach, but it can often be too late.

Unfortunately, there is no easy way to work out individual media requirements beyond experience and asking a lot of questions. Some people like to receive proof copies and emails, while others want finished books and prefer to talk on the phone. Again, the Publishers Publicity Circle can be a good place to find and share information about what people like when.

Most publicists contact the media by telephone or email. Ringing up can get you an instant response, but busy people often prefer an email to which they can reply when they have time. If you phone, work out what you want to say in advance and keep it to the point. If you email, make the approach personalized rather than sending a circular message.

Following up on everything you send to the media is essential. If you've emailed an idea and haven't heard back, phone to politely enquire if it is of interest. The worst that can happen is they say no—sometimes, admittedly, rudely—and it will often help to jog the memory and prompt some coverage. Phoning also helps to establish yourself as a contact and make you better known. Don't be afraid of rejections from the media, and don't take them personally.

Remember that exclusivity is often important to the media. If you have a story or idea that you think will be of interest to more than one outlet, you might have to decide who to offer it to first. National newspapers are particularly keen on having sole rights to a story, and will often check with you that this is the case. You are perfectly entitled to offer something to more than one channel if you like, but your contacts may be irritated if something they thought was exclusive then appears in another outlet at the same time.

PRESS RELEASES

A key ingredient in most publicity campaigns is the press release. This is used to alert the media to your book, but is also—like the AI sheet—a useful resource to have, to send to anyone who enquires about it.

Releases are sometimes used by publishers to announce the acquisition of a new book, but they are more likely to be sent around publication to help spread the word about it or persuade people to review it. Most publishers develop a simple press release template that they can work from, but each one needs to be sharp and focused. Start by making a list of people you want to target with your release, then bear them in mind as you write it. If you are sending it to different sectors—to both national and local media, for instance, or both specialist and general magazines—tweak the release for each. Whoever you send it to needs to feel that you have considered their needs and requirements.

Media outlets are deluged with press releases, so you will have to work hard to make yours stand out. Keep it as short and snappy as possible—no more than a page in length if you can help it. The headline and first paragraph are absolutely vital: good ones will prick up readers' ears but dull ones will be sent straight to the bin. Use these to highlight the main theme or angle of the book, but also to entice people to read on.

Break up the text regularly and insert covers or author photos if you can. Press releases also usually have a few quotes from the book's author or publisher; these are handy for journalists to use in their stories. Also make sure you include prominent contact details, including phone numbers, email addresses and any websites where more information can be found. Avoid all jargon throughout, and check for mistakes in spelling or grammar; both are irritants to journalists. Check the formatting before you distribute it, and produce an electronic version as a Word or PDF file to send via email. If any of the material in the release is embargoed, note the date prominently in your release. The vast majority of journalists understand the need for embargoes and can be trusted to respect them.

Time the distribution of your press release carefully. Unless you have promised someone exclusivity, you will usually want to send it to everyone at the same time so they have equal opportunities to cover it. If you stagger release and one newspaper knows that a rival has already covered it, they will not give it much attention.

REVIEWS

Getting review coverage is a big part of the publicist's job. Most publishers submit copies of their books to the media a month or two ahead of publication, giving writers plenty of time to read and review. Finished copies are usually sent, but proofs or even PDF versions might be acceptable if they are not yet available. If you have one, enclose a press release or AI sheet along with the book and, ideally, a personalized letter introducing it and outlining why the publication's readers would be interested in it. Distributors may sometimes be used to send out review copies on a publisher's behalf.

Posting multiple copies of books can be expensive, so be sure that a newspaper or magazine is going to be interested in it before you dispatch. Use directories or your database of contacts to identify likely reviewers, and get to know key review editors and any freelancers specializing in your field (many national papers use dedicated crime or audio reviewers, for instance). If you have a specialist book, ask your author and colleagues for ideas about places it might be reviewed—they may know outlets that you don't. If you are not sure if someone will be interested, post or email them your press release or AI sheet instead, noting that review copies are available on request.

Don't forget online reviewers. Bloggers are becoming increasingly influential, and if you know of any in your particular field, drop them a line to see if they would like a review copy. Reviews on Amazon.co.uk can also be a major influence on prospective purchasers there. It would be unethical to review your own titles here, but there is nothing wrong in encouraging known fans of the book to post some positive comments.

Don't forget review—or rather preview—coverage in *The Bookseller* magazine either. This will be the first opportunity you have to publicize your books to retailers, so try to get your books featured in the magazine's rolling programme of new release round-ups. Remember that these tend to run three or four months before publication to tie in with retailers' buying patterns, so you will have to send out material even earlier than that. See the Marketing chapter for more on this.

TV AND RADIO

Valuable though reviews are, any publicity you can get for your books on national television or radio will probably reach many more people. Unless you have lots of celebrities among your authors, it's not easy to achieve—but with hard work, imagination and a bit of luck it can be done. There's certainly no harm in trying.

The key to securing broadcast coverage for any book is to find a good hook. Any TV or radio coverage will require an entertaining or topical angle and, probably, an author who is happy to talk and can stimulate opinion and debate (see below for more on working with authors to this end). If you have an author who is an expert on a subject that is suddenly newsworthy and who is available to talk to the media, for instance, put him or her forward for comment on news channels and in newspapers. If you have books that somehow reflect a current trend or fashion—on a popular diet or holiday destination, for example—offer up their authors to discuss that trend on shows.

Aside from celebrity-focused slots, good opportunities for TV coverage include chat or magazine shows and the rolling news channels. Radio slots include *Front Row*, *Start the Week*, *In Our Time* and *Loose Ends* on BBC Radio 4, plus *Night Waves* on Radio 3, though other specialist publishers might find other opportunities (travel publishers might get their books on to the *Excess Baggage* show, for instance). Books-dedicated strands on Radio 4 include *Book of the Week*, *Book at Bedtime*, *Open Book* and *Book Club*. The *Thinking Allowed* programme is an excellent opportunity for academic or specialist publishers.

For coverage on these or other slots, publishers need to contact the relevant producer or booker. Look for their names and numbers on the programme's website—most can be easily tracked down on the BBC's umbrella site—and get to know a little bit about the show you are pitching for space on. Bookers will soon be put off if it is clear you haven't done your homework. They are generally frantically busy, so keep pitches short and to the point. Email contact is usually best. Think about exclusivity—some shows will not want to touch a story if someone else has already covered it, and the BBC's radio programmes are wary of overlapping or clashing schedules with each other, so it's usually best to pitch to just one of them and, if you've offered it elsewhere, to mention that fact. If you have more than a few books that you think a TV or radio slot might be interested in, try to arrange a lunch or coffee meeting to discuss your list. If and when you do succeed in getting coverage, pester to make sure that the book is plugged on screen or air.

OTHER MEDIA COVERAGE

Getting media coverage for your books doesn't necessarily have to mean a review or TV or radio appearance. Try to think laterally and imaginatively about ways to get the media interested, and keep your eyes and ears open for opportunities.

Getting to know the publications where you want coverage can help you drum up some coverage. Look out for regular features or little columns featuring different contributors from week to week or month to month, and pitch your authors to appear there. Newspapers have dozens of slots like 'A Day in the Life' or 'My Favourite Holiday' that need filling. You might also consider running some competitions with newspapers or magazines, offering a few copies of your books as prizes in return for some free editorial space.

Media coverage can also be secured by allowing newspapers or magazines to publish one or a series of extracts from your books, sometimes, but not always, in return for a fee. Pitch for these well in advance of publication—a couple of months is about right, and perhaps longer for monthly magazines. As with media appearances, always insist that any extracts are accompanied by a prominent plug for the book. See the Rights and Copyright chapter for more on serial deals.

Newspapers and magazines often maintain lists of publicity contacts whom they can approach if they have general requests for material or specific subjects to fill. Try to get your name added to these, and also keep an eye on the website of the Publishers Publicity Circle, where media outlets sometimes post ad hoc requests for content from publishers.

When planning media coverage, don't overlook local media. While obviously reaching far fewer readers than their national equivalents, local or regional newspapers can be much more receptive, usually agreeing to review or feature a book if it has a connection with their area, however tenuous. The BBC's network of local radio stations is also generally very responsive too; many stations are desperate for locally-oriented material to fill their schedules and will welcome approaches, and syndicated coverage across the BBC may be possible.

With so many media channels to fill, measuring the coverage you generate can be difficult. If you have lots of books and publicity, you might consider hiring a media monitoring or clippings agency like Durrants to collect reviews and other media mentions on your behalf.

AUTHORS AND PUBLICITY

In the past, authors tended to be in the background when it came to publicity—but now they are an essential part of the story. Media-savvy writers understand the value of the media and how it works, and will be prepared to work hard to promote their book in whatever way they can. Unless they are exceptionally talented writers, you might ask whether authors who are bad at publicity and unwilling to help out are really worth publishing at all. Given that budgets for publicity are invariably tight, it is not unreasonable to expect authors to contribute to campaigns by giving up some time and contributing ideas. Increasingly in publishing, it is a question of selling the author as much as the book, and in sectors with tight-knit audiences in which the writer is well known, he or she can be a powerful publicity tool.

Well ahead of publication, assess all of your authors for publicity potential. Many publishers do this via a standard questionnaire, asking authors about their time commitments around publication and ideas for media coverage, as well as some standard biographical information that can be used in marketing or publicity. Ask authors what they see as the appeal and main selling points of their books; which newspapers, magazines and journals might review it; and, if it's for use in education, which particular courses it is appropriate to. Look for things in your authors' background that might be interesting to the media. Do they have an interesting life story that you could link in to the book? Are they particularly renowned in their field? Are they members of groups or institutions that might be interested in their book? Do they have any useful contacts in the media? Ask authors to make the most of any connections, and see if they are prepared to write pieces or appear on television or radio if the opportunity arises.

Try to work out how confident they will be in any media or public appearances. If they are in education, see if they will be prepared to run workshops or talks at exhibitions and conferences. To some this sort of activity will be second nature, but others might need some help, either through formal media training or, more likely, through friendly advice and encouragement from yourself.

Don't underestimate the power of your author's brand. If he or she is well known in a particular field, make the author rather than the book the focus of your publicity campaign. Ask authors to include on their email signatures a link to somewhere people can purchase their book—either your own website or one of the online retailers. If they have one, use authors' websites as a publicity tool too, displaying the book prominently on their homepages or blogs.

BOOK SIGNINGS, EVENTS AND LAUNCH PARTIES

Signings have traditionally been the most popular sort of author event in bookshops. But they are only really appropriate to a handful of books, and unless you have a celebrity author you will invariably have to work hard to get an audience. Putting up a poster is not enough to guarantee a crowd, and you will probably have to get either advertising or editorial coverage in local media. Try to make as many people as you can aware of your event. Publicize it via newsletters or web groups relevant to the book or author. Spread the word among local societies or reading groups. Ask your author to invite all his friends and contacts. Check with the venue to see who will be responsible for supplying books—there's nothing more likely to rile an author than a signing with no books. Just about every publicist in publishing has a story of a signing to which no one came, so try not to take it personally if it happens to you. But do consider whether it's really worth doing it again.

For some books like fiction or poetry, readings can be better than signings in publicity and sales terms. Again, you will have to work hard if the author isn't well known, so don't charge much, if at all, for any events, and consider incentives to get people along. The promise of a free glass or two of wine, for instance, can do wonders for turnout. Think about joining forces with local organizations or groups. If it's a local history book, for instance, ask societies in the area if they would be interested in hosting a joint event. And think about other angles on events. Could you organize a quiz around the book? A discussion or question and answer session? A lecture? Or perhaps an evening themed around its subject?

In trade publishing at least, there was a time when a launch party was an integral part of any publicity campaign. Nowadays they are much rarer, with publishers seeking a measurable return in publicity or sales on any outlay.

Launches can be good for specialist markets where you can be confident that everyone who attends will either buy the book or publicize it in the media, but in others they can be an expensive extravagance. As with all events, hold one only for sound commercial reasons and not because your author demands one. Make books available for sale and, unless you're feeling exceptionally generous, be wary of giving them away to guests free.

FESTIVALS

Book festivals can be another good way of publicizing your books. The biggest three in the UK are Cheltenham, Hay and Edinburgh, but below these are many dozens more in all corners of the country. Most will be glad to hear from you if you have an established name or celeb to offer, but they may well also be open to ideas if you can think of a good topical angle for an event. Local-interest books are particularly popular—if you have a book about, set in or somehow connected to Yorkshire, for instance, scour the festivals in that county.

Most festival events involve authors reading or discussing their work, so make sure yours are confident enough to do this before committing them. And all but the largest will not normally pay authors to attend or, sometimes, even meet expenses, so you need to be sure either that your author would like to do it for its own sake or that you can sell some books at the event. This can be done, but you will have to decide if the work and expense involved in setting everything up will be worthwhile. Festival appearances can be good for the author's ego but not necessarily for the publisher's bank balance.

PRIZES

There are dozens of literary awards in the UK, and no matter how specialist your publishing there is probably something to suit your books. Unless you win the Booker or the Orange prize, these awards do not tend to have a massive impact on sales, but they can be useful for publicity purposes and do have a cumulative effect. They are also great for the egos of authors and publishers alike.

Research which awards are relevant to your publishing and make a diary note of deadlines and submissions policies. Booktrust has a very useful online database of major and minor awards. Don't be shy of entering; many specialist awards have surprisingly low entry fields, and you may well stand a good chance of winning.

If any of your books win—or even if they are shortlisted—use it as an excuse to publicize the book in question. Draw up a brief press release and circulate it among your media contacts. Whenever you refer to the book in the future, make sure the words 'award-winning' are in close proximity, and consider flagging up the fact on the book, either via the cover of a new edition or a sticker. Don't forget about prizes for your company as a whole too—there are plenty of local, regional and national awards for businesses and start-ups of all shapes and sizes, but the premier prizes are, of course, the IPG Awards!

STAFF, SKILLS AND OUTSOURCING

Many independent publishers will not have a dedicated publicity person, instead either doing the job themselves or relying on sales and/or marketing specialists to add it to their responsibilities. Whoever is doing the job will need the ability to think creatively and imagine fresh and different ways of generating coverage. But given the need to plug away at media contacts, hard work and organizational skills are probably even more important. Enthusiasm, calmness under pressure and a thick skin are essential, as is flexibility and the capacity to respond to sudden changes in schedules and media demands.

People skills are vital when it comes to cajoling and placating authors or working with other publishing functions in the company. It's particularly important to have good communications with whoever is selling and distributing your books—whether that is in or out of house—as a good publicity campaign can increase sales, and it helps if you can forecast extra demand a little in advance. Tell your sales reps about any substantial media coverage so they can make sure retailers have a good supply of your books ready.

Publicity can be a good job to outsource to freelancers or agencies. It is something that new publishers, without the contacts that are so important in publicity, might especially consider. There are plenty of freelancers, many of whom have previously worked in large publicity departments and who should have good contact books. Some are service members of the IPG, and some of your fellow members will be able to supply recommendations. The Publishers Publicity Circle is another useful resource, offering a database of freelance members and a notice board for recruitment. Larger and recommended publicity agencies specializing in publishing include Colman Getty and Midas, both of whom have long track records in books and excellent contacts.

Whoever you work with, ask for endorsements; look for evidence of hard work as well as flair; brief very closely on what you want; and consider negotiating fees based on success—perhaps paying extra if media coverage exceeds expectations, for instance. If possible, test out potential freelancers or agencies before you hire them for the first time, perhaps by asking them for their initial ideas on a particular project.

RESOURCES
TRADE GROUPS
Publishers Publicity Circle
A professional and social group for book publicists, with regular speaker events and an awards programme, plus a useful directory of members including free-lancers. An excellent source of publicity advice and support.
Web www.publisherspublicitycircle.co.uk
Tel 020 8994 1881

MEDIA CONTACTS
Arts Media Contacts
Subscription service offering a useful directory of contacts and various tools for planning and managing campaigns. Free trials are available.
Web www.artsmediacontacts.co.uk
Tel 01273 488996

BBC
Search here for contacts at the TV or radio programmes you want to pitch to.
Web www.bbc.co.uk

BBC Local Radio
Helpful listings of the BBC's network of local radio stations across England.
Web www.bbc.co.uk/england/radindex.shtml

Daryl Wilcox
Provider of databases of media contacts.
Web www.dwpub.com
Tel 0845 370 7777

Durrants
Agency monitoring media coverage on behalf of clients.
Web www.durrants.co.uk
Tel 020 7674 0200

Media UK
Very useful free online database of contacts in TV, radio, newspapers and magazines—a good starting point if you need to find someone.
Web www.mediauk.com

The Newspaper Society
Useful database of local newspapers across the UK and their contact details.
Web www.newspapersoc.org.uk
Tel 020 7632 7400

Publishers Publicity Circle
Has an online notice board where media contacts regularly request content.
Web www.publisherspublicitycircle.co.uk

UK newspapers and magazines
Handy database of print media contacts to try if you want to sell serial rights.
Web www.mediauk.com

FESTIVALS

Edinburgh International Book Festival
Runs for two weeks each August as part of the city's wider arts festival.
Web www.edbookfest.co.uk
Tel 0131 718 5666

The Guardian Hay Festival
In the second half of May each year.
Web www.hayfestival.com
Tel 0870 787 2848

The Times Cheltenham Festival
Over ten days in October.
Web www.cheltenhamfestivals.com
Tel 01242 774400

Literary Festivals in the UK
A useful round-up of some of the country's other leading festivals.
Web www.thewordtravels.com/literary-festivals.html

PRIZES

Booktrust
Handy directory of book prizes in the UK.
Web www.booktrust.org.uk
Tel 020 8516 2977

British Book Industry Awards
Prizes across the publishing and bookselling industry, including an award for Independent Publisher of the Year.
Web www.britishbookindustryawards.co.uk
Tel 0203 089 4460

The IPG Awards
The IPG's annual prizes, presented at the Annual Conference in March. All members are warmly encouraged to enter!
Web www.ipg.uk.com/awards
Tel 01437 563335

AGENCIES AND FREELANCERS

Angela Martin PR
Tel 020 7701 4723

Annabel Briggs Publicity
Tel 01273 400406

Arts and Books PR
Web www.artsandbookspr.co.uk
Tel 07968 352213

Booked PR
Web www.bookedpr.com
Tel 01730 233885

Cameron Publicity and Marketing
Web www.cameronpm.co.uk
Tel 07903 951957

Claire Bowles PR
Web www.clairebowlespr.co.uk
Tel 01858 565800

Colbert Macalister
Web www.colbertmacalister.co.uk
Tel 01494 434548 and 020 8671 6615

Colman Getty
Web www.colmangettypr.co.uk
Tel 020 7631 2666

Emma O'Bryen
Tel 020 7619 0098

Flora Littlejohn
Web www.floralittlejohn.com
Tel 020 7371 9283

FMcM Associates
Web www.fmcm.co.uk
Tel 020 7405 7422

Gotch Solutions
Tel 020 7733 0882

Macdougall Gabriel Associates
Web www.mga-pr.com
Tel 020 7836 4774

Maria Boyle Communications
Web www.mbcomms.co.uk
Tel 020 8876 8444

Midas PR
Web www.midaspr.co.uk
Tel 020 7584 7474

The Oxford Publicity Partnership
Web www.oppuk.co.uk
Tel 01327 357770

Platypus PR
Web www.platypuspr.com
Tel 01273 692215

Publicity and the Printed Word
Tel 0131 337 9724

Publishing Services
Web www.publishing-services.co.uk
Tel 020 8222 6800

Riot Communications
Web www.riotcommunications.com
Tel 020 3174 0118

Stonehill Salt PR
Web www.stonehillsaltpr.co.uk
Tel 01620 829800

Sue Blake Media Relations
Web www.sueblakemedia.co.uk
Tel 020 8979 5220

BOOKS

1700 Ways to Earn Free Book Publicity by Anne Hart (iUniverse.com, $17.95, 9780595385539)

Effective Media Relations by David Wragg, Alison Theaker and Michael Bland (Kogan Page, £16.99, 9780749443801)

How to Market Books: The Essential Guide to Maximizing Profit and Exploiting All Channels to Market by Alison Baverstock (Kogan Page, £25, 9780749450205)

The New Rules of Marketing and PR: How to Use News Releases, Blogs, Podcasting, Viral Marketing and Online Media to Reach Buyers Directly by David Meerman Scott (John Wiley, £9.99, 9780470379288)

Planning and Managing Public Relations Campaigns by Anne Gregory (Kogan Page, £16.99, 9780749429911)

Plug Your Book: Online Book Marketing for Authors by Steve Weber (Weber Books, £9.49, 9780977240616)

The Publicity Handbook by David Yale (McGraw-Hill, £13.99, 9780844232423)

Public Relations for Dummies by Richard Kirshenbaum (John Wiley, £13.99, 9780471772729)

The Public Relations Handbook by Alison Theaker (Routledge, £22.99, 9780415428026)

The Reading Groups Book by Jenny Hartley (OUP, £7.99, 9780199255962)

Media 08 edited by Janine Gibson (Guardian Books, £19.99, 9780852650912)

7 DISTRIBUTION

CONTENTS

Doing your own distribution or working with a third party / What distributors do / Choosing the right distributor / Negotiating contracts / Working with a distributor / Reviewing and switching distributors / Coping with crises / Distributors and the environment / Overseas distribution / Resources

Distribution isn't exactly the most glamorous aspect of publishing, but it is one of the most important. Get it right and you will keep your existing customers happy while finding new ones; get it wrong and you will lose them. Distribution is the engine that keeps publishing's wheels turning.

DOING YOUR OWN DISTRIBUTION OR WORKING WITH A THIRD PARTY

All new publishers must decide if they want to distribute their books themselves or outsource the job to someone else. Doing it yourself means you can control everything and provide the levels of customer support you want while also keeping your costs down. And on a very small scale, with a handful of books and a limited number of wholesale or retail channels to supply, distribution can be done from your home or office. To start with, at least, you may have no other option, since distributors may not take on new clients until they have a minimum number of books or turnover. Doing it yourself can also be a good way of getting to know your customers and what they want. Doing it well will help to promote your brand and books.

But the time and cost of managing stock, processing orders, co-ordinating dispatches, invoicing, handling returns and keeping up with all the administration involved should never be underestimated. If you have multiple routes to market and lots of small volume orders, distribution can soon take over your life and your property. Keeping your customers happy means supplying them with books promptly and accurately, so you need to be confident that your business is equipped to do so, both now and in the future if you grow.

The advantages of outsourcing to a specialist books distributor should be obvious. They take care of all the logistical challenges of supplying books around the country, and will be able to cope with the fluctuations in demand from your customers. They will improve the chances of your books getting into chains and other outlets since they will be easier and quicker to obtain. They have excellent contacts to help smooth your path to the people you want to trade with, and they give you access and accreditation to things like Electronic Data Interchange and PubEasy that would be costly and time-consuming to achieve on your own. Above all, they leave you free to concentrate on the things in publishing that you will do best—producing, marketing and selling books—secure in the knowledge that your distribution is being looked after by professionals. Unless your sales are very low, the costs of working with a distributor will always be outweighed by the benefits to your business. New publishers with ambitions to be successful and profitable are strongly recommended to outsource distribution as soon as they can.

Of course, it needn't be a straight choice between doing distribution yourself and getting someone else to do it for you. Some publishers combine the two, fulfilling some orders like direct sales themselves and getting distribution partners to do others—perhaps trade or export ones—on their behalf. If you use print-on-demand specialists to produce your books, another way of organizing distribution is to use your printer to dispatch orders on your behalf after printing them. Many now offer this service, and it can be a good way of keeping costs down for very small new publishers in particular, since it requires few upfront expenses beyond setting up the book for printing.

WHAT DISTRIBUTORS DO

Book distributors are either independently owned or part of a larger publishing group, offering services to other companies as well as their own. They supply books to the people who want to buy them, whether individuals or retailers who will sell them on. They take delivery of your books from yourselves or your printers, storing them securely in their warehouses. They then receive orders from your customers and fulfil them by picking, packing and dispatching your books, by road, rail, air or sea. They keep detailed records of all sales, including where, when and how your books have been sent out.

Beyond this, distributors offer a wide menu of extra services to pick and choose from. These can range from a few basic sales-related jobs to just about everything outside of editorial, but they generally tend to include things like invoicing, credit control, returns processing, marketing, sales representation, accountancy, royalties and the supply of review or inspection copies or books for fairs. You will have to pay for each extra service, of course, but many small companies find it is a relief to have them taken off their hands so they can concentrate on their publishing.

Of all the add-on services, credit control in particular is something best done at the point of distribution. But tread carefully before you sign up to any sales representation or marketing services. These are key parts of your business that it might be better to do yourself, or hand over to a freelance or agency specialist. Be wary of putting all your eggs in one distributor's basket.

Some distributors are now offering their own print-on-demand facilities— in effect making themselves your printer as well as your distributor. For small publishers intending to use POD for all their books, this can seem a neat and appealing way of doing things. But be wary of committing yourself to an exclusive POD deal with a distributor. Because this sector is changing so fast, it's best to leave your options open so you can work with other POD specialists and, often, get better rates. Remember that distributors will take delivery from other POD providers too.

CHOOSING THE RIGHT DISTRIBUTOR

Choosing a distributor is one of the most important decisions a publisher will ever have to make. So it is worth spending plenty of time to get it right.

Start by working out exactly what you want from a distributor and which of their menu of services you would like to use (see above). Next, draw up a shortlist of companies to approach. The leading companies are listed in the Resources section, but also ask around in the IPG and elsewhere for feedback on any partners you are considering. Distributors quickly develop reputations, good and bad, and between them IPG members have a vast amount of experience of just about every company. Most will be very happy to talk—perhaps in confidence—about the pros and cons of their arrangements. Try also to assess the robustness of your shortlisted companies. Check their latest accounts to see if they are in good shape. A reliable indicator of their prospects is whether they are taking on clients or shedding them. Steer clear if it's the latter.

Some distributors specialize in particular fields like educational or trade publishing, so research their client lists and decide which companies look most suitable to your list. A good one will know your market intimately; will be able to help you identify new routes to your customers; and might even have ways of helping you get your digital content onto the right platforms. Think too about which would be a good 'fit' for your company. Do you want to work with the distribution arm of a large multinational publisher, or would you feel happier partnering a smaller independent? Look for signs that a distributor is interested in your business and your books and sees you as more than just another customer.

Try to visit as many distributors as you can at the shortlist stage. Doing so will tell you so much more about your potential partner than websites or phone calls ever can—and it will also help you understand how distribution works. Publishers don't need to be experts in warehousing, picking and packing and logistics, but they should at least appreciate the basics.

While visiting a distributor, talk to as many people as you can. Talk to their customer service team, and ask to sit in on a few of their calls to see what kind of service they deliver. Good distribution and good customer service should be joined at the hip, since your distributor will be the most important point of contact for anyone buying your books. Also get to know the credit control people and work out how hard they would work to chase your money. Across the company, look for a can-do, flexible and hardworking approach.

Ask for a tour of the warehouse to see the company in action. Look at the technology. Chat to the IT people and ascertain whether the systems they use are compatible with your own; headaches may lie in store if they are not. Check that they are compliant with industry standards and initiatives like e4books and Batch. If they are not, ask why not.

Many distributors now have very high-tech systems and machinery to make their dispatches faster and more accurate, putting them light years ahead of their counterparts even ten years ago. Fancy technology doesn't necessarily make things better, of course, but if your distributor is still working on manual systems then they will have to introduce new technology sooner or later. Since switch-overs are a common cause of crises in distributors, you need to be confident they can manage any change. Ask too about the carriers that distributors work with to deliver books.

The location of a distributor may or may not be important to you. Having one near by obviously means you can visit often, but its geographical position doesn't really have any impact on its ability to supply books effectively, and distributors can be found all over Britain. More important is making sure that your distributor can cope with highs and lows of demand. If you have a crucial month when demand tends to peak, make sure they'll have plans in place to deal with that. Many have hotlines for the peaks of Christmas or academic buying seasons, for instance.

After making contact, distributors will want to know lots more about you, too. They will ask you to fill in a pile of forms outlining things such as your sales history and channel breakdown, top accounts, number of books, average net price, levels of returns, forward publishing plans, print runs and much more.

These will take time to complete but are worth filling in rigorously and honestly so that both sides know what they are committing themselves to. If you are just starting out in publishing and can't point to any sales history, present all your relevant information and projections in detailed business, publishing, marketing and sales plans. Distributors are used to dealing with these, and will be looking for sound, realistic forecasts rather than optimistic guesses.

The information you provide will influence a distributor's decision about whether to take you on. Doing so is not automatic, and if one decides to turn you down it will probably be for reasons that make sense to both of you. It is up to you to demonstrate your worth and potential as a publisher, and to prove that a distributor will be able to make money with and from you. Demonstrate your professionalism and outline your ambitions for the future. But don't feel intimidated. Distribution is generally a buyers' market, and whatever your size you should at least get a fair hearing from all potential partners.

NEGOTIATING CONTRACTS

Once you have assessed your shortlisted distributors, try to reduce them to two. It's now time to start interrogating firms a bit further and to knuckle down to draft contracts. Distributors should at this stage be happy to put you in touch with their existing clients too so you can get their opinions if you have not already done so.

Distributors' fees tend to be calculated as a percentage of total projected turn-over and/or a commission on sales. Other models of payment may be available, but try to avoid a flat rate across all distribution services. Rates should be different, for instance, for the distribution of books sold on consignment or printed on the distributor's own POD facility. Rates tend to be between 10 and 15%, and while small publishers might not have huge clout, competition for clients is such that there is often room to negotiate. Don't be afraid to play distributors off against one another. And don't assume that cheapest is always best. The old rule that you get what you pay for is usually true in distribution.

Discuss when you will be paid for your sales and how your money will be handled. Most distributors now hold their clients' money in ring-fenced accounts that are protected in the event of the former falling into difficulties, but double check that this is the case. Also check proposed fees very carefully to make sure there will be no surprise extras. Add-on charges may include carriage, the cost of processing returns and any bank charges incurred from handling credit and debit cards, unless they are covered by an all-in fee. Look out for stealth clauses penalizing you for holding excess stock in a distributor's warehouse; for distributing more than an agreed number of inspection or review copies; or for excess credit notes. These charges can stack up, so go through contracts with a fine toothcomb and query anything you're not happy with. Ask a lawyer to do so if you are worried about missing anything.

Distribution contracts give security to both sides, but try to push for rolling, renewable contracts rather than long-term agreements. Three years is about right in the first instance, since this gives both sides enough time to get to know each other without committing you for too long if you're not happy with the relationship.

Remember that you may want or need to adjust your own terms to customers to reflect your distribution costs. If you are selling direct, it's not unreasonable to add a small surcharge that you can bill as 'carriage', 'post and packing' or 'handling' fees. If you are selling via distributors to retailers, factor in your distribution costs when setting your discounts. Your pricing structure is entirely up to you rather than your distributor, even if they have a standard policy. If they refuse to implement your prices and follow your wishes, look elsewhere.

WORKING WITH A DISTRIBUTOR

Communication and good personal relationships are paramount in distribution. Get to know your potential partners thoroughly before you sign any deal with them, and be sure that you will be confident and happy working with them. Establish at least one contact to whom you can address your queries. Visit often, or use book fairs to meet with other key contacts like credit control and customer service managers.

Good data and systems are crucial for both sides. Before you sign any contract, check that you will be able to get the reports you want, and make sure the systems are in place for you to receive it. If you are selling books from your own website, make sure the feeds are set up to pass the orders on to your distributor. Don't underestimate the time it takes to learn new systems and tackle any glitches.

Distributors' records should be able to tell you in real time how many orders have been received for any title, as well as everything you need to know about cash flow, levels of stock and returns. Keep a particularly close eye on credit control and bad debts. Properly used, data can also identify your leading customers and inform your future publishing strategies as well as printing decisions. Distributors' reports should be web-based and secure so you and your colleagues can access them at any time. Publishers should be drilling down into their distributors' data at least weekly, if not daily.

Make sure that your distributor knows your company inside out. Its customer service staff in particular need to be regularly briefed about your books so they know what they are talking about when dealing with customers. Invite key contacts at your distributor to any sales presentations, staff away days or social occasions you have. Think of your distributor as part of your business, not outside of it.

REVIEWING AND SWITCHING DISTRIBUTORS

Monitor your distributors' performance carefully and make sure they are meeting all their obligations and your expectations. And make sure you are getting value for money. Regular joint reviews of the way you do things—ideally once or twice a year—can identify areas where you can make savings and improve efficiencies.

Unless there is a compelling reason, switching distributors is something to be avoided. Beyond the time and costs of physically transferring stock, there are the burdens of retraining on new systems, informing customers of changes and all the processes of selection and negotiation outlined above. Avoid it unless your distributor is in danger of going bust, seriously neglectful or in breach of contract. Instead, try to address any grievances and don't be afraid to re-negotiate terms if you don't think you're getting a good enough deal.

If you do have to move, start researching new partners and planning handovers about a year before your distribution agreement is due to end. Involve your whole company in any decision to switch—they will have valuable contributions to make, and morale can plummet if the upheaval of a move is imposed on them without warning. Talk to your new partner about the practicalities of a switch well in advance, and factor in plenty of time for delays and disruption. Good distributors will make the transition from bad ones as smooth as possible for you, but it will inevitably entail a lot of hard work.

COPING WITH CRISES

For some unlucky independent publishers, the biggest challenge they can ever face is the failure of their distributor. At worst, this can mean that a publisher's stock and cash goes down with it, with no means of retrieving it once the administrator has taken charge.

It is difficult to work out if your distributor will be good in a crisis, but you at least need to trust them to be honest and communicative about any difficulties. Check also that your money is being kept in ring-fenced accounts that cannot be raided in a crisis (see above). Ask your distributor about any crisis contingency plans they might have, and try to imagine and plan how you would cope if you were left without a distributor.

Warning signs to watch for include a distributor trying to hold on to your money for longer than usual, or losing clients. Word soon gets around if a distributor gets into difficulties, so keep your ear to the ground and stay in touch with others on your distributor's client list. If you have concerns, run a credit check with an agency or do a spot check on their latest accounts at Companies House. Trust your instincts, and if you think a distributor is in serious trouble, stop supply and minimize your risk. If it is clear that administration is imminent, try to retrieve your stock from a distributor's warehouse, and make contact with a receiver or administrator as soon as they are appointed. Keep hold of your shortlist of preferred distributors so you can quickly go back to one in the event of a crisis.

DISTRIBUTORS AND THE ENVIRONMENT

Distribution isn't exactly the most environmentally friendly part of publishing, but pressure from publishers means that more and more specialists are having to think about their green policies. If they matter to you, it's worth adding them to the list of things to investigate when talking to potential distribution partners. Most will be able to talk about what they are doing to reduce their carbon footprint, packaging and book miles, and you should be wary of anyone without an environmental action plan. See the Publishing and the Environment chapter for more about this.

OVERSEAS DISTRIBUTION

If you are selling books overseas, you will need to decide how you want to fulfil your orders: by doing it yourself; getting a UK distributor to do it for you; or getting a local wholesaler or distributor in each of your markets to do it for you.

If your overseas orders are fairly small, one of the first two options will probably suit. More and more publishers are choosing to distribute overseas from the UK, and carriers are now so fast and efficient that most orders can be fulfilled within a reasonable time. If you have a UK distributor offering worldwide distribution, it usually makes life easier if you nominate them as your point of contact for any overseas customers.

The costs of setting up local distribution are prohibitive for most small publishers. But if your sales are increasing overseas, fulfilling orders via a local distributor or wholesaler will have the advantages of improved delivery speed and more local customer service. Some publishers like in particular to set up distribution arrangements in North America, where sales can be high and the market benefits from local attention. Popular distributors for IPG members here include the Independent Publishers Group and Publishers Group West.

Terms of trading with overseas distributors are similar to those with UK ones, though you will also have to remember to allocate the costs of getting your books to them in the first place. These are usually borne by the distributor, though the UK publisher might pay for books to be delivered to the distributor's shipping agent or local port.

Finding a good overseas distributor requires much the same research and interrogation as it does if you are looking in the UK (see above). The difficulty, of course, is that you cannot easily visit prospective partners, unless you set aside a special trip to see candidates. You might also not be able to learn as much about them as you would your UK partners, so tread very carefully. Some IPG members have experience of overseas distribution and some salutary lessons from the US in particular, so ask around at events or on the forum.

RESOURCES
UK DISTRIBUTORS
BEBC Distribution
Web www.bebcdistribution.co.uk
Tel 01202 712934

Bookpoint
Web www.bookpoint.co.uk
Tel 01235 400400

The Book Service (TBS)
Web www.thebookservice.co.uk
Tel 01206 256000

Booksource
Web www.booksource.net
Tel 0845 370 0063

Book Systems Plus
Web www.booksystemsplus.com
Tel 01223 894870

Central Books
Web www.centralbooks.com
Tel 0845 458 9911

Combined Book Services (CBS)
Web www.combook.co.uk
Tel 01892 839819

Gazelle Book Services
Web www.gazellebookservices.co.uk
Tel 01524 68765

Grantham Book Services (GBS)
Web www.granthambookservices.co.uk
Tel 01476 541000

Inpress
Web www.inpressbooks.co.uk
Tel 020 8832 7464

Littlehampton Book Services (LBS)
Web www.lbsltd.co.uk
Tel 01903 828500

Macmillan Distribution
Web www.macmillandistribution.co.uk
Tel 01256 329242

Marston Book Services
Web www.marston.co.uk
Tel 01235 465504

NBN International
Web www.nbninternational.com
Tel 01752 202300

Orca Book Services
Web www.orcabookservices.co.uk
Tel 01202 665432

Portfolio Books
Web www.portfoliobooks.com
Tel 020 8326 5620

Publishers Group UK
Web www.pguk.co.uk
Tel 020 8804 0400

The Trade Counter
Web www.tradecounter.co.uk
Tel 01449 766629

Turnaround
Web www.turnaround-psl.com
Tel 020 8829 3000

Turpin Distribution
Web www.turpin-distribution.com
Tel 01767 604951

Vine House Distribution
Web www.vinehouseuk.co.uk
Tel 01825 767396

INDUSTRY STANDARDS AND INITIATIVES
Batch
The industry system to help everyone trade electronically; most distributors are
signed up to it.
Web www.batch.co.uk
Tel 020 7802 0847

E4books
Initiative to promote better use of e-commerce in the book supply chain. Check
if your distributor is accredited.
Web www.bic.org.uk/e4books
Tel 020 7607 0021

US DISTRIBUTORS
Independent Publishers Group
Web www.ipgbook.com
Tel 00 1 312 337 0747

Publishers Group West
Web www.pgw.com
Tel 00 1 212 614 7888

8 BIBLIOGRAPHIC AND IT

CONTENTS

ISBNs and ISSNs / Bar codes / Producing bibliographic data / Classifying books / Supplying bibliographic data / Legal deposit / ONIX / Electronic trading / e4books and e-commerce strategies / IT and systems / Resources

They are unlikely to be anyone's favourite subjects, but good bibliographic data and solid IT are cornerstones of successful publishing. If you can supply your bibliographic data accurately and on time, you may be surprised how many orders you receive without having to lift a finger. But get it wrong and your books will be far less likely to be put on sale by retailers in the first place, scuppering their chances of success from the start. Wherever you are aiming to sell your books, compiling and feeding good data can make as much as 25% difference to your sales, and if you're not interested in getting it right, it's probably not worth publishing books.

Fortunately, producing great data isn't rocket science, and requires only sound organization and planning. In the same way, reliable IT systems will drive an efficient business, making day-to-day life much simpler and leaving you free to get on with the fun stuff, like producing great books.

ISBNS AND ISSNS

Although it is not a legal requirement, the vast majority of books published in the UK carry an International Standard Book Number (ISBN)—a unique 13-digit code to identify them to the people who want to buy them. Without one, retailers are very unlikely to stock your book, or even to know that it exists. Every book needs one.

ISBNs are usually printed above a book's bar code—for which it forms the basis (see below)—and on the title verso in the preliminary pages. To get one, new publishers need to register with the UK ISBN Agency, run in the UK by Nielsen. Registration gives all publishers a unique ISBN prefix, which will appear towards the front of each of your books' ISBNs and identify you as the publisher of them. When registering, publishers can buy ready-to-go ISBNs in blocks of either 10, 100 or 1,000. Single ISBNs are not available. You can then allocate each of your ISBNs as you like for any book you publish, completing a registration form for each to indicate basic information like title, author and price. Reprints can carry the same ISBN as their original, but new editions with substantial changes require a new one.

Register each ISBN as far ahead of publication as you can, since it will be a key ingredient in the bibliographic data you will need to supply later. Processing time for applications is usually no more than ten working days, though a fast-track service is available for anything urgent. For application forms and prices, contact the ISBN Agency, which can also help with any queries you have about getting or using ISBNs.

Journals or other serial publications are identified by an eight-digit International Standard Serial Number (ISSN) rather than an ISBN. These are available from the ISSN UK Centre, run by the British Library.

BAR CODES

Like its ISBN, a bar code is a non-essential but extremely useful element of any book. The parallel black lines of the bar code contain the book's ISBN and indicate key pieces of information about it. The code can be scanned at every stage of the supply chain and makes life much easier for distributors, booksellers and others. Most retailers are unlikely to stock a book that doesn't have one.

Bar codes come in a few different formats, but are generally positioned on a book's back cover, often at the bottom. Any publisher making them less prominent risks the ire of retailers who subsequently have to hunt around for them. Bar codes need to be printed carefully to ensure accuracy, though all popular digital or litho printing methods will do the job adequately. If you are using one, a designer will usually generate a bar code for you, and distributors and printers will also be able to advise. Specialist companies are available to help produce bar codes or sell software that will enable you to do the job yourself, while Book Industry Communication (BIC) has a very useful downloadable guide to all bar code issues that includes contact details for suppliers.

PRODUCING BIBLIOGRAPHIC DATA

Getting ISBNs for your books is the first step towards obtaining and managing professional bibliographic information for them.

When producing it, all publishers should as a minimum aim to reach BIC BASIC, a very useful set of standards developed by BIC to outline how product information should be compiled and communicated between people in the book trade. To comply with BIC BASIC standards, you will need to produce the following nine pieces of information for each of your books:

13-digit ISBN
Title (in full and without abbreviations)
Type of product and format (hardback, paperback, audiobook, etc.)
Subject classification (see section below)
Publisher and supplier (your details, including any imprint the book is published under, plus details of where a bookseller can obtain your book—your distributor or a wholesaler, for instance)
Publication date
Price (remember to include VAT for non-book items)
Availability status (whether in or out of print or awaiting a reprint, for instance; often updated by your distributor, if you have one)
Rights (in which territories you are entitled to sell the book; be as specific as you can, as per your contracts)

This is the mandatory data that all publishers should provide for all books. In addition, publishers might include details of a book's authors; its edition and whether it is part of a series; its extent, dimensions and weight; its language; its intended readership; details of any prizes it has won; and its jacket. The more information you can offer, the richer will be the picture of the book that is obtained by anyone searching for it.

To help manage all this information, new publishers should start and maintain a spreadsheet or database for their data, containing all the bibliographic information about all books. Manage it in a single place so that you have one official source for your data, and update it as often as necessary. If you don't already have one, consider a publishing system that has a built-in repository for your data (see below for more on this). Aim to have at least the basic bibliographic data for each book ready in whatever system you use at least six months before publication so you can meet deadlines for supply to Nielsen BookData and others (see below). Accuracy is absolutely essential, since any wrong information can wreck a book's chances of selling. No matter how confident you are, scrupulously double-check any bibliographic data you key in.

BIC has lots of useful downloadable guides to meeting the BASIC standards, and runs a Product Data Excellence Scheme, which all publishers should aim to complete. Bronze, silver and gold awards are given according to levels of compliance with data supply and ONIX (see below), and the award helps to demonstrate to others in the industry that you are serious about data. Details of the scheme and how to apply are available from BIC.

CLASSIFYING BOOKS

To meet BIC BASIC standards, you will need to learn and use a few codes for identifying things like the availability of books. In particular, you will need to classify and code each book you publish by subject. This is important because it will influence how a book is searched for and how it is categorized and shelved by booksellers. Subject codes are on various levels, beginning with broad categories before drilling down into more specific fields. A historical romance novel, for instance, might be classified first as F (Fiction); then FR (Romance Fiction); and then FRH (Historical Romance Fiction).

While categories are numerous and sophisticated they can never be perfect, and you may find it tricky to work out which of them is right for your book. It can help to think about classification from the point of view of the people you want to buy your books. Consider how a shopper, rather than you, would classify the book. If it is about the history of cooking, for instance, would they be likely to look for it in the cookery section of a bookshop or on the history shelves?

Long lists of the subject codes are available from BIC's website. So too is a very handy tool for helping to classify your books, developed by HarperCollins but available to use for free by all publishers. Remember that when you come to submit your classifications to bibliographic agencies, retailers, wholesalers and others, they may be subject to vetting and possible change. If you think a book's classification might be contentious, check to see how it has finally been registered.

SUPPLYING BIBLIOGRAPHIC DATA

All publishers need to supply bibliographic data to various aggregating agencies. Doing so will ensure your books are visible to the thousands of bookshops, libraries and others who use these agencies' products for identifying and buying books. Feeding your data into these agencies greatly increases the sales potential of your books at a stroke.

The leading bibliographic agency in the UK is Nielsen BookData, whose database holds some six million records of books and is used by individuals and organizations in the book industries in the UK and more than 100 other countries around the world to search for the books they want. Nielsen BookData's basic listings service is free, and any book that has an ISBN and is available to purchase is entitled to be included. Print-on-demand, audio and e-books are all eligible, as are novelty books or mixed products like book and CD packs. Beyond this free basic service, fees are payable to list more detailed information like descriptions, author biographies, reviews and promotional details. Fees are charged on an annual subscription basis, calculated according to how many new titles you add. The enriched service does beef up your book's presence on Nielsen BookData's database, and may well improve the chances of it being bought by anyone who reads the entry. It also gets you a named editor contact at Nielsen BookData, which can be useful. But you will have to decide if the benefits justify the expense.

In order to fit in with retailers' buying patterns and allow a bit of time for processing, product information should ideally be supplied to BookData around six months before publication, and closer to nine if you can manage it. Data for it should comply with BIC's BASIC standards (see above), and can be supplied electronically or via paper. Electronic supply is much preferred, and will save time for you as well as BookData. And since this may well become the only means of supply in the future, it is worth trying to set up systems to make electronic feeds as easy as possible.

If you are able to master it, the easiest method of data supply is via the ONIX standard (see below). Other formats may be acceptable if they are properly structured and can be easily imported into Nielsen BookData's database; check with staff there for guidance. Another option is PubWeb, BookData's portal for adding and updating data about your books. This is straightforward to use and ensures swift upload of your information, though you'll need to register to use it. It is probably the best option for small publishers.

Paper-based supply of bibliographic data is slower, and must be via either one of BookData's new titles forms, available to download from its website (these must be typed rather than handwritten); or your own Advance Information (AI) sheet (which must be kept to a single page and checked to make sure it includes all the required information). Paper-based material can be posted or emailed, and jackets supplied on disks or as email attachments.

However you choose to supply product information to Nielsen BookData, set yourself schedules and reminders to get the job done. Though it is a simple chore, its impact on sales means it is also one of the most important in publishing. If you have more than a few staff, allocate the job to someone and make sure they know their responsibilities. If you have more than a few books on your list, set aside a specific time each week or month to do the task.

Remember also to update your data should any details change. This might be done if the price or availability of a book changes or it wins a prize, for instance. Updates can be processed in the same way as original notifications, but you might find PubWeb the easiest way of viewing and changing details. If you have one, your distributor can update a book's availability and price on your behalf. To see how your data is actually presented to the world by BookData, you will need to subscribe to its products. Free trials are often available if you want to assess how useful it is. For any queries about this or any other aspect of data supply, Nielsen BookData's dedicated Publisher Helpdesk can help.

Publishers should also register their data with Bowker, the leading ISBN and bibliographic data provider in the US and an increasingly important aggregator worldwide. Its Global Books in Print service lists books published in the major English-language territories including the UK. Bowker used to take its British data from Nielsen BookData, but now compiles its own locally, so publishers need to submit to them separately. Like its rival, Bowker has guidelines for the supply of data, and a website—BowkerLink—via which it can be uploaded. Providing data to Bowker is free.

A third bibliographic agency with whom to register is Bibliographic Data Services (BDS), which provides data to libraries in particular. BDS is used by the British Library to administer its Cataloguing-in-Publication (CIP) programme, which records all new and forthcoming books for the British National Bibliography. The CIP programme is used by libraries to keep track of books they should be stocking now and in future, and many publishers include a note that they are registered with it on the copyright pages of their books. BDS updates the CIP database with information it receives from publishers, either on pre-printed forms or in the shape of AI sheets. BDS requires much the same bibliographic information as Nielsen BookData, at least four months before the publication date. Inclusion is free.

LEGAL DEPOSIT

A final bibliographic consideration for all publishers is the system of legal deposit, whereby copies of all new books published in the UK and Ireland are supplied free of charge to six designated national archives. These legal deposit libraries, sometimes known as copyright libraries, are the British Library, the Bodleian Library in Oxford, Cambridge University Library, the National Libraries of Scotland and Wales, and Trinity College Library in Dublin, Ireland.

The British Library is entitled to its copy of each of your books within one month of its publication, while the other five have the right to claim it within one year. Most publishers pre-empt that claim, arranging to supply all six promptly on publication or getting their distributors to do so on their behalf. Fortunately, five of the six libraries—all but the British Library—are represented by the Edinburgh-based Agency for the Legal Deposit Libraries, which accepts deliveries of books on behalf of all five, saving on multiple postings. No forms or fees are required. The British Library is in ongoing consultations with various groups about the legal deposit status of digitally published material. The British

Library and the Agency for the Legal Deposit Libraries can both help with any queries.

Supplying multiple copies for legal deposit can seem like a chore and expense, but it does guarantee that your books will be catalogued and preserved in national archives for generations to come, alongside those published over the last four centuries—a nice feeling for any publisher or author. It also means your books are listed on the British National Bibliography, used by individuals and organizations in the UK and worldwide to identify and obtain books.

ONIX

The days when publishers, booksellers and others in the supply chain used to communicate their data, orders and invoices by paper and post are long gone. Nowadays, all publishers need at least to some extent be able to present information and trade electronically. And the worldwide gold standard for doing this is ONline Information eXchange—ONIX.

ONIX is used to structure and transmit product information in an agreed, standard way. Devised specifically for the book business, it is maintained worldwide by EDItEUR and in the UK by BIC. Written in eXtensible Markup Language (XML), among many other things it enables publishers to create product 'files' containing all the essential information about a book outlined above. It is useful to publishers because it creates a single standard by which to structure and store information; and is useful for bibliographic agencies and booksellers because they can use it to receive and update product information quickly and accurately. Skilfully handled, ONIX can also be used to automatically flow information out of databases and into websites, catalogues, AI sheets and other materials.

Publishers can build platforms on which to use ONIX from scratch, using the technical guidelines provided by EDItEUR. A far more common solution, though, is to buy and use a publishing management system that is ONIX compliant. These give you ready-made ONIX feeds to send your data to agencies like Nielsen BookData and Bowker. See below for more about these systems, and in Resources for ones that are endorsed by BIC as ONIX-compatible.

Even if you use it via an off-the-shelf system, ONIX is undoubtedly daunting, requiring time and research to master. New publishers may not consider it a priority. But the rewards of ONIX are usually well worth any effort you put in, providing you with excellent data and brilliantly easy workflows that will save you a lot of time and be much valued by the people you work with. And there is plenty of help to bring you up to speed. BIC has comprehensive guides to ONIX and can advise on where to find more guidance, while BookData will provide advice and testing to make sure ONIX feeds it receives are properly set up.

ELECTRONIC TRADING

Providing accurate data gets publishers half of the way towards successful electronic trading. If you want to process orders from retailers and distribute books yourself—as opposed to getting a distributor to do the jobs for you—the second step is to make yourself familiar and compatible with the electronic channels through which booksellers, distributors and others can communicate and trade with you.

The most important channel is Nielsen BookNet, which provides a host of electronic ordering, trading and messaging services to the book trade. Its long established TeleOrdering system allows orders from booksellers, wholesalers, libraries or other purchasers to be routed to the correct publisher—or the distributor or supplier acting on its behalf—while its newer BookNet Web platform routes them instantly via the internet. Publishers can then acknowledge them, indicate the availability of the books required and supply invoices and credit notes electronically. Delivery notes, required for orders to Waterstone's stores, can also be generated. All the information is communicated from computer to computer via Electronic Data Interchange (EDI).

BookNet pledges to support publishers of any size wanting to trade electronically. Its most basic Online Collection Service allows small suppliers to pick up orders when they are placed, free of charge for the very smallest. At its simplest, BookNet Web needs no new software, though it can be integrated into systems you already have. BookNet also offers its own software package—DesktopEDI— to support its trading platforms, and this can be a good option for those with fairly small volumes of traffic. Any publisher can register with Nielsen BookNet, and staff there can provide more information about the set-up and costs of its electronic trading. Fellow IPG members will be able to offer advice on getting started with it too.

Other facilities for e-commerce in the UK include PubEasy, an online service for placing and fulfilling orders, run by Bowker as a rival to BookNet and used mainly by larger publishers and distributors. Smaller publishers can subscribe to PubEasy Exchange, an off-the-shelf package that provides a dedicated web page to which booksellers can send their orders for books. This can be a cost-effective way of beginning e-commerce.

Batch, meanwhile, is a web platform for booksellers and suppliers to send, receive, pay and query invoices online, cutting the time spent doing them separately and trimming piles of paper transactions. It also makes it easier for both sides to deal with returns by providing simpler, online authorization, and has affordable options for small publishers to get involved.

Most e-commerce platforms identify the various components of the supply chain—booksellers, publishers, wholesalers, distributors, libraries, printers and so on—by means of a seven-digit Standard Address Number (SAN) or 13-digit Global Location Number (GLN, sometimes also called an EAN). They are particularly useful for publishers or distributors who want to identify the locations of booksellers in order to deliver books to them. SANs and GLNs are allocated for a small fee by the SAN Agency, run in the UK by Nielsen.

Another way of encouraging greater electronic trading in the supply chain is to sign up to BIC's Industry Returns Initiative, or to get your distributor to do so. This shifts the process of authorizing returns online, cutting the considerable use of time and paper that it has previously involved.

E4BOOKS AND E-COMMERCE STRATEGIES

The best way to get to grips with the various e-commerce platforms is to get involved with e4books—the cross-trade initiative run by BIC to promote the wider use of electronic trading in the book supply chain. It aims to encourage publishers and booksellers to use electronic channels to share bibliographic information, place and acknowledge orders, invoice and request and authorize returns. The e4books scheme was launched to try to get as many companies as possible enabled for e-commerce by an official 'E-Day' in 2008, but its aims and resources continue to be valid.

BIC's e4books website has masses of useful resources to help publishers master their electronic trading, including case studies and step-by-step user guides. BIC also runs an accreditation scheme that allows publishers to display their e-commerce credentials via an e4books logo. To pass, publishers have to show that they can supply their bibliographic data in an electronic format that meets the BIC BASIC standard (see above); and use an accredited third party distributor (or else meet other, detailed criteria if they distribute books themselves). The process is confidential, and BIC can help publishers who don't yet meet the required standards to pull themselves up to the required level. Many IPG members are already accredited, and whatever your size, the scheme is highly recommended.

Not all trading is electronic, of course, and publishers still receive plenty of orders for their books by telephone, fax and post. It is still possible to get by without adopting systems and standards for electronic communication. But it may not always be, and through BIC the industry is gradually making e-commerce the standard. E-commerce can save all sides a lot of money in the printing, processing and posting orders to and fro, and when it works smoothly it saves time and cuts down on laborious administration and rekeying. By making ordering painless for retailers, it increases your chances of sales, too. Efficient electronic trading is something all new publishers should aspire to.

For now, though, the extent to which new small publishers embrace electronic trading and the ONIX standard will depend on how much time and money they have to invest in it. Independents will not be able to match larger companies' investment, but any efforts you can make will increase your chances of selling books and competing with larger rivals. The complexities of e-commerce and the likelihood of it becoming even more widespread in the future also increases the incentive for new publishers to get an e4books-accredited distributor to handle transactions and logistical headaches on their behalf. This is probably the easiest single step you can take towards e-commerce. See the Distribution chapter for tips on finding a good distributor and making the relationship work.

IT AND SYSTEMS

For help in e-commerce and managing bibliographic data, some publishers use software systems. These can certainly make day-to-day life easier in these respects, automating processes and saving time and effort. They can also help publishers manage their budgets and workflows, allowing the progress of a book to be logged and monitored through the publishing processes.

Systems divide publishers. Some IPG members swear by them as ways to stay on top of their work, while others think that a good memory and a pile of reminder notes serve just as well. Which side you stand on will probably depend on your size. Most small start-ups with only a handful of books will not need an expensive system, but larger companies may well find them useful as they expand, especially if they are serious about e-commerce.

As with any major business purchase, shop around for the product that suits you best. Draw up a list of things you want your system to do, rather than changing your existing workflows and habits to suit an existing system. Check that systems you consider can cope with the demands of ONIX and e-commerce by looking for BIC accreditation. Check that they can dovetail with any systems you are already using—this is particularly tricky when it comes to generic accounting packages. Above all, check carefully how much back-up support the deal includes. No matter how high your levels of technical expertise, you will need help implementing the system, tailoring it to your requirements and troubleshooting any difficulties that crop up. Think of it as buying an ongoing relationship rather than a piece of computer kit, and get to know the people behind the software.

There are plenty of options on the market, so hunt around for a good deal. Get recommendations from systems users within the IPG by asking for tips on the forum or the e-bulletin. Look closely at the small print in any contract before you sign it, since this will often reveal extra charges beyond the basic quote. And remember that introducing a new system from any of these companies will take time, money and commitment, and may often involve a great deal of upheaval and disgruntlement from staff.

Beyond your systems, the only IT equipment publishers should need is a good computer with broadband access. Macs are widely used in publishing, but if you plan to use one it might be worth checking that all your intended systems and applications are compatible with it, since some were built only with PCs in mind. See the Print and Production chapter for more on the design function of computers.

IT support can be a big issue for small publishers. Without the resources to employ specialist IT staff, publishers have the option of buying it in from agencies or consultants or doing it themselves. Given the likely importance of e-commerce and systems in the future, it is worth trying to learn as much about IT as you possibly can. It's not particularly exciting, but it is probably as important a part of running a successful publishing company as editing books or managing finances.

RESOURCES

NIELSEN BOOK

Handy gateway to all of Nielsen's services, including the ISBN Agency, BookData, BookNet and BookScan, all of which may well be used by publishers at some point.
Web www.nielsenbook.co.uk
Tel 01483 712200

ISBNS AND ISSNS

ISBN Agency
The UK office of the worldwide ISBN Agency, run by Nielsen.
Web www.isbn.nielsenbookdata.co.uk
Tel 0870 777 8712
Write to UK International Standard Book Numbering Agency, 3rd Floor, Midas House, 62 Goldsworth Road, Woking, Surrey GU21 6LQ

ISSN UK Centre
The UK office of the ISSN agency is run by the British Library.
Web www.bl.uk/issn
Tel 01937 546959
Write to The ISSN UK Centre, The British Library, Boston Spa, Wetherby, West Yorkshire LS23 7BQ

BAR CODES

Agamik
Provides software to help you make your own bar codes.
Web www.agamik.co.uk
Tel 01506 650163

BIC Guide
Free, downloadable guide to bar codes for books, containing all you could ever wish to know about the subject.
Web www.bic.org.uk/30/Barcoding-RFID

Computalabel
Another bar code software specialist.
Web www.computalabel.com
Tel 0116 270 0881

BIBLIOGRAPHIC DATA

Book Industry Communication (BIC)
The industry's leader on bibliographic matters, with lots of useful resources to help you master data organization and supply. Also runs BIC BASIC, the industry's data standards to which all publishers should aspire.
Web www.bic.org.uk
Tel 020 7607 0021

Bibliographic Data Services
Leading provider of data to libraries, and responsible for the Cataloguing-in-Publication programme.
Web www.bibliographicdata.com
Tel 01387 702251
Write to Publisher Liaison Department, Annadale House, The Crichton, Bankend Road, Dumfries DG1 4TA

Bowker UK
The leading bibliographic data provider in the US, with an increasing UK presence.
Web www.bowker.co.uk
Tel 01342 310450
Write to 1st Floor, Cantelupe Road, East Grinstead, West Sussex RH19 3BJ

Nielsen BookData
The UK's leading bibliographic services agency.
Web www.nielsenbookdata.com
Tel 0845 450 0016
Write to 89–95 Queensway, Stevenage, Hertfordshire SG1 1EA

PORTALS FOR SUPPLYING BIBLIOGRAPHIC DATA

BowkerLink
Bowker's website to help publishers upload data about their books.
Web www.bowkerlink.co.uk

PubWeb
Nielsen BookData's website to help publishers upload data about their books.
Web www.nielsenbookdata.com/pubweb

CLASSIFYING BOOKS

BIC Subject Categories
Details of subject category codes and a useful online tool to help you identify the right ones for your books.
Web www.bic.org.uk/7/Subject-Categories

LEGAL DEPOSIT

Agency for the Legal Deposit Libraries
One-stop shop for five of the six legal deposit libraries—excluding the British Library—and a good source of help for publishers.
Web www.legaldeposit.org.uk
Tel 02131 623 4680
Write to 161 Causewayside, Edinburgh EH9 1PH

British National Bibliography
The country's official bibliography, recording details of books supplied under the legal deposit scheme.
Web www.bl.uk/bibliographic/natbib.html
Tel 01937 546548

Legal Deposit at the British Library
The point of contact for all publishers.
Web www.bl.uk/aboutus/stratpolprog/legaldep/
Write to Legal Deposit Office, The British Library, Boston Spa, Wetherby, West
Yorkshire LS23 7BY
Tel 01937 546268

Legal Deposit and Digital Acquisitions
For enquiries about digital deposits, currently the subject of much discussion by
the British Library and stakeholders.
Tel 01937 546535

ONIX

BIC
Very helpful introductions to ONIX, its benefits and getting started with it.
Web www.bic.org.uk
Tel 020 7607 0021

EDItEUR
The agency responsible for ONIX worldwide, offering lots of information about
using it, plus technical specifications.
Web www.editeur.org
Tel 020 7503 6418

ONIXCentral
Very useful guide to the wonders of ONIX, including video demonstrations.
ONIXCentral also offers consultancy support to other publishers wanting to use
ONIX for specific projects.
Web www.onixcentral.com

WebGuild
Consultancy building ONIX-compliant websites for publishers—as well as the
IPG.
Web www.webguild.co.uk
Tel 0161 428 1102

Yahoo Group
Web group dedicated to ONIX chat.
Web http://groups.yahoo.com/group/ONIX/IMPLEMENT

ELECTRONIC TRADING

Batch

The Booksellers Association's initiative to make electronic communication between publishers and booksellers on orders and returns easier.
Web www.batch.co.uk
Tel 020 7802 0847

Industry Returns Initiative

BIC's project to reduce the costs and numbers of returns.
Web www.bic.org.uk
Tel 020 7607 0021

Nielsen BookNet

Runs the established TeleOrdering service and the BookNet Web platform providing electronic trading services to publishers and booksellers.
Web www.nielsenbooknet.co.uk
Tel 0870 777 8710

PubEasy

Bowker's Online trading platform to link booksellers and suppliers.
Web www.pubeasy.com
Tel 01342 310481

SAN Agency

The place to get a Standard Address Number (SAN) or Global Location Number (GLN), used to identify your business in the e-commerce supply chain.
Web www.san.nielsenbookdata.co.uk
Tel 0870 777 8712

E4BOOKS

e4books

BIC's initiative to improve e-commerce in the book supply chain. The website is full of useful resources to help all publishers improve their performance.
Web www.bic.org.uk/e4books
Tel 020 7607 0021

Yahoo discussion group

Forum for exchanging news and views on the e4books project—a little outdated now but still a useful port of call for any questions you may have.
Web http://tech.groups.yahoo.com/group/e4books

SYSTEMS

BIC

Downloadable guides to accredited system suppliers and a checklist of requirements for small publishers.
Web www.bic.org.uk/e4books/7/Systems-Suppliers

Systems providers marked with an asterisk below are acknowledged by BIC as ONIX-compliant.

Anko*
Web www.anko.ie
Tel 00 353 51396764

Avatar*
Web www.avatar-software.com
Tel 020 7516 2200

BooksoniX*
Web www.booksonix.com
Tel 01883 343000

Focus*
Web www.focusservices.co.uk
Tel 020 8469 4000

IBS
Web www.ibs.net
Tel 020 8207 5655

Klopotek
Web www.klopotek.de
Tel 020 7716 5500

Publishing Technology*
Web www.publishingtechnology.com
Tel 01865 397800

Schilling
Web www.schilling-ltd.co.uk
Tel 020 7868 1648

Sweetens
Web www.sweetens.co.uk
Tel 01772 641140

Trilogy*
Web www.trilogygroup.com
Tel 01242 222132

VirtuSales*
Web www.virtusales.com
Tel 0845 458 4020

9 RIGHTS AND COPYRIGHT

CONTENTS

Rights audits / Foreign rights / Co-editions / Selling strategies and techniques / Contracts / Book club rights / Serial rights / Electronic rights / Other rights / Book fairs / Buying rights / Staff and skills / Sub agents / Copyright / Licensing and collecting agencies / Permissions / Legal issues / Copyright in the digital age / Resources

For small independents with hard-pressed resources, the job of selling rights can seem either overwhelming or a low priority. In practice, though, it is not nearly as daunting as many seem to think, and it's something that can, with sound planning and hard work, be achieved by anyone. It can be great for business too, producing income that costs little to generate and goes straight to the bottom line. Other publishers and media around the world are hungry for content, and whatever your field there is almost certainly someone interested in it. Roll up your sleeves and get stuck into rights—you'll be glad you did.

RIGHTS AUDITS

Before dealing in rights, publishers need to be sure which are theirs to sell. If you are starting from scratch, conduct an audit of your contracts and work out which subsidiary rights—the rights beyond the basic agreement to publish and sell a printed book in the UK—are held by you and which are kept by your author or his or her agent. As well as making this very clear, contracts should also indicate the agreed splits in any rights deals, which can vary considerably. If you have signed a book from an agent, you may find that many rights have been kept back. Some authors also like to retain the right to approve any rights deal before it is signed. But most small publishers, dealing largely with unagented authors, will seek to retain all world rights in all books they publish.

Securing rights is just one more reason why new publishers should spend some time and money getting every line of their standard author contract exactly as they want it. For more on this, see the Editorial chapter. As a rule, the more rights you can retain in a book the better—but be sure you are likely to sell them before you pay extra for them. It is inadvisable to pay over the odds for rights that you will never sell on.

Once you have worked out which rights you can sell, assess each of your books as honestly and realistically as you are able. Consider all the rights options outlined in this chapter against each of your books. Can you think of any particular country in which any of them might be popular? Could they sell in the US as well as the UK? Is there anything newsworthy about their content that might help you to sell serial rights? Would they work in large print or audio format? Might book clubs be interested? Think about the rights potential as far ahead of publication as you can, in order to give you maximum time to sell rights. Ideally, think about rights even before drawing up a contract.

FOREIGN RIGHTS

The most popular sort of rights deal for UK publishers allows an overseas equivalent to publish an edition of a book in a particular territory. That overseas publisher bears the cost of printing and publishing, and pays an advance and royalties to the UK publisher or, in some cases, a flat fee for the rights to print and sell a set number of copies. The balance between the advance and royalties varies, but a good rule of thumb is to set any advance to about 60% of the total royalty that you expect to be earned from the first print run. Standard royalties are between 6% and 10%. All income is shared by the UK publisher with the author of the book, according to the terms of their contract. The overseas publisher will probably seek to translate and/or alter the book before publishing in order to make it appropriate to its market, but in some cases it may simply be reprinted untouched.

Because of the costs involved in translating a book, a lot of overseas rights deals are done to fellow English-language markets like the US. But if the book is popular enough, translation deals can be a useful source of income for small publishers. When dealing with these rights, be careful to specify which markets they are for. If you are selling Spanish rights to a Spanish publisher, for instance, you may wish to exclude the right to sell the book in Latin America. If you agree a royalty deal, also make sure you are going to receive accurate sales figures from the publisher you have sold rights to; this isn't always the case in developing markets. Overseas rights don't always have to be in translation, of course, and publishers can also sell the rights to publish a book in the English language in foreign territories.

CO-EDITIONS

Another way of selling a book to another publisher is to produce a co-edition. This sees a UK publisher working with one in another country to print editions of the same book for both markets.

Co-editions can reduce costs for both sides as they get to share a large print run of books. They work well for illustrated books or children's picture books where the text is of less importance and can be easily altered for different markets, and they are sometimes done on academic books too. Because they use the same language, co-editions are particularly common among UK and US publishers. If they have the idea for one, UK publishers usually sell it by presenting mock-up examples of the book to their overseas counterparts, at book fairs, in private meetings or via email.

Selling co-editions is as much about production as it is about rights. Schedules and contracts need to be carefully negotiated and watertight. Publication dates and cover prices need to be set, and the territories where each side has the right to sell the book agreed (in a UK–US co-edition, for instance, the US publisher usually sells into Canada while the UK publisher takes the Commonwealth and European territories). Royalties must be set—they are often included in the cost price of the book rather than calculated according to sales—and serial and book club rights must be allocated. The prices you agree should be all-inclusive, covering all 'extras' like distribution costs. UK publishers working with foreign partners also need to keep an eye on the exchange rate between the pound and their partner's currency, which at its extremes can make co-edition deals either juicily lucrative or prohibitively expensive. One way of balancing out fluctuations is to buy and sell in the same currency.

Whoever you are working with it pays to get to know them a bit, since good personal relationships are often the key to successful co-edition publishing. Set a clear design spec and production timetable that you are both happy with, and make sure you know who is supposed to be doing what and when. Put in place a sign-off system that gives both sides the opportunity to tick off all work on a co-edition as it is done; otherwise you risk arguing later on about who made a mistake and is liable for extra costs.

SELLING STRATEGIES AND TECHNIQUES

Whether you want to sell foreign or co-edition rights, a thorough strategy is vital if you want to maximize your revenue. Start by working out which territories around the world might be interested, and keep an eye in particular on emerging markets (China and India, for instance, have both become more and more important to publishers). Then scour publishers in these territories for ones that might be interested in the books you have to offer. Book fairs are ideal for this (see below) and the online or print International Literary Marketplace and the UK *Writers' and Artists' Yearbook* are good starting points from your desk.

Literary scouts—people who seek out good books on behalf of publishers around the world—can be useful conduits into overseas markets; ask around in the IPG for recommendations, or again consult the *Writers' and Artists' Yearbook*. Follow industry news in *The Bookseller*, BookBrunch and elsewhere to get an idea of who is buying what from whom. Search for books similar to your own on Amazon or Google to see who is publishing them around the world. Keep notes of any publisher you think might be interested, and start building these up into a database of contacts, annotated with each of their particular interests and tastes. No matter how specialist your subject, you will soon find plenty of relevant publishers who will hopefully become regular partners.

Publishers can sell at different stages of a book's life—at acquisition, draft or even publication, for instance, though the latter is usually too late—but generally the earlier you pitch the better. Whenever you do it, try to pick out the books that each of your prospective buyers will be interested in rather than throwing everything at everyone and hoping something sticks. Think about each of your books' key selling points and why they might appeal to your buyers' market. Put yourself in your counterpart's shoes and try to imagine what he or she is looking for.

Supply buyers with finished or proof copies if you can, or Advance Information (AI) sheets, jackets and samples if you can't. Email PDF versions if you are not meeting in person, as this saves time and a lot of money in postage. Provide evidence of the author's track record if he or she has one. Produce as many review quotes, UK sales figures and details of other rights deals around the world as you can, since these all help to create a positive impression about a book. Be enthusiastic and passionate about your books, but at the same time avoid hyperbole—publishers around the world will have heard it all before. Remember that rights buyers very rarely read anything twice, so you have to make sure that the first impression is as dazzling as possible.

Stay patient when it comes to selling. You may have to wait a long time for your prospective buyer to read or review a book and make a decision about taking it on. Putting a price on deals is difficult, and the only safe rule is that a book is only worth what someone is prepared to pay for it. In an ideal world, you will have competition for your books and be able to auction rights until there is one buyer left standing. In this situation, make the auction rules clear at the outset and don't disclose the names of any bidders to anyone else. Stay calm, be organized in letting each bidder take their turn to offer, and be honest with everyone. In all sales negotiations, keep good records of all your contact with prospective purchasers so you can see at a glance where you stand on a deal. There's nothing worse than selling rights to two different people by mistake and having to let one of them down.

CONTRACTS

Contracts for English-language rights deals are usually drawn up by the buyer, but you may prefer to offer your own templates. For help with these—as with all things to do with contracts—buy a copy of *Clark's Publishing Agreements*, an essential guide to deals and licences with templates that you can adapt and use. The book is edited by rights and copyright expert Lynette Owen and available to IPG members at a special discount; see the website for details. If you use them, local sub agents (see below) may also be able to help with contracts, and IPG members will often be prepared to share their templates.

If you are handed a contract from a publisher buying rights, scrutinize it carefully. The golden rule is to limit eventualities so you have confidence that your content will be used only in ways you are happy about. Make sure all clauses cover what is possible rather than what is probable, leaving you both in no doubt where you stand in relation to rights. Limit the length of any licence agreements; be clear on the publication date; outline the terms of payment; and settle the time when any rights will revert back to you. Ensure you have an exit route from the contract if you become unhappy with the deal. And monitor all rights business at regular intervals. Unlike straightforward sales, rights deals do not stop when the contract is signed, but can go on earning money until interest dwindles or the rights that you have sold revert back to you.

BOOK CLUB RIGHTS

Plenty of subsidiary rights can be sold domestically, too. Some publishers, usually in popular fiction or non-fiction, strike deals with book clubs to sell special editions of their books. Clubs sell to their members at large discount, so usually request, in turn, a heavy discount from the publisher of up to 80% off the cover price. Book clubs usually buy copies on firm sale, so it helps to sell these rights in advance of printing the book so that publishers can add the order on to the print run it is commissioning for copies that will be sold elsewhere. Some book club rights deals are done on a royalty basis, whereby the club pays a fixed royalty—usually 5 to 10%—on each copy sold, to be shared by the publisher and author.

Book club deals are often high volume but low profit, and publishers need to decide if they are willing to accept lower margins on their book in return for the advantages of firm sale, heavy sales and widespread exposure. It is also important to consider if selling a book through clubs will compromise its sales elsewhere. Opinion on this is divided, but clubs usually argue that their sales are in addition to trade sales rather than instead of. Book clubs in the UK are led by Book Club Associates.

SERIAL RIGHTS

Large trade publishers with a celebrity or politician on their hands can often sell serial rights to daily newspapers or glossy magazines for large sums. These rights will never make a fortune for most small publishers, but they might still be worth considering if you think a media outlet might be interested in running excerpts. Specialist publishers might be able to suggest book-based features to magazines in the same subject, for instance, or a local newspaper might be interested in running extracts from a local-interest book. Another option is Reader's Digest, which condenses books for its magazines. Try to negotiate at least a nominal sum for any serial or digest rights, but think of any such deals more as a publicity tool than a way to make money. Anything that is earned will have to be shared with your author, as per your contract.

Be careful how much material you allow the media to take from your book. You want to give away enough to fire readers' interest but not enough to leave them thinking they have read all the best bits. Always insist on a very prominent plug for the book in question, together with a picture of the jacket if possible and details of where it can be bought. If you think a book has serial potential, start pitching it to newspaper or magazine editors a couple of months before publication. Send them copies so they can choose for themselves the extracts that might be of interest to their readers. If it is important that no information from the serial is leaked before publication, draw up an embargo agreement.

ELECTRONIC RIGHTS

Electronic rights are an increasingly important avenue for publishers in all areas, but in academic, reference and STM publishing in particular.

If they decide to sell rights to their digital content rather than exploit it themselves, publishers usually use third parties who have better expertise in using digital content and better access to the people who will pay for it. The companies buying rights are often new media specialists, looking to fill their various electronic platforms with content. Aggregators—companies who bundle together content from various publishers to sell on to academic libraries or institutions—are also on the hunt for electronic rights, as are e-book specialists and websites. Digital content is particularly popular in education, where new e-learning providers are emerging. Mobile phone specialists are also seeking content.

Because many of them are from outside publishing, finding buyers for electronic rights can be tricky, and some publishers hire consultants or specialist agents to do so on their behalf; ask around the IPG or on the forum for recommendations of good ones. If you do it yourself, be prepared for some long hours researching the market. First of all, check to see which electronic rights you actually own—author contracts should stipulate this, though older ones may not—and check that your content is ready to be adapted for electronic environments (see the E-publishing and Print and Production chapter for more about this). Then try to imagine where you can see your content being useful. Would it convert nicely into an e-book? Would mobile phone users like to access it?

All agreements for electronic rights need to be carefully stipulated, restricting use of publishers' content to a set audience for a set time on a set platform. Be sure that you know where and how the content is to be used, or you risk damaging your publishing brand. Ensure that the rights buyer is properly protecting your copyright from piracy and misuse. And be wary of tying yourself into long-term or exclusive deals on just one electronic platform. Electronic channels are changing fast, and you don't want to find your content stuck in one where sales are dying. Payments for electronic rights are sometimes on a royalty and advance basis, as with traditional book rights, but might also be in the form of a set licensing fee.

It is also important to consider if selling rights to your digital content will compromise your own sales of books in print form. If someone else is offering your content for free online, will that hurt your print sales? Or will it act as an advert for your material and actually encourage more people to buy your books? When deciding, look around publishing at companies similar in size and specialism to your own. If you're confused, take comfort that no one really knows the answers to many of the questions about electronic publishing. For the time being, stay open minded about it and keep a close eye on where it's heading.

For more on using and selling digital content, see the E-publishing chapter.

OTHER RIGHTS

Though less common than they once were, **reprint rights** are still being sold and bought. This is where publishers license rights to their books in different formats. Having published a book in hardback, for instance, a small publisher might sell rights to publish the paperback edition to another company. This obviously means the original publisher will miss out on sales, but it may consider that a book has a better chance of success with another company—perhaps because it is larger and better connected and has greater selling power. Reprint rights deals usually involve the buying publisher paying the original publisher a royalty on each sale, which the latter then shares with the author.

Publishers with popular fiction or non-fiction books may be able to sell **audio rights** to either a specialist audio company or a larger publisher with its own list of audiobooks. Audio rights can be either abridged—where the book is condensed from its full length into something more manageable—or un-abridged; the former is more popular among booksellers and the latter among libraries. The rising popularity of digital downloads to iPods and other MP3 players means this is a developing market, though it is only suitable for certain books. The alternative to selling rights is to produce an audio version of your book yourself, and while this can be done by hiring a studio, producer, reader and manufacturer, most small publishers prefer to save the headaches and let someone else do the hard work.

For generic fiction in particular, **large print rights** can sometimes be sold to a specialist publisher like Ulverscroft. They sell largely to public libraries. If you think you have material that would translate well to either audio or large print, get to know the key players—there aren't many, and the Audiobook Publishing Association and the Large Print Bookshop are good places to find them—and pitch ideas to them regularly, perhaps once or twice a year. Audio and large print fees are generally quite standard, leaving little room for negotiation. **Braille rights** can be sold too, though these are usually granted for free to help improve access to books for visually impaired people. Access to copyright works is now a statutory right of the visually impaired since a change to the law in 2003. This does not mean publishers are obliged to provide material in an accessible format (for audiotape reproduction, for example), but it does mean that they cannot restrict access to it. The RNIB is putting pressure on rights holders to make this process easier for the visually impaired. The Publishers Licensing Society has up-to-date information about what publishers can and should do to help.

If you are lucky enough to get TV or film **screen rights** interest in one of your books, enjoy the extra money but don't raise your hopes that a movie is on the way. These rights are usually sold on an option basis, meaning that a film studio or production company pays to reserve exclusively the chance to buy the full rights to turn a book into a movie. The option lasts for a fixed amount of time, but more often than not it will never be taken up. The money paid for the option is non-refundable though, and there is nothing to stop publishers selling a second option once the first has expired. Because dealing with Hollywood film studios is not among publishers' common skills, screen rights are usually only sold when an approach is made to the publisher or via a specialist sub agent in London or Los Angeles.

Radio dramatization rights may be another occasional earner; these are mostly handled by the BBC's Readings Unit and command standard, fairly low fees. Contact the Unit for details of how to submit, something that usually needs to be done around the same time you pitch for serial rights.

In educational publishing, it is increasingly common to license content to institutions for use in **coursepacks** or **customized books**. Instead of supplying students with a dozen books that they use only in part, higher education institutions are keen on the idea of bundling together content in a pack tailored for the course, photocopied or sometimes bound into a proper book. Fees for this will be much lower than the revenue gained from selling a full book, but some publishers consider it to be better than no revenue at all. Remember to register with the Publishers Licensing Society in order to receive payments for the copying of your material and, in the US, with the Copyright Clearance Center.

Some publishers are able to license **artwork** from their books for other publishers to use, or charge **offset fees** to allow other publishers to base the design of pages on their own templates. Beyond this there are even more rights to be sold; if you think, for instance, that a children's character from one of your books would be popular as a doll or on a duvet, seek out appropriate merchandisers and try to interest them in rights. There's no harm in being ambitious, but small businesses must also be conscious of the time it takes to chase rights deals and realistic about what they can achieve with limited experience and hours in the day.

BOOK FAIRS

Selling rights is often best done face to face, when publishers can present and inspect books and discuss deals openly. This can be done by extensive travelling, visiting each potentially interested party in turn—or it can be done under one roof at one of the international book fairs.

For most UK publishers, the big two fairs of the year are London, held each April, and Frankfurt, staged in October. Children's publishers usually add Bologna in March, while publishers with a particular interest in the US market might visit BookExpo America, held each June in rotating US cities. All these fairs are ideal for buying and selling overseas and co-edition rights, and they also claim to be forums for doing rights business with TV and film companies and electronic media too. They are by no means essential for all publishers, but if you want to sell rights they are the perfect place to start.

They can also be expensive, the costs of hiring space there added to by travel and hotel bills. Publishers can and do visit without renting space, instead touring the halls or meeting in cafés, though this is very hard work and can create an unprofessional impression. If you can afford it, take a small stand, or a table in the dedicated Rights Centres of the fairgrounds, something that saves leg-work, creates a good impression with your contacts and gets you listed in the all-important fair directories. You can also keep costs down by exhibiting on the IPG's collective stand, where you can display books, hold meetings and share advice with fellow members. Look out for booking details on the website and e-bulletins several months in advance. Other ways of saving money include staying out of a fair's central town, where hotel prices will be extortionate, or travelling by train or car rather than flying.

Whether exhibiting with the IPG or on your own, preparation is key to suc-cess at book fairs. Be clear on what you want to sell well before you go. Prepare all the material you need: presentation packs (or programmed laptops) to show the titles you want to sell, samples of books and lots of catalogues to hand out, clearly indicating which rights you have available to sell for each of your existing and forthcoming books. If you have more than a few books to sell at a fair, draw up a special rights list. Get all your publishing material filed and ready to email if anyone requests it.

Send your materials out to contacts and ask them for an appointment well in advance of any fair you will be visiting (booking for the London Book Fair often starts as early as January, and for Frankfurt as early as June). Don't rely on spontaneous or random meetings; most publishers are so busy that without a pre-booking you may never get to see them. Remember too that much buying and selling goes on in the week or two before big fairs—another reason to start thinking about strategies well in advance.

Fairs can be overwhelming and dispiriting if you don't achieve the business you hope for. But don't be put off—it can take several years to build up contacts and see a return on your investment. Even if only one in ten of your meetings leads to direct business, many more of those you meet may prove useful in future years. Fairs are a great way to get your company known around the world, even if you don't immediately sell lots of rights. Build in a bit of time to explore the halls and get inspiration from publishers around the world. Pick up any catalogue that looks interesting or relevant to your line of work, and leave your card and a note with any publisher that catches your eye, even if you can't get an appointment.

If you are lucky enough to have lots of interest in a book at a fair, try to arrange an auction between bidders. You may also consider selling books on exclusive option, allowing the buyer time to consider a deal rather than shaking hands on it at the fair. Most publishers now wrap up many more deals once everyone is back home than they do at fairs—another reason not to worry if you don't sign on the dotted line there and then. Make careful notes about every single contact you make at the fair, and follow up promptly with an email or call on your return.

If you have extensive rights to sell and a potentially large income from them, it may well be worth visiting other book fairs around the world. Choose those which are relevant to your target markets: the Beijing Book Fair for the Far East, for instance (held each September); Abu Dhabi for the Middle East (March); Cape Town for Africa (June); and Warsaw for Eastern Europe (May). Ask around in the IPG and elsewhere for recommendations and tips on making the most of each fair. Government grants are sometimes available to fund UK publishers' visits; the IPG will notify you of these.

BUYING RIGHTS

Most small publishers will be interested in selling foreign rights to their own books rather than buying rights to someone else's. But if you are seeking to pick up books, much the same advice as above applies. Research your market and make contact with leading players around the world. Arrange to meet them at London or Frankfurt if you can. Shop around and don't snap up the first book you see. If you are presented with a book you like at a fair, avoid the temptation to make a bid on the spot and wait until you get home when you will have a clearer idea of whether it will work. Negotiate hard. Unless you are buying in very popular genres or books by established names, the chances are that the rights seller will be more desperate for a sale than you are for a purchase. As with all acquisitions, consult with colleagues as widely as you can to make sure a book is going to work for you. If you are considering a book in a foreign language, don't forget to factor in the costs of translating it into English, which can be considerable. To offset these costs, investigate the possibility of grants, which might be offered by a government agency in the seller's country; the seller should be able to brief you on the opportunities and the processes you need to follow to obtain the money. See the Editorial chapter for more tips on acquiring books.

STAFF AND SKILLS

Selling rights requires good negotiation skills and the ability to understand different ways of doing things around the world, both culturally and publishing-wise. The ability to identify opportunities—often in unlikely places—is crucial, and while direct experience of publishing is not as essential as it is in, say, editorial, a knowledge and passion for books certainly helps. Although most negotiations at book fairs and elsewhere are done in English, competency in French, German or Spanish can only help to open doors. Rights dealers also need an appreciation of changing media, and particularly the new world of electronic rights.

Beyond the actual deal-making, selling rights entails lots of admin, so a meticulous approach and ability to juggle projects both help. Attention to detail is vital in contracts to make sure no potentially adverse detail slips through. Numeracy is obviously handy when it comes to fee negotiations and currency conversions. Stamina and the ability to talk enthusiastically for hours on end without losing your voice is an advantage when it comes to book fairs.

For anyone new to rights, training can help improve your confidence and tactics. The best provider is the Publishing Training Centre, while the London Book Fair has sessions for beginners.

SUB AGENTS

Because selling is time-intensive, many publishers seek some sort of help with rights. Freelance sub agents are available in the UK and in all overseas markets, and while they will take a cut of your deals they can maximize the value of your rights and save you a lot of legwork.

Recommended UK-based agencies selling foreign rights on behalf of publishers include the Andrew Nurnberg, Christopher Collier, Marsh and ILA agencies. Each can provide expert advice as well as a wealth of trading contacts, but check that your books are suitable for them before you make an approach. Individual freelance agents are available too, adding your list to other publishers in their portfolios.

Alternatively, if you think your books will appeal to a particular market overseas it may well be worth hiring an agent there to sell rights on your behalf. Outsourcing can be a particularly good idea in countries or regions where the deal value might be small; where the markets are complex to an outsider; or where the culture of doing business is very different and best left to locals. All but the very biggest publishers use sub agents to sell in the Far East, for instance, since getting proper introductions to these markets is next to impossible for outsiders.

However you choose to subcontract your rights, ask around in the IPG for recommended agents. Word of mouth soon spreads about good and bad ones, and you will get to know the reputations of the operators in overseas markets. In territories you are interested in, see who other publishers use—most websites will list the contact information. Another source of names is the Publishers Association's Global Publishing Information database.

When considering whether or not to hire help, consider the balance you need to strike between product knowledge, of which you will have the best, and market knowledge, which local agents can offer. And try to consider any sub agents you use as part of your team. Don't pressure them with unrealistic targets, but keep them supplied with as much information as you can about the books they are trying to sell for you. Meet them at book fairs if you can. Sub agents will represent many different publishers, but if they feel like a valued member of your company they are more likely to make selling your books a priority.

There are also various publishing contract specialists who can advise on agreements and draw up templates for you, though copies of Lynette Owen's *Clark's Publishing Agreements* and *Selling Rights* are much cheaper and probably more helpful. Buying these books is by far the best investment any publisher can make in their rights business and sales strategies. Publishers with a lot of rights business might also consider using a rights database to keep track of their trading and contacts.

COPYRIGHT

Copyright is the legal right of publishers and writers to control and protect the use of their original works. It is a framework by which publishers and others can use and trade intellectual property—essentially words and ideas. Copyright owners have the sole right to sell, distribute, copy and adapt their work, and anyone who does any of these things without express permission commits an infringement. Copyright is set out by legislation, and thanks to worldwide agreements and conventions, UK copyright holders are also protected around the world. Without this protection, books and journals could be shared freely and for free, and publishers would make very little money indeed.

Any material that can be defined as original—in so much as it does not draw heavily from previously published work—is eligible for copyright protection. From the moment it is created—in publishing terms set down on the page—it automatically qualifies for this protection without the need to apply for it.

Publishers need to be clear on the balance of copyright between themselves and authors. In most instances, they must choose between licensing content from authors or asking to be assigned all copyright, in both cases via the author contract. Authors of books may also retain moral rights, entitling them to be identified as the creator of the work and for it not to be distorted by anyone, though publishers sometimes ask these to be waived in contracts. If your books do not involve an author and have been created by you or the people you employ as part of your day-to-day work, they become your copyright—again, automatically. If a book has been created for you on a contractual, freelance or collaborative basis, you need to make sure that copyright has been expressly assigned to you by whoever has contributed.

However it is organized, notice of copyright should be made at the front of all books, together with the international copyright symbol ©. Protection from copyright in the UK (as well as the US and Europe) lasts for 70 years after the death of the author. After that, copyright ends and publishers can reproduce material without permission and without paying royalties.

LICENSING AND COLLECTING AGENCIES

The use of publishers' copyright material by companies, academic institutions and other third parties is monitored by the Copyright Licensing Agency (CLA), which collects and distributes fees on publishers' behalf. It was set up jointly by the Authors' Licensing and Collecting Society (ALCS) and the Publishers Licensing Society (PLS). The CLA gives permission to third parties to copy material in return for an annual licence fee, distributed among publishers according to levels of use of their material. You don't have to join the scheme if you don't wish to, but if your material is likely to be copied by third parties it is worth your while. To be eligible, publishers must give a mandate for licensing in this way to the PLS.

Use of copyright material in public libraries—in other words the borrowing of books—is covered by the Public Lending Right, which pays authors, but not publishers, for the use of their work.

PERMISSIONS

Publishers and agents are often approached by other firms or authors seeking permission to use copyright material from their books elsewhere. Unless the request is for a large amount of information or it is particularly sensitive, this is fairly commonly given. Fees are usually paid, though since there are no agreed rates for these, they are entirely at the copyright holder's discretion, varying according to the author's status and the commercial purpose to which the extract is being put. Though they are usually small, they can add up to useful income if you are granting a lot of them. Fees are shared equally between publisher and author. As a matter of courtesy you should ask your author's permission before granting or rejecting it on his or her behalf. When granting, insist on the user making clear acknowledgement of the source. Put a limit on all permissions—to one print run or one year, for instance. Keep a record of the fees you charge so you can build up a scale to work from.

If you are seeking permission to use someone else's copyright material, identify the holder and put your request in writing, stating very specifically the material you wish to use and where you want to use it. Do so as far in advance of your deadlines as you can—three months is an advisable minimum—since permissions are a low priority for many large publishers. You must request permission whenever the material you require is a 'substantial' part of copyright work, unless it can be justified under 'fair dealing' exemptions where it has been used for criticism or review. Unfortunately, the interpretation of substantial is entirely subjective—it was commonly taken to mean more than 400 words, but it all depends on the context of the work in which it appears. A handful of words from a poem might be argued to be substantial, for instance, but several paragraphs of a long novel may not. If in doubt, always ask permission.

If you are struggling to trace a copyright holder, the WATCH (Writers, Artists and Their Copyright Holders) File or the Society of Authors may be able to help. If you still can't find someone to grant permission, you will have to decide whether to omit the extract or risk it going unchallenged.

LEGAL ISSUES

The chances of a serious infringement of copyright that someone will feel strongly enough to complain about it are low, but it is best to be as scrupulous about obtaining permission as possible. Doing so avoids all risk of potentially costly and laborious legal disputes later on.

Another legal risk publishers may face is libel—the act of making false and damaging statements about an individual or organization. Believing something to be true is no defence against libel, and laws in the UK frequently punish transgressions. Small companies without the resources to fight legal battles can easily be intimidated by libel complainants, and some publishers fear this is damaging the right to free speech. Again, the best advice is to be extremely cautious, having any contentious material checked carefully by lawyers before publication. Author contracts also commonly require writers to indemnify publishers against any legal action for copyright infringement and libel, and if you have any concerns over these then this can provide reassurance.

Publishers also have liability for anything in their books that is wrong or could lead their readers to harm. This might apply, for instance, to books with medical information, where the need for total accuracy is obvious. Data protection is another legal minefield for publishers, and anyone holding personal information about customers via things like databases or mailing lists will need to make sure they are meeting legal obligations. The Information Commissioner's Office is the best place to start investigating this.

Highly recommended for more information about all aspects of the law is Hugh Jones and Christopher Benson's book *Publishing Law*.

COPYRIGHT IN THE DIGITAL AGE

The use and abuse of copyright has become much more complicated in the digital age, when material can so easily be copied, communicated and plagiarized. The music industry has suffered from its content being copied, shared and downloaded for free, and publishers fear that their material could be equally vulnerable. The means by which it is protected is called Digital Rights Management (DRM), whereby publishers can encrypt and tag their copyright material to protect against misuse. DRM software can protect against material being cut and pasted, for instance, but it can be circumvented by hackers and will not completely protect work. Publishers can also protect their digital content by imposing tight licences on those who read it, stipulating where, when and how it is used and who by.

As electronic use of content increases, publishers may have to change attitudes to copyright. One alternative may be more open licence arrangements like Creative Commons, whereby authors offer their work to publishers and readers on terms very different from traditional copyright, allowing freer use of material while reserving some rights. The advantage is that work published under this licence becomes far more widely known; the disadvantage is that far fewer people might be inclined to pay for it. In journals publishing, the open access model of publishing makes material available to view for free, with the costs of publishing it met by the author or institution behind it.

RESOURCES

RIGHTS CONTACTS

Audiobook Publishing Association
Useful database of specialist publishers if you are interested in selling audio rights.
Web www.theapa.net

BBC Readings Unit
Gateway to getting your book considered for reading or dramatization on the BBC.
Web www.bbc.co.uk/writersroom/writing/submissions_other_readingsunit.shtml
Write to The Readings Unit, G12 East Wing, BBC Bush House, The Strand, London WC2 4PH

Large Print Bookshop
Large print and audio retailer—a good place to identify people you might sell rights to.
Web www.largeprintbookshop.co.uk
Tel 01763 252687

Literary Market Place
Useful database of worldwide publishers to help you begin the search for rights buyers.
Web www.literarymarketplace.com
Tel 00 1 800 300 9868

UK newspapers and magazines
Handy database of print media contacts to try if you want to sell serial rights.
Web www.mediauk.com

RIGHTS NEWS

BookBrunch
Daily updates on rights deals involving UK publishers.
Web www.bookbrunch.co.uk
Tel 020 7242 9972

The Bookseller
News of rights deals.
Web www.thebookseller.com
Tel 020 7420 6000

BOOK CLUBS

Book Club Associates (BCA)
Umbrella group of various UK book clubs.
Web www.bca.co.uk
Tel 0844 499 0000

The Book People
The UK's leading direct bookseller.
Web www.thebookpeople.co.uk
Tel 01483 861144

RIGHTS TRAINING

The Publishing Training Centre
Its courses on rights and copyright are particularly useful for non-specialists.
Web www.train4publishing.co.uk/guideto/rights
Tel 020 8874 2718

The London Book Fair
Runs a workshop each year to introduce newcomers to rights.
Web www.londonbookfair.co.uk
Tel 020 8910 7910

BOOK FAIRS

Beijing International Book Fair
Asia's biggest fair, held each August or September.
Web www.bibf.net
Tel 00 86 10 6586 6995

Bologna Book Fair
The main annual event for children's publishers, held each March or April.
Web www.bookfair.bolognafiere.it
Tel 00 39 051 282361

BookExpo America
America's most important book fair, hosted by a different city each year.
Web www.bookexpoamerica.com
Tel 00 1 203 840 5890

Frankfurt Book Fair
The autumn equivalent of London and the largest book fair in the world. The IPG takes a collective stand here.
Web www.book-fair.com
Tel 00 49 69 21020

London Book Fair
The book world's main spring fair, held each April usually at Earls Court. The IPG offers members space on a collective stand here.
Web www.londonbookfair.co.uk
Tel 020 8910 7910

BOOK FAIR FUNDING AND ASSISTANCE

AMK
Specialist in book fairs, providing help to publishers with transport and logistics.
Web www.amk.org
Tel 01545 571190

The British Council
Runs occasional delegations to fairs around the world and may be able to help with costs.
Web www.britishcouncil.org
Tel 0161 957 7755

UK Trade & Investment
Provides intermittent funding to help small- and medium-sized publishers attend book fairs, plus plenty of advice about doing business overseas.
Web www.uktradeinvest.gov.uk
Tel 020 7215 8000

SUB AGENTS

Andrew Nurnberg Associates
Web www.andrewnurnberg.com
Tel 0203 327 0400

Christopher Collier
Web www.collier-international.co.uk
Tel 020 8894 9777

Global Publishing Information
The Publishers Association's database of country profiles can help identify people to sell your rights locally.
Web www.publishers.org.uk
Tel 020 7691 9191

Intercontinental Literary Agency
Web www.ila-agency.co.uk
Tel 020 7379 6611

The Marsh Agency
Web www.marsh-agency.co.uk
Tel 020 7493 4361

RIGHTS DATABASES

Bradbury Phillips
Specialist producer of databases for rights, permissions and royalties.
Web www.bradburyphillips.co.uk
Tel 020 8202 0903

COPYRIGHT

British Copyright Council
Advisory and lobbying body for copyright owners.
Web www.britishcopyright.org
Tel 01986 788122

Copyright, Designs and Patents Act
The text of the legislation from which British copyright is drawn.
Web www.opsi.gov.uk/acts/acts1988/UKpga_19880048_en_1.htm

Copyright Toolkit
Very useful advice on using and clearing copyright content, plus sample contracts, funded by EduServ.
Web www.copyrighttoolkit.com

Copytrain
Recommended consultancy offering advice and training on copyright issues.
Tel 01844 279345

Creative Commons
New copyright licensing method offering freer access to authors' work while retaining some rights.
Web www.creativecommons.org
Tel 00 1 415 369 8480

Information Commissioner's Office
Advice on data protection issues.
Web www.ico.gov.uk
Tel 08456 30 60 60 (Helpline)

Intellectual Property Office
Government agency responsible for intellectual property rights including patents, trademarks and copyright.
Web www.ipo.gov.uk
Tel 0845 9500 505

COPYRIGHT LICENSING AND COLLECTING AGENCIES

Authors' Licensing and Collecting Society
Protects and promotes the copyright of authors, and redistributes money paid in licences to use their content.
Web www.alcs.co.uk
Tel 020 7264 5700

Copyright Clearance Center
Publishers with content available in the US should register with the CCC, the agency responsible for licensing content to third parties.
Web www.copyright.com
Tel 00 1 978 750 8400

Copyright Licensing Agency
Promotes and protects publishers' copyright in the UK, arranging licences for organizations to copy or scan their work in return for fees. It has an enforcement arm, Copywatch.
Web www.cla.co.uk
Tel 020 7400 3100

Design and Artists Copyright Society
Artists' equivalent of ALCS.
Web www.dacs.org.uk
Tel 020 7336 8811

Public Lending Right
Co-ordinates payments to authors for the loan of their books from public libraries, funded by a government grant.
Web www.plr.uk.com
Tel 01642 604699

Publishers Licensing Society
Co-ordinates payments for the use of publishers' copyright by individuals and organizations. Also leads the industry on copyright and licensing issues, including publishers' obligations on making content available to visually impaired people.
Web www.pls.org.uk
Tel 020 7079 5930

PERMISSIONS

Society of Authors
May be able to advise on tracing copyright holders and has a useful quick guide to permissions.
Web www.societyofauthors.org
Tel 020 7373 6642

Writers, Artists and Their Copyright Holders (WATCH) File
Database of copyright contacts in the UK and US.
Web www.watch-file.com

BOOKS

Clark's Publishing Agreements: A Book of Precedents by Lynette Owen (Tottel, £85, 9781845927851). A discount on this book is available to IPG members buying direct from Tottel; see www.ipg.uk.com for details.

The Copyright Book: A Practical Guide by W.S. Strong (MIT Press, £25.95, 9780262194198)

Digital Rights Management by Christopher May (Chandos, £39.95, 9781843341246)

A Handbook of Copyright in British Publishing Practice by J.M. Cavendish and Kate Pool (Continuum, £47.50, 9780304326356)

International Literary Market Place 2009 (Bowker, $259, 9781573873253)

Patents, Registered Designs, Trade Marks and Copyright for Dummies by John Grant et al. (John Wiley, £16.99, 9780470519974)

Publishing Forms and Contracts by Roy Kaufman (OUP US, £79, 9780195367348)

Publishing Law by Hugh Jones and Christopher Benson (Routledge, £29.95, 9780415384278)

Quick Guide to Copyright and Moral Rights (Society of Authors, £2 to non-members, available direct from the Society)

Selling Rights by Lynette Owen (Routledge, £29.95, 9780415386524)

Writers' and Artists' Yearbook (A&C Black, £14.99, 9781408102640)

10 E-PUBLISHING

CONTENTS

The argument that the future of publishing is electronic rather than print has been around for some time. And it is true that there has been something of a digital revolution in areas like academic, professional and journals publishing, where people want content in digital formats and on the move. But in many other consumer sectors, the change is a much slower evolution. That's partly because so many new electronic channels have emerged without one model establishing itself as the standard for publishing. If you feel baffled by the myriad fast-changing channels and uncertain about what you should be doing with them, don't worry—every publisher, large or small, feels exactly the same. For most, it is enough at this stage to understand the e-publishing options available to you and to be ready to capitalize on them in the future. The good news is that doing so is not as daunting a job as many think, nor as expensive.

STRATEGIES

How you decide to approach electronic publishing will depend on the sector of publishing you are in; the quality and quantity of the content you've got; and how much money you want to invest. So far at least, everyone has many more questions than answers when working out their strategies.

Most of these questions revolve around the balance between your print and electronic content. Do you see e-publishing as an opportunity or a threat? Will making content available electronically compromise sales of your print books or improve them? Will readers of the future want your books in print or digital form or both? Should you publish content in both forms at the same time, or stagger the release?

Publishers must also decide how they want to approach electronic markets— either by sticking a toe in the water or diving straight in. As the options below show, they must also work out whether to go it alone and sell content themselves; or team up with third parties to tackle the market together. Unless you have a high level of technical expertise and bottomless resources to pour into web platforms, it is likely that you'll be doing the latter. Most small publishers are so far taking a cautious approach, making their content available in a number of ways while waiting for the channels to settle down, and getting help from experts to prepare and sell their content in the digital world.

Whichever way you decide to approach e-publishing, a good way of staying on top of trends is to attend the IPG's Digital Quarterly Meetings, designed to keep members updated in this fast-changing aspect of publishing. Keep an eye on the website and bulletins for details of forthcoming meetings.

MAKING E-BOOKS

It need not be too difficult for publishers to get their content ready for electronic channels. E-books have generally been made available as PDF (Portable Document Format) documents, a simple way of making and sharing material that replicates the look of the printed page. Other, more sophisticated formats are based on XML (eXtensible Mark-up Language), which allows content to be tagged and structured so it can flow into various reading devices. This is an increasingly popular, versatile way for publishers to get their content digitized, and something that is well worth exploring for all publishers. See the Print and Production chapter for more on XML.

Because many e-books will be searched by readers, they need to incorporate metadata—information about a chunk of a book's content or, put simply, data about data. The industry's standard for communicating information about a book electronically is Online INformation eXchange (ONIX); see the Bibliographic and IT chapter for advice on making the most of this. There are also registration agencies for Digital Object Identifiers (DOIs)—unique codes by which digital content like a chapter or table of a book can be tagged and identified on the internet. DOIs are administered around the world by the International DOI Foundation, which has a list of registration agencies including CrossRef. The International Standard Text Code, meanwhile, is a way of identifying textual work around the world; registration agencies for it in the UK are run by Nielsen and Bowker.

Some publishers have become experts in XML and now produce all their books with it, leaving them ready-made for various e-book formats. The widely accepted industry standard for this format is EPUB, created by the International Digital Publishing Forum. But because few publishers have the time or expertise to master XML, DOIs and metadata, most prefer to outsource the job. There are plenty of companies around the world who offer varying degrees of help with this—anything from tagging a single book to digitizing an entire backlist, making it ready for any number of e-book platforms and even selling it for you. If you envisage selling a lot of your content electronically in the future, it may be worth setting up a partnership to get all of your new books digitized like this.

While some digitization specialists can be found in the UK, many operate from cheap labour markets like India and China. Companies come and go at quite a rate, so ask around in the IPG for recommendations or talk to companies at the London or Frankfurt Book Fairs. Get three or four quotations for the work you want done, preferably from companies with good track records and endorsements from the UK. Agree contracts carefully, and insist on performance and penalty clauses.

Whatever form they take, e-books need software or hardware to make and read them. E-books can be read on computers or as standalone devices, and formats in the UK are changing all the time. Some of the leading ones are listed in the Resources section. E-books are now listed alongside print books on bibliographic databases by Nielsen BookData and Bowker, and suppliers and wholesalers have followed suit in listing them available for purchase. So publishers need to catalogue their electronic titles and obtain ISBNs for them just as they do for their print titles. Each different digital version of a title should have a different ISBN, or customers will struggle to find the one they want.

SELLING DIRECT

Once your content is digitized and ready to distribute, there is a choice to be made between selling it yourself and getting someone else to do it for you.

Selling direct to users has the advantage of keeping everything you do in your control. It generally involves asking users to pay to download the whole or part of a book, to be read either on their computers or handheld devices like Sony's Reader, Apple's iPad or Amazon's Kindle. That means investing in a web platform from which to sell, something that done properly can be expensive and time-consuming. There are plenty of specialists who will help you build a store for your e-books, and they will be able to advise on how to secure the use of your content and how to monitor it. But remember that however much help you get, you will ultimately be responsible for every aspect of your site and the fulfilment of all your orders. Your publishing brand and reputation will suffer if users experience any difficulty using your site.

There are variations on this direct sales model. Some publishers 'slice and dice' or offer 'chunking'—selling parts of their books instead of the whole text, perhaps chapter by chapter or even page by page. This is particularly popular for educational texts, suiting students who are not prepared to pay for a book of which they use only part, or teachers and academics who want to put together material for coursepacks or Virtual Learning Environments (VLEs). Other publishers might offer text on a 'read only' basis, whereby it cannot be printed; or on a rental basis, whereby users pay to access it by the hour, day, week or month.

Don't forget that supplying content direct to people can be a good marketing tool as well as a sales model. It is particularly good for inspection or review copies, and costs can be cut substantially by emailing an e-inspection copy instead of posting a printed book. Some publishers also offer free 'tasters' of e-books for a limited time, hoping that readers will be interested enough to buy the whole text.

Even if high-spec transactional sites are beyond your budget, any investment in your website is invariably money well spent. As web usage increases, more and more people will seek out your content direct, even if they eventually buy it in print rather than digital format. Fill your website with as much content as you can that demonstrates your publishing personality, and use it as a shop window from which to promote your brand. Look around at competitors' sites to get ideas, and ask around in the IPG for recommended consultants or designers to build sites for you. Websites are increasingly seen as complements to books too; in reference publishing, for instance, a site can act as a good place to get the latest updates to a book's content.

SELLING VIA THIRD PARTIES

Because investment in a web platform to sell from can be expensive, many independents get their electronic content to readers via third parties—usually institutions or aggregators. This is particularly prevalent in academic, professional and STM sectors and publishing, where libraries and organizations are increasing their e-book spends. And there are a growing number of companies putting together content for use on mobile phones, too, though the market here is still tiny.

As with selling direct, deals with intermediaries can be structured in a number of ways. Publishers can sell a single 'copy' of an e-book to, say, a library, so that it can be inspected by users in much the same way as a print one could. A 'maintenance' fee is sometimes attached to these sales to prolong the library's access to the material and allow the publisher to update the material if need be.

Another way to generate income from libraries is to rent material rather than sell it. Libraries can, for instance, pay an annual subscription to get access to anything from a single book to a publisher's entire archive, with fees worked out according to the number of books and number of library users involved. They might also rent access to a publisher's website for a more limited time—by week, month or academic term.

Because of the admin involved in agreeing deals with individual publishers, libraries often prefer to get their content from aggregators, sometimes known as Digital Asset Distributors (DAD)—a catch-all term for platforms offering material from more than one source. These third parties gather together content from various publishers and sell or rent it on, and they use much the same models for getting it to end users as the publishers' ones described above.

Aggregators can be a very good proposition for publishers without the re-sources, know-how or desire to get their electronic content onto their own web platform or to market and sell it themselves. Some aggregators are library suppliers like Dawson and Coutts who have started to deliver electronic content just as they do printed books, but many are new start-ups, and the field is quite competitive. See Resources for some of the leading aggregators.

Agreements between publishers and aggregators vary and are still evolving. Some aggregators will purchase e-books at a discount from publishers—in much the same way that booksellers buy print books from them—and then charge libraries or other users the list price of the e-books if they want to buy them outright. Other aggregators offer subscription models, bundling together lots of content into single packages for their customers, perhaps divided by subject or tailored to needs. Publishers then share in the subscription proceeds according to the amount of content they have contributed to the package or the levels of usage. Another payment model is to ask the end-user—students and academics—to buy on a pay-per-view basis rather than charging their academic institutions.

It is important to scrutinize the way an aggregator proposes to use and sell your content, since this will be out of your control once a contract is signed. Check what security measures an aggregator has in place to protect your copy-right, and ask how it monitors and regulates usage of content once it has sold it. Ask how you will be paid, how often, and how it will be calculated. Find out how the aggregator will market and publicize your content, or whether you are expected to do so yourself. Assess what contact a third party has with the people they will sell to; for this reason you might consider it better to work with one of the established library suppliers, known and trusted by their customers, than one of the new aggregators. Licensing deals should never be exclusive and ought not to tie you in for too long a period, given the pace at which the digital market is changing.

Be particularly careful if you are working with an overseas aggregator—many are based in the US—and be sure that terms are sound and legal in the UK. Research aggregators thoroughly and trial their websites. Ask around in the IPG for feedback, both good and bad, and ask librarians or other customers of the aggregators too. Although many of these companies are now well established and profitable, others are new and might not have proven business models. Make sure your contract has get-out clauses in place in case the arrangement doesn't work.

Publishers wanting to sell through an aggregator will have to deliver content in a suitable way, though often all that is needed is the same PDF of the text that is used to produce the print version of the book. Some aggregators will also bear the costs of digitizing text or converting it to XML themselves; check before you agree any deals. As a rule, the better you can prepare your content for e-publishing via metadata and XML structuring, the more value it will have.

Just as wholesalers offer print publishers a way of selling to a host of retail customers, so they are becoming a useful intermediary in e-publishing. Through the Gardners Digital Warehouse and Bertram Digital schemes, both of the UK's main trade wholesalers are developing routes to sell electronic material. Again, while sales are still small, it is worth most publishers' while to keep an eye on these markets and be ready to sell through them in the future.

Help in mastering the various routes to market in e-publishing is offered by the Digital Supply Chain Group run by Book Industry Communications.

PRICING AND VAT

Until the market for them settles down, pricing electronic products is tricky. Many customers assume they will be cheaper than their print equivalents—and even free—since there will be fewer costs in physically producing the material. But this overlooks publishers' other expenses in preparing the content in the first place. So far, some publishers have priced at the same rate as their print books, while others price a little cheaper. Pricing the chunks of books sold in the slice and dice way is even more difficult, but is generally driven by the market rather than the publisher. Look around at larger publishers' pricing structures to see what you might be able to charge.

Pricing decisions will be influenced by the fact that VAT is payable on e-books while it is not on print ones. So if you want to sell an e-book at the same rate as a print one, you will have to absorb the VAT charge yourself. Remember that VAT is charged at the rate of the country where it is bought rather than sold, so you will need to check rates in whichever markets you are selling into. To make life easier, most publishers will not alter costs according to different VAT rates, but you may still need to indicate the VAT rate on invoices to libraries or suppliers.

RIGHTS AND ROYALTIES

Protecting your content and copyright from piracy or misuse is just as important in the digital world as it is in the print one—and many think the risk of it happening is far greater here. Publishers need to protect all digital content, via encryption, password protection and, particularly if it's being used in libraries, limiting access to it. Most UK libraries will ensure this by bolting protection systems on to the digital products they offer users, but check contract terms carefully. Negotiate how many users the content will be available to and for how long.

Publishers' own Digital Rights Management (DRM) systems are still evolving. Software systems designed to protect content can be dismantled or circumvented by hackers, and as yet there is no single, common way of protecting content. One protection against misuse of content is the Digital Object Identifier, which helps publishers track use of their content (see above).

Publishers also need to be confident they have the right to use authors' content electronically before they sell it. Most standard contracts nowadays will give publishers electronic rights, but some agents will try to exclude them and older contracts may not address the issue, so check. Selling digital content is quite straightforward if you have world rights in it, but if there is another publisher involved—holding North America rights, for instance—you may have to strike a deal with that publisher or else restrict access to the content to the territories for which you hold rights. Publishers and authors also need to clarify whether electronic income is sales rights or subsidiary rights, since the rates for each will be different.

Publishers generally aim to make royalty rates for electronic content the same as they are for print. Authors, on the other hand, think rates should be higher as publishers' costs are lower. The Society of Authors has been urging authors to press for better rates, but how much you are prepared to negotiate will depend on how much wider—if at all—your margins are on electronic content compared to print. For more on digital rights, see the Rights and Copyright chapter.

WORKING WITH GOOGLE

Any publisher using the web to sell content will sooner or later have to work out how to deal with internet superpower Google.

Google's Book Search project—formerly known as Google Print—allows users to search inside all the books it has scanned and archived, which amounts to millions of titles. Users who click through can then search through the scanned pages that are available to view, download it for free if it is out of copyright, or order a print copy from a bookshop if it is in copyright. Google pledges to respect the copyright of authors and publishers, and will limit the amount of content it displays for free according to their wishes. Publishers have to opt in to Book Search by sending Google their books to be made available.

Depending on your view, Google Book Search is potentially either the world's greatest ever archive of information or the greatest ever threat to publishing as we know it. All publishers must decide how much of their text—if any—they want Google to display or withhold. The question is whether making content available in this way is a useful marketing tool and an incentive for customers to buy it, or simply a big giveaway.

Perhaps the best proof of its success is in the subsequent sales of books featured in Google Book Search, though these can be difficult to monitor, and in the share of advertising sales that publishers can obtain if users click through on advertising that is displayed against its content. What can't be disputed is Google's size and power, and this will make it either a major ally or threat to publishers in the future. Google thinks it is an ally.

Publishers of scholarly books and journals must similarly weigh up the pros and cons of Google Scholar, a search engine that pulls together scholarly information from print and digital sources. Publishers can work with Google to have their information indexed and searched, but must decide if doing so contributes to sales or compromises them.

Another useful tool offered by Google is AdWords, which allows publishers to advertise on the results page their content, website or third party sellers when certain keywords are searched for. Fees are payable every time an ad is clicked by a searcher rather than every time it is displayed, and advertisers can set limits according to their budgets. AdWords are particularly effective for publishers of very specialist content for which web users are likely to search.

RESOURCES

IPG Digital Quarterly Meetings
A great way to stay up to date with the latest e-publishing issues.
Web www.ipg.uk.com
Tel 01437 563335

TRADE GROUPS

Association of Online Publishers
Trade group for digital publishers.
Web www.ukaop.org.uk
Tel 020 7404 4166

Book Industry Communication (BIC)
Promotes standards in e-commerce and has a Digital Supply Chain Group to discuss issues at meetings and workshops.
Web www.bic.org.uk
Tel 020 7607 0021

Digital Content Forum
Cross-industry group set up to discuss issues around digitization and electronic content.
Web www.dcf.org.uk

The Independent Digital Publishing Forum
Looks after standards across digital publishing; formerly known as the Open Ebook Forum.
Web www.idpf.org
Tel 00 1 905 235 4373

CREATING WEBSITES

WWW Web Pack
A very good guide to many aspects of working with the web, compiled by Aberdeen University.
Web www.abdn.ac.uk/webpack

METADATA AND DOIS

Bowker
Provides DOIs for publishers to help identify their content on the internet.
Web www.bowker.co.uk
Tel 01342 310450

CrossRef
US-based independent, publisher-founded agency registering DOIs for research content.
Web www.crossref.org
Tel 00 1 781 295 0072

EDItEUR
Co-ordinates and promotes universal standards in e-commerce for books, and administers the ONIX standard.
Web www.editeur.org
Tel 020 7503 6418

International DOI Foundation
Administers DOIs worldwide and keeps a list of agencies able to register them.
Web www.doi.org

International Standard Text Code
The means by which textual work can be identified by publishers, booksellers
and libraries around the world.
Web www.istc-international.org

ISTC Agency
Registers ISTCs in the UK on behalf of publishers.
Web www.istc.nielsenbook.co.uk
Tel 0870 777 8712

EBOOK READERS

Adobe Reader
Web www.adobe.com/products/reader

Amazon Kindle
Web www.amazon.com

Apple iPad
Web http://www.apple.com/uk/ipad/

iRex iLiad
Web www.irextechnologies.com/products/iliad

Microsoft Reader
Web www.microsoft.com/reader

Mobipocket Reader
Web www.mobipocket.com

Sony Reader
Web www.sony.co.uk/reader

AGGREGATORS

Blackwell Digital Reference
Web www.blackwell.com

Books24x7
Web www.books24x7.com

Content Reserve
Web www.contentreserve.com

Credo Reference (formerly XRefer)
Web www.credoreference.com

Cyberlibris
Web www.cyberlibris.com

DawsonEra
Web www.dawsonera.com

Ebooks Corporation
Web www.ebooks.com

Ebook Library
Web www.eblib.com

Ebrary
Web www.ebrary.com

EBSCO
Web www.ebscohost.com

Ellibs
Web www.ellibs.com

Knovel
Web www.knovel.com

MyiLibrary
Web www.myilibrary.com

NetLibrary
Web www.netlibrary.com

ProQuest
Web www.proquest.com

Questia
Web www.questia.com

WHOLESALERS

Bertram Digital
Web www.bertrams.com
Tel 0871 803 6600

Gardners Digital Warehouse
Web www.gardners.com
Tel 01323 521777

GOOGLE

Google AdWords
Google's advertising.
Web www.adwords.google.com

Google Book Search
Including an overview of the project, FAQs for publishers and instructions for getting involved.
Web www.books.google.com

Google Scholar
Google's search engine for scholarly information, much of it from books and journals.
Web www.scholar.google.com

EVENTS

Online Information
Annual fair around e-publishing, held each December in London.
Web www.online-information.co.uk
Tel 020 7316 9572

CONSULTANTS

Attwooll Associates
Web www.attwoollassociates.com
Tel 01865 422230

BOOKS

Adapting to E-books edited by William Miller and Rita Pellen (Routledge, £75, 9780415483773)

Books in the Digital Age: The Transformation of Academic and Higher Education Publishing in Britain and the United States by John Thompson (Polity Press, £19.99, 9780745634784)

From Entrepreneur to Infopreneur by Stephanie Chandler (John Wiley, £13.99, 9780470050866)

The Future of the Book in the Digital Age edited by Bill Cope and Angus Phillips (Chandos, £39.95, 9781843342403)

Get Into Bed with Google: Top Ranking Search Optimization Techniques by Jon Smith (Infinite Ideas, £8.99, 9781905940493)

Get to the Top on Google: Tips and Techniques to Get Your Site to the Top of the Search Engine Rankings and Stay There by David Viney (Nicholas Brealey, £14.99 9781857885026)

11 STAFF

CONTENTS

Qualities and qualifications / Recruitment / Pay / Diversity and equality /
Keeping hold of staff / Dealing with staff issues and employment law /
Training / Work experience / Outsourcing and freelancers / Resources

More than most, publishing is a people industry. Aside from a bit of luck with
books, getting and keeping the right staff is probably the most important factor
in determining the success or otherwise of any publisher. But this is emphatically
the case for small independents in particular, where staff will often have to turn
their hands to most disciplines at one time or another.

Many small publishers operate perfectly well with just one or two personnel.
But should you need any more, you are unlikely to be short of good staff.
Publishing has always been one of the most popular of the creative industries,
and unless you are in a particularly remote rural location, competition for jobs
is likely to be high. You should be able to get good calibre candidates for even
the most junior or lowly paid of posts. But quantity doesn't always mean quality,
of course, and sifting out the right people for your business is absolutely crucial.

QUALITIES AND QUALIFICATIONS

It is difficult to define the qualities needed to work in publishing, and they will
in any case vary from department to department. See the relevant chapters for
some thoughts on the skills that suit each discipline. For further guidance about
the skills good staff should have in publishing, SkillSet offer free, useful and very
comprehensive guidelines for just about every role a publisher might require.

A passion for books is obviously important, but all candidates will profess
this and it won't tell you much about their skills. A commercial nous is much
more important, along with a basic understanding of how the book trade
works and how books are sold (bookshop experience can be very useful). Good
communication skills, the skills to negotiate and cajole and the ability to manage
projects and finance are handy in most roles, as is computer literacy. For such

a creative industry, numeracy is surprisingly important—all staff should at least be able to work out the percentage of something in their day-to-day work, for instance. Technological know-how is becoming more and more valued as electronic forms of publishing expand. If you are a specialist publisher, a sound knowledge of your subject is obviously essential, and you should be wary of anyone who can't demonstrate at least an interest in your field.

In small companies, a can-do attitude and adaptability are probably the most important qualities of all. This is especially so at entry level, since staff will probably have to turn their hands to many aspects of what you do. Look for flexibility, a willingness to learn and enthusiasm.

People generally work in publishing because they enjoy it, and it is relatively rare for staff to leave the industry altogether, or for people to join it above the entry level. As a result, more senior posts are usually recruited from within the industry. There are exceptions to this, especially in specialized areas such as ELT or scientific publishing, where you may be better advised to seek staff who have picked up subject knowledge in other careers like teaching rather than publishing.

Some publishers like to maintain a blend of youth and experience, but age should be less of a factor when recruiting than finding the right person for the job. Opinion is also divided on the value of professional or vocational qualifications. Because competition for jobs is so fierce, most publishers tend to insist on degree qualifications for all but the most menial of jobs. But others think that if a candidate can demonstrate good work experience, adaptability and the right attitude, these might be worth much more to a business than a piece of paper. One discipline where most agree that a degree is not essential is sales, where personal qualities, work experience and general know-how are more important.

There are plenty of higher education courses now offering degrees or diplomas in publishing, and some of the leading ones are listed in the Resources section. Some of these prepare their students very well for a career in publishing, and for small publishers in particular, the value of recruiting someone with a solid grounding in all aspects of publishing can be very high. It certainly saves on training. But the quality of publishing courses varies, and a qualification does not automatically mean that a candidate is going to be suitable. Treat publishing qualifications with respect but also with some caution, and don't let them blind you to personal skills and attitudes.

RECRUITMENT

New publishers will have to start by working out very clearly what staff support they need. This can be difficult if you are not sure how many books you are going to publish or how successful they are going to be, and in the early days you may wish to outsource a lot of your work to freelancers or agencies (see below). But if you can project workflows and output accurately from the outset and hire the in-house personnel to help you with it, your company will have a much better chance of growing quickly and smoothly.

There are plenty of avenues when it comes to advertising for staff. The IPG offers free recruitment ads on its website and e-bulletin, and this can turn up very good candidates. If you are seeking to fill junior positions, you could also consider a free ad with the website and newsletters of the Society of Young Publishers, read by a large number of newly qualified people in search of their big break in publishing. Word of mouth can be useful too, so spread the word around fellow publishers and IPG members if you are trying to recruit. They won't thank you if you try to poach their staff, but they may well be able to tell you about former colleagues, work experience placements or students seeking full-time positions.

For more senior positions, *The Bookseller* magazine is publishing's leading recruitment channel. Advertising there is not cheap, but its job pages are read by the majority of publishers as well as plenty of people seeking to get in, and discounted or repeat ad deals can sometimes be negotiated. Another popular media option for publishers is the *Guardian*. This can be a good source of high calibre candidates and you are guaranteed a high response, but rates here are out of the reach of many small companies and many of the applications will be speculative non-starters. The *Guardian* runs media industry job ads on a Monday, and you could consider the equivalent sections in the *Independent* (Monday), *The Times* (Thursday) and *Daily Telegraph* (Thursday) too.

Cheaper options for junior roles are local or regional newspapers. These are particularly effective outside London, especially in cities with strong universities and relatively high concentrations of publishers like Oxford, Cambridge, Edinburgh and Bristol. If you can, time your ads for the summer, when floods of new university graduates return home looking for work. If you have one near by, you might also approach a university or college direct—their career services welcome approaches from employers and can often produce some great candidates or help you distribute an ad to their students.

Wherever you post your ad, be realistic and honest in what you ask for and in your job description. Most new publishers will be looking for assistants to help with a bit of everything, so don't be afraid to ask for exactly that rather than dressing up roles in exaggerated job titles or descriptions. Remember that job ads (and interviews) must not be discriminatory, so focus purely on the qualities needed to do a job. Check with the guidelines of the Equality and Human Rights Commission if you are worried about the phrasing of any ad.

One final option is to go through an agency, though this is generally used by larger companies seeking senior staff rather than by small ones for junior roles. Agencies specializing in publishing include Inspired Selection, Judy Fisher Associates, JFL Recruitment and KP Publishing Recruitment. Similarly, job websites like TotalJobs and CVPoster can occasionally turn up good candidates, but these will probably be of limited value to smaller independent publishers. If you use an agency, ask around in the IPG for recommendations, and make sure you understand the terms of any deal before you agree to it.

When reviewing applicants, treat all CVs with appropriate caution and scepticism, and set your sensors for jargon and exaggeration to high. Since attention to detail and good writing skills are fundamental in publishing, badly written or error-strewn applications can go straight in the bin. Be wary of any application that is not tailored to your company, since the same letter and CV has probably been sent to dozens of others. Look instead for proof that applicants have done their homework and taken the trouble to understand your business. It might be a good idea to ask prospective employees to do some sample work for you so you can get an idea of their skills in action. Watching people in a working environment often tells you much more about them than a CV or interview. A good question to ask all applicants is where they see themselves in five years' time—a useful indication of their ambition and commitment.

If you find your business is growing rapidly and you need some help with staff recruitment and management, it may be worth hiring an HR consultant. A brief internet search will turn up plenty of local candidates to help you.

PAY

Pay is a thorny issue in publishing. High demand for jobs means publishers have historically been able to pay relatively low salaries for highly skilled jobs. There is some evidence that this is changing as publishing realizes that low pay is beginning to turn graduates away from the industry. With exceptions, the old adage about peanuts and monkeys generally holds true.

Pay will vary substantially from region to region, and small publishers are generally able to pay less the further they are from London. Whatever your size, try to get an idea of the market rate for staff at various levels, by scouring recruitment channels and advertisements. If you have a medium to large staff, it may be worth benchmarking your pay. This can be done informally if you are close enough to other publishers to be able to share information about salaries. If you are to stay competitive, you should be aiming to pay at least roughly as much as your rivals. If you don't, you may well find that staff soon move on— bad news for the stability of your company.

Useful external benchmarks include an annual salary and benefits survey by *The Bookseller*, which found in 2008 that average earnings in the industry were £26,577. (Well over half of all employees were paid in the £20,000 to £40,000 bracket, and a quarter earned less than £20,000.) The IPG's survey of members' salaries in 2009 found that pay varied widely from company to company—in the case of managing directors or proprietors, from as little as £2,000 to as much as £218,000, with an average of around £56,000. The survey found that the most common pay bracket for directors was £60,000 or more, while for managers it was £25,000 to £30,000; editors, executives or coordinators £20,000 to £25,000; and assistants £15,000 to £20,000. But starting salaries outside London are usually much less than this, and salaries in the £10,000 to £15,000 region are not uncommon (if you are paying at the low end of the scale, bear in mind the minimum wage). Consultancy BookCareers also runs an annual salary survey, and plenty of general consultancies and websites provide tools to help you benchmark rates, though not specific to publishing.

Try to keep your pay structure simple but logical, especially as you take on more people. When setting salaries, bear in mind tax thresholds and avoid paying wages just above a threshold. A sound rule of thumb for publishers large enough to have distinct tiers of staff is for people on each rung of the ladder to earn two-thirds the salary of those on the rung above.

You could also consider bonuses, commissions or other incentives, but make sure that any targets you set staff are realistic. Keep them SMART—Specific, Measurable, Achievable, Relevant and Timed. In small, developing companies, you might consider offering staff shares in the business that could—if it is successful—prove to be valuable in the future. Share option schemes can motivate staff to work hard and sharpen their commercial sense, and are tax efficient when shares come to be sold. A formal profit-sharing agreement is another alternative, perhaps made open to staff who have served a certain number of years. Benefits like pensions, cars, mobile phones, subsidized meals, good holiday allowances and staff parties are also highly valued by employees and might also be used as incentives. Whatever you pay, review it on at least an annual basis and outline the reasons for any changes to salary carefully. Try to base increases on performance rather than inflation so that you are rewarding the best people.

If you are a new employer, you will need to register as such with HMRC by calling the New Employer Helpline. Employers should also hold employers' liability insurance to cover against accidents or illnesses as a result of work.

DIVERSITY AND EQUALITY

Few in publishing would claim that it is the most diverse of industries. Rightly or wrongly, it has been regarded as a preserve of white middle-class professionals, and surveys of the industry have discovered low levels of representation from many minority ethnic groups compared to other sectors. Nor, despite some improvements and the rise of some prominent female chief executives, is it a completely gender-equal industry, with salary surveys regularly revealing lower average pay for women than for men.

The IPG is a wholehearted supporter of diversity and equality in publishing, encouraging people of all races and backgrounds to work in publishing and supporting full gender equality and equal opportunity rights for disabled people. It has a sub-committee dedicated to diversity issues, an action plan and a Diversity Award as part of the annual IPG Awards. It is always looking for new ways to promote the interests of members and staff from minority ethnic groups, and welcomes all input from members. Publishing in the UK can only benefit from becoming a fairer and more diverse industry, and the IPG warmly encourages all publishers to do their bit to achieve it.

Information about the IPG's work in diversity plus some useful other resources and links can be found on the website.

KEEPING HOLD OF STAFF

Fortunately, given the generally low salaries, pay and other financial incentives are not the only way to reward staff and keep them motivated. A good working environment counts for a lot, so make sure all staff have the tools they need for their job and are comfortable in the office. Scrimping on IT or tea bags might save businesses a few pounds, but it risks alienating and losing their most valuable asset. Try to think of little, inexpensive ways to make people's day to day jobs a bit more fun.

Treat staff as individuals and accommodate their needs and requests if you can. Flexible working patterns are not always possible in small companies, but they are better suited to publishing than many industries. Allowing people to work from home on a regular or occasional basis can save you money in overheads too, and you may well find that you are rewarded for being accommodating by increased loyalty and commitment. Make sure you are fully aware of employers' obligations on flexible working, which are changing but which currently require you to consider seriously any request for it. The Department for Business, Innovation and Skills will have the latest guidelines.

Honest, frequent communication with all staff is essential. Appraise staff at least once a year, but let them take the lead in discussions. In any company with fewer than 50 or so staff, there is no excuse for not having regular staff meetings and, if possible, a company away day to talk about day-to-day matters and longer term strategy. Even if people don't want to raise issues directly at the meeting, they will feel more disposed to do so afterwards. Be open about the state of the business, whether it's good or bad. Give credit where it is due—it is amazing how much difference a simple 'thank you' or 'well done' can make to staff morale and motivation.

In small publishers many people—particularly those just starting a career— will appreciate the opportunity to work across the business and pick up lots of experience very quickly. Encourage staff to follow their interests and contribute wherever they are able. A good boss empowers their staff, delegating jobs and backing colleagues up even when they get things wrong. A medium-sized business should be able to run perfectly well without you, leaving you free to concentrate on working *on* the business rather than *in* it.

No matter how rewarding and considerate you are as an employer, it is inevitable that some staff will at some point want to leave. For small companies, this can be a real challenge. To ease the transition, try to get your key staff on long notice periods so you have time to cope with their departure. For anyone employed for longer than three years, a three-month notice period is fair enough on both sides, allowing you time to recruit a member of staff's successor and plan for a handover.

DEALING WITH STAFF ISSUES AND EMPLOYMENT LAW

The best advice for dealing with bad staff is not to hire them in the first place. But no matter how scrupulous you are in your recruitment, most managers will encounter unsatisfactory staff at some point.

If you need to take disciplinary action or terminate someone's employment, do things strictly by the book. Employment tribunals are to be avoided at all costs: they can be very messy and time-consuming, and they can often rule that the fault lies with unscrupulous employers rather than employees. Once you start recruiting staff, draw up discipline and grievance guidelines, perhaps borrowing a template from a fellow publisher. Even better, incorporate them into a staff handbook outlining all your employment terms and policies, so that everyone knows where they stand when they join you. A good, transparent staff policy reflects the professionalism of a company, and gives new staff confidence that they are joining a responsible employer.

Sticking to employment law is one of the trickiest parts of running a business. Make sure you are clear on all relevant aspects of it before you start dealing with issues. Key areas to focus on when it comes to staff and the law include discrimination—by age, race, nationality, gender, sexual orientation, disability, religion, marital status, pregnancy or beliefs. Swot up on the basics of contracts (all employees must have one, outlining at least hours, pay, job title, holiday entitlement and notice period); working hours (no more than 48 per week); pensions (you must provide access to a stakeholder scheme if you have more than five members of staff); statutory sick and maternity pay; tax (see Financial chapter for more on this); and redundancy. Remember that you need a valid reason to dismiss someone, and check the statutory procedures you need to follow. But remember also that all businesses have employment rights too, including the right to terminate the contract of any new member of staff within an initial trial period.

Get expert help on legal issues if necessary. Consult the Croner Business Support Helpline—free to IPG members—for up-to-date advice. Online, the government's guide to law for businesses is comprehensive, covering terms, conditions, pay, rights, discrimination, health and safety, and trade unions among many other issues, as well as helpline telephone numbers in various subjects and advice for finding more help. ACAS is another useful resource, especially when dealing with grievances, and so too is the Institute of Directors. Beyond this, endless consultancies and solicitors will offer help with legal issues, but their costs can quickly pile up.

TRAINING

Compared to many industries, publishing does not take training as seriously as it should. Money for training is often the first to be cut if budgets are tight, but this is usually a false economy. Improving staff skills and showing that you are committed to their professional development is essential if you are to reduce the risk of staff feeling disgruntled and looking elsewhere for work.

Publishers of a decent size might develop their own on-the-job training, delegating experienced staff to teach junior personnel as they go. For companies wanting external help there are plenty of options, many of them accessible even to small budgets. A leading specialist in book and journal publishing training is the highly recommended Publishing Training Centre at Book House in southwest London. It provides numerous packages of open, in-company, distance and online training, and covers every conceivable aspect of the industry, benchmarked against National Occupational Standards. It has particularly good introductory courses, offering publishers a grounding in the industry; and an ongoing programme of events with the IPG includes excellent packages on financial management, rights and marketing, tailored to the needs of independents. Keep an eye on the IPG's website and e-bulletins for the latest events.

Choosing the right sort of training is important. If you have a decent number of staff who all want to train in the same field, it might be more cost-effective to hire the Publishing Training Centre or others to come to you and run some in-company training. For small publishers who find it difficult to spare staff for a day away from the office, online or distance learning can be better options, allowing staff to learn at their own pace.

Other good sources of training include professional societies like the Society for Editors and Proofreaders, which offers members thorough courses and qualifications in both those careers. If you are a member, the Association of Learned and Professional Society Publishers, the Society of Young Publishers and Women in Publishing also run courses. More recommended training providers include Marketability, Chapterhouse Editorial Training, Imago and Nelson Croom. Some higher education institutions run evening or distance learning courses for staff too. The Institute of Paper, Printing and Publishing (an amalgamated institute that includes what used to be known as the Institute of Publishing) can be useful, offering professional qualifications and recognition. For business directors and managers, the Train to Gain scheme from the Learning and Skills Council provides useful training to help companies sharpen up their competitiveness and profitability, and sometimes has free courses brokered by the IPG for members.

Funding is sometimes available to help small businesses in particular to offer training. The Publishing Training Centre offers discounts for new and small businesses among many others, and has a useful guide to other sources of grants and discounts. It also administers grants from the Unwin Charitable Trust for small publishers, which have been greatly appreciated by many independents over the years. Government agencies can sometimes help with grants or advice, and Arts Council England has been a useful source of help too, though the money available is subject to the vagaries of funding.

WORK EXPERIENCE

Work placements are seen by some as offering easy access to cheap casual labour, but most publishers are more ethical about their schemes than that. It is better to regard work experience as a service to the community, offering young people valuable insights into the industry. Unless the company is very large, it is best to limit the number of placements you offer and to restrict them to one at any one time; otherwise it will be an unsatisfactory experience all round. Employment legislation stipulates that placements must be connected to recognized courses that are relevant to people's studies, and it is certainly worth making sure that all people on placements have an aptitude and interest in the business. If you have a university or college with publishing-related courses near by, it might be worth working with them to identify suitable candidates.

Unless they express an interest in one particular aspect of publishing, try to give placements a taster of several jobs, and set them specific projects so they are able to work on their own as well as under supervision. Plan and structure days as closely as you can. Offer them a good experience and don't expect your business to get anything in return—that way you can only be pleasantly surprised if placements contribute anything of value or turn out to be worth a full-time job. Plenty have found good staff this way. Most publishers reimburse work experience placements for travel costs and perhaps lunch if they can afford it.

OUTSOURCING AND FREELANCERS

Because of all the processes a book goes through before it is finished, outsourcing is particularly common in publishing. The first and most important job of all— writing a book—is, course, itself outsourced to an author, and the industry could not survive without its army of freelancers.

A good rule of thumb is to keep any creative jobs in house but consider outsourcing anything that is more repetitive or laborious. As soon as you start to substantially outsource any creative tasks like editorial or marketing, you start to lose control of your products. But typesetting, proofreading, indexing and other time-consuming jobs are examples of the kind of things that publishers find easiest and most cost-efficient to outsource. Many prefer to outsource sales to an agency or other publisher, and all but the smallest or largest of publishers will outsource their distribution. See the relevant chapters in this guide for more on outsourcing in particular disciplines.

Finding freelancers is often best done via the publishing network. Ask fellow publishers if they can recommend anyone for the work you're seeking, or ask around at IPG meetings or online via the forum. *The Bookseller* carries some advertisements from freelancers in its classified section, and professional societies such as the Society for Editors and Proofreaders and the Society of Indexers are obvious starting points for finding good people. The Publishing Training Centre has a useful directory of freelancers who have completed one of its courses. If your publishing is particularly specialized, experience of your subject may be more important than experience of publishing. In a scientific book, for instance, a proofreader's understanding of the subject might well be more important than a long background in proofreading, so it might be best to recruit from schools or academic institutions for candidates. Again, see the relevant chapters in this guide for more recommended sources of freelancers or agencies in each discipline.

Reliability is essential in deadline-driven work like publishing, so be sure that any freelancer you hire will be able to deliver on time. Ask for references and samples of previous work, and trial someone before you hire them for the first time, perhaps by setting them a short project to test their competencies.

See if you can negotiate on rates if your budget is tight. Competition for work is usually quite high, so you should be able to find good value. Setting your own rates and sticking to them can be a good tactic if you are going to seek freelance help regularly. Once you've found a network of good, reliable freelancers, do your best to keep hold of them. But don't be afraid to review them as you would any supplier or partner—systematically and regularly. Review performance and pay every year or so if you can. Check to see you are getting good rates, and use the wealth of competition to negotiate better ones if need be. The supply of freelancers is such that you will usually be able to find someone cheaper, though not necessarily better.

More and more publishers are now looking to developing countries for their outsourcing, and India is a particularly popular destination. With low labour costs, widespread English and generally high standards, the attractions are obvious, and it is now possible to get just about any publishing job done in Asia—from copy-editing to translation to typesetting to digitizing and much in between. But the pitfalls are obvious too. Outsourcing so far from home takes the work well out of your control, and while some companies are reliable, you may find out that others are not up to the required standards when it's too late. So choose carefully, and ask around in the IPG and elsewhere for recommendations—word of mouth spreads quickly about both good and bad companies. Events like the London Book Fair can be good places to identify and meet outsourcing specialists. Ask for samples of work before you commission, and check companies' client lists to see if they match your field of work. If you are going to send regular work to a country like India, it is worth visiting to get to know the people doing it for you—or you could hire a local agent to keep on top of projects for you. And when comparing quotes for work, remember that cheapest isn't always best. Put the emphasis on reliability and quality rather than price.

RESOURCES
RECRUITMENT
IPG
Use the e-bulletin and job vacancies section of the website to advertise for new staff.
Web www.ipg.uk.com
Tel 01437 563335

Bookcareers
One-stop shop for publishing careers offering various services for staff at all levels and lots of practical advice. The CV clearing house is a useful way of finding staff and advertising your own skills if you want to move on.
Web www.bookcareers.com

The Bookseller
The industry's leading source of job advertisements.
Web www.thebookseller.com
Tel 020 7420 6065 (recruitment advertising number)

The Guardian
A popular port of call for recruiting publishers.
Web www.guardian.co.uk/jobs
Tel 020 7611 9111 (recruitment)

Inspired Selection
Recruitment consultancy specializing in publishing, with offices in London and Oxford.
Web www.inspiredselection.co.uk
Tel 020 7953 4060

JFL Recruitment
Recruitment agency with interests in publishing.
Web www.jflrecruit.com
Tel 020 7009 3504

Judy Fisher Associates
Media recruitment agency with a publishing department.
Web www.judyfisher.co.uk
Tel 020 7437 2277

KP Publishing Recruitment
Publishing specialist.
Web www.kppublishing.com
Tel 0845 389 2289

Society of Young Publishers
Has an online database of vacancies—a good way of finding people wanting to break into publishing, work their way up the ladder or get some work experience.
Web www.thesyp.org.uk

PAY

Bookcareers Salary Survey
An annual salary survey that could give you useful benchmarks for pay.
Web www.bookcareers.com

The Bookseller
A long-established annual survey of pay and benefits in the publishing industry.
Web www.thebookseller.com

Minimum wage
HMRC guide to the UK minimum wage guidelines.
Web www.hmrc.gov.uk/nmw

DIVERSITY

IPG
The IPG's policy and action plan on diversity, plus information about the Diversity award and some useful links.
Web www.ipg.uk.com/cgi-bin/scribe?showinfo=pp050

Arts Council England and Books for All
ACE's downloadable report into diversity in the publishing industry.
Web www.artscouncil.org.uk/aboutus/project_detail.php?rid=7&id=466

Diversity in Publishing Network
Forum promoting the status of new and existing publishing professionals from diverse ethnic groups.
Web www.diversityinpublishing.com

Equality and Human Rights Commission
Guidelines and advice about good practice for employers in diversity and equality issues and law.
Web www.equalityhumanrights.com
Tel 0845 604 6610

EMPLOYMENT LAW AND ADVICE

IPG Croner Helpline
Available to help answer your queries on employment law.
Tel 08445 618 133 and quote your members' scheme number

ACAS

Lots of advice about employment issues and arbitration in cases of dispute.
Web www.acas.org.uk
Tel 08457 47 47 47

BBC

Straightforward, impartial guide to employers' and employees' rights.
Web www.bbc.co.uk/consumer/guides_to/employment_index.shtml

Business Link

Practical advice for businesses, including tax, payroll, employment law and obligations to staff.
Web www.businesslink.gov.uk
Tel 0845 600 9006

Chartered Institute of Personnel and Development

Professional advice on employment and legislation.
Web www.cipd.co.uk
Tel 020 8612 6200

Department for Business, Innovation and Skills

Government guidance on working issues, including flexible working rights.
Web www.bis.gov.uk
Tel 020 7215 5000

Emplaw

Online guide to employment law, with a directory of solicitors.
Web www.emplaw.co.uk
Tel 01904 471492

Employment Tribunal Service

Hopefully never needed, but a useful introduction to tribunals.
Web www.employmenttribunals.gov.uk
Tel 08457 959775

Health and Safety Executive

All the information you need about keeping the workplace safe and secure.
Web www.hse.gov.uk
Tel 08453 450 055

HMRC
Advice on the tax and payroll obligations of new employers.
Web www.hmrc.gov.uk/employers
Tel 0845 60 70 143 (New Employer Helpline)

Institute of Directors
Useful advice on staff issues.
Web www.iod.co.uk
Tel 020 7766 8866

The Pension Service
Government tips on pensions and the responsibilities of employers.
Web www.thepensionservice.gov.uk
Tel 08456 060265

UK Government
Comprehensive portal for all aspects of employment law.
Web www.direct.gov.uk/employment

SKILLS AND TRAINING

Publishing Training Centre
A partner of the IPG and an excellent one-stop shop for training for book and journal publishers. Offers in-house, open, distance and online training options on all aspects of publishing.
Web www.train4publishing.co.uk
Tel 020 8874 2718

Arts Council England
May be able to provide help with training.
Web www.artscouncil.org.uk
Tel 0845 300 6200

The Association of Learned and Professional Society Publishers
Training for and by members.
Web www.alpsp.org
Tel 01275 856444

Chapterhouse Editorial Training
Face-to-face or correspondence courses for copy-editors and proofreaders.
Web www.chapterhousepublishing.co.uk
Tel 01392 499488

Copytrain
Consultancy offering in-house training. An IPG member.
Tel 01844 279345

Department for Education and Skills
Government advice on staff training and lifelong learning.
Web www.dfes.gov.uk
Tel 08700 002 288

Government grants
Advice on where to look for grants and subsidies for training.
Web www.direct.gov.uk/en/educationandlearning

Imago
Relatively new publishing trainer, specializing in print and production.
Web www.imago.co.uk
Tel 01844 337000

The Institute of Paper, Printing and Publishing
Professional body offering certification in the industry.
Web www.ip3.org.uk
Tel 08707 500 332

Investors in People
Best practice advice on training.
Web www.investorsinpeople.co.uk
Tel 020 7467 1900

Literature Training
A database of training support, mostly for writers but also intended for those who support new literature.
Web www.literaturetraining.com

Marketability
Publishing consultancy offering training across a wide range of disciplines.
Web www.marketability.info
Tel 020 8977 2741

Nelson Croom
Online learning specialist with a portfolio of publishing courses.
Web www.nelsoncroom.co.uk
Tel 020 7582 3309

SkillSet
Sector Skills Council for the creative media, with useful downloadable guidelines
for the skills staff should have in just about all of the publishing disciplines.
Web www.skillset.org/publishing
Tel 020 7713 9800

Train to Gain
A free service from the Learning and Skills Council that offers training to help
businesses improve their competitiveness and profitability. The IPG sometimes
brokers courses especially for members on the scheme's behalf; look out for news
of forthcoming sessions.
Web www.traintogain.gov.uk
Tel 0845 600 9006

Society for Editors and Proofreaders
Offers training and accreditation for members.
Web www.sfep.org.uk
Tel 020 8785 5617

Unwin Charitable Trust
Offers grants for small publishers' training.
Web www.train4publishing.co.uk/discounts

Women in Publishing
Organizes frequent courses for members.
Web www.wipub.org.uk

HIGHER EDUCATION

Centre for Publishing Studies at Stirling University
Teaches an M.Phil in Publishing Studies.
Web www.pubstd.stir.ac.uk
Tel 01786 467510

City University London
Offers an MA/Diploma in Publishing Studies.
Web www.city.ac.uk/journalism/courses/postgrad/publishing
Tel 020 7040 5060

Kingston University
Offers a MA/PgDip in Publishing with guaranteed work placements for students.
Web www.kingston.ac.uk/pgpublish
Tel 020 8547 8361

London School of Publishing
Offers short, mostly evening courses in lots of aspects of publishing.
Web www.publishing-school.co.uk
Tel 020 7221 3399

Oxford Brookes University
Long-running and respected MA in Publishing.
Web www.brookes.ac.uk/studying/courses/postgraduate/2008/publishing
Tel 01865 484848

Robert Gordon University
Runs a Publishing MSc course.
Web www.rgu.ac.uk
Tel 01224 262000

School of Printing and Publishing at the London College of Communication
Offers short courses in publishing, including new multimedia and digital skills.
Web www.lcc.arts.ac.uk/printing_publishing_school
Tel 020 7514 6700

UCL Centre for Publishing
Major London centre for publishing training and research.
Web www.publishing.ucl.ac.uk
Tel 020 7679 2473

BOOKS

The Definitive Job Book: Rules from the Recruitment Insiders by Anne Watson (Capstone, £12.99, 9781841127811)

Employment Law Made Easy by Melanie Slocombe (Lawpack, £11.99, 9781905261468)

The Essential Guide to Recruitment: How to Conduct Great Interviews and Select the Best Employees by Margaret Dale (Kogan Page, £18.95, 9780749444747)

Essentials of Employment Law by David Lewis and Malcolm Sargeant (Chartered Institute of Personnel and Development, £35.99, 9781843981626)

How to Get a Job in Publishing: A Really Practical Guide to Careers in Books and Magazines by Alison Baverstock et al. (A&C Black, £9.99, 97807136805039)

Inside Book Publishing by Giles Clark and Angus Phillips (Routledge, £19.99, 9780415441575)

12 FINANCIAL

CONTENTS

Funding / Forecasting and budgeting / Costing your books /
Book-keeping and accounting / Monitoring performance /
Tips for cash flow / Tax / Help / Resources

Among publishers with a passion for books, it is not unusual for the financial side of the business to be neglected. It can seem much more enjoyable to concentrate on producing great books and to leave money matters to one side for a while. But this is invariably a mistake, and it is just as important—if not probably more so—to be as on top of your financial books as it is to be on top of your printed ones. The most successful members of the IPG are great business managers as well as great publishers. As with most sorts of small businesses, worries about money will probably never be far away—this is not the industry in which to make a fast million, after all—but staying on top of your finances will save a lot of headaches in the long run, and give you a much better chance of flourishing.

FUNDING

Most publishers will rely at least in part on their own money or that of a private investor to get their business going (see the Getting Started chapter for more on this). But there are countless other sources of financial help for new companies.

Common sources among IPG members include Arts Council England and its three sister councils. These support in particular publishers of literature and genres that are otherwise under-represented in the UK—as well as the IPG. Whether through regular funding or one-off programmes, the Arts Council has been a strong supporter of independent publishing over the years, offering resources and advice as well as money. Its Grants for the Arts, funded by the National Lottery, are great for projects over a set period of time—a particular book or series or events, for instance. If you are considering seeking funding from ACE, first research its aims and policies thoroughly to see if you might be eligible, and download an application pack online.

Other supporters of publishing include the Paul Hamlyn Foundation, set up by the legendary independent publisher to support arts, learning and social justice related projects in particular; various government departments and agencies (a good place to search them all is the Government Funding website); and, for people under 30, the Prince's Trust. Look for help from regional development or enterprise agencies too, especially in areas that have been earmarked for regeneration money. Overseas, the British Council can help publishers establish trade links, and sometimes works in partnership with the IPG on projects, while UK Trade & Investment can sometimes offer assistance getting into overseas markets.

When searching for grants and awards, don't forget that there are other types of financial or in-kind support available, like interest-free loans, training bursaries and free consultancy, mentoring or seminars. In all there are hundreds if not thousands of different sources, and the best place to start working out which ones might be available to you both locally and nationally is the Business Link web portal, which has a massive list of sources and a tool to help you search them. Also make contact with your local Business Link office—there are nine across England—as they will know about funding schemes specific to your area. Other useful tools are the print *Directory of Grant Making Trusts* and various regional guides published by the Directory of Social Change; and the GrantsNet, GrantsOnline and FunderFinder websites, each offering searchable databases, the latter two in return for a subscription.

Grants and awards are hugely valuable and valued by small publishers, but they are not without their responsibilities and conditions. Funding organizations will generally be very supportive of your work, but they will want to see that the money they give is being properly used. Any publishers getting funding will have to set aside plenty of time to manage and measure how money is being spent, and to complete forms and attend meetings to review its use.

Publishers also need to be wary of relying too heavily on individual sources of funding. Even well established grant providers are not guaranteed to last for ever, and the vagaries of funding and budgets mean that payments can be vulnerable to change, or might even disappear altogether. In some sectors of publishing it is never the aim to turn a profit, and it may be impossible to do so—but all companies should try to become as self-reliant as they can so that they are not suddenly threatened by cuts in funding. Many IPG members have had to deal with the threat or reality of funding drying up, and it is well worth talking to them about their experiences.

FORECASTING AND BUDGETING

Planning your finances is as important as planning your books, especially in the first few years when you may well not see much money coming in. It should start with your business plan (see the Getting Started chapter), which needs to include detailed month by month financial forecasts for at least the first three years. If you project these realistically and stick to them, you will have a much better chance of succeeding in the long run. Forecasting can be laborious, but time spent doing it well will repay itself many times over.

Project your net receipts month by month, according to your planned schedule of book releases. Predicting sales is very tricky in publishing, but try to do as much market research as you can. Segment them by channel, noting what you expect to sell direct, through chains, through independents and online, for instance. Take into account seasonal fluctuations—if you have books that would make good gifts, for instance, sales should accelerate towards Christmas, but if you are in the academic market, summer and early autumn may be your peaks. Remember that most customers will expect credit of 30, 60 or even 90 days, so sales made in January might not translate into cash until March or April. Don't forget to factor in the discounts that you will have to give your customers, often underestimated by new publishers. If you have any other likely sources of income—from selling rights or licensing deals, for instance—include those too.

Now tot up all your outgoings. The costs incurred in producing a book are outlined below, and whatever is left after these are deducted from your projected sales is your predicted profit. This will be a rough and ready figure, but it should tell you if your business is viable. Break down month by month your costs and overheads—things like staff, rent, insurance, office equipment, tax and loans, as well as your own salary—and add when direct costs like printers' bills and royalties are likely to be paid. Any net profit that is left over after these deductions usually goes back into the business or is used to build up a cash 'buffer'—money to keep aside in the event of larger than expected bills or months where sales are poor. Having even a small cash buffer can be very reassuring when it comes to cash flow (see below), and will save having to dip into overdrafts or loans.

When forecasting, be wary of falling into the common trap of underestimating costs and overestimating sales. Be pessimistic rather than optimistic, and you won't be disappointed.

COSTING YOUR BOOKS

Each book that you intend to publish should have its own financial mini-plan. This helps to focus minds on the strengths and weaknesses of a project, and will give you an idea of how much it will cost, what it might earn for you and the consequent risk involved in publishing it. These plans need not take too long to prepare—many publishers have standard forms or spreadsheets that can be completed in minutes—but a little time spent budgeting can save you a lot of money further down the line. Systems can help you with this budgeting (see below), and other publishers might share their template forms or spreadsheets with you.

Once you have a design spec for a book, calculate as accurately as you can the costs that you will incur in publishing it. Include the following: the costs of printing; advances and royalties to the author; editorial and design costs like permissions, artwork and freelance editors, proofreaders, designers, typesetters and indexers; sales, marketing and publicity spends; distribution costs; and a small provision for books that might be given away or returned.

Break all these down in as detailed a way as you can. The allocation of costs varies widely from sector to sector and format to format. But the revenue from a book might typically be accounted for in the following splits: production costs of 30%; editorial and design costs of 10%; author royalties of 10%; distribution costs of 10%; sales and marketing costs of 5%; promotion and publicity costs of 5%; a write-off against returns and unsold stock of 10%; and an allocation for general business overheads of 20%. Dividing your total costs by your print run will give you a unit cost—the amount a book will cost you per copy printed.

Now project your net sales receipts for the book over its projected lifespan (see above). Compare this forecast to your costs. Does it show a profit or a loss? What is the break-even point—the number of copies you will need to sell to start making money? Is this achievable or too risky? Most publishers begin to develop a net profit margin to which all books will ideally work—typically 10% to 20%, though it may well be lower for trade publishers and higher for academic or journals publishers or big bestsellers. Publishing is much too unpredictable a business to be certain about your projections, but your forecasts should give you a good idea of whether or not a book is likely to be profitable for you. If it is not, consider how you might tweak the forecasted costings and sales to improve the margins, perhaps by raising the cover price or cutting the price per unit by printing more copies. But always bear in mind the knock-on effects of any changes—will raising the price reduce sales, for instance, or will you really be able to shift those extra books that you print? Over-printing in particular is a very common mistake. It might help to picture unsold stocks of books in a warehouse as piles of banknotes tied up and inaccessible to your business. In the worst-case scenario, if you decide in the end that you'll never be able to sell them, then these banknotes will simply be shredded.

Forecasting sales and costs is difficult for new publishers, but gets easier with experience. The golden rule is to be ruled by your head rather than your heart. Give everyone involved in a book some input into the estimate, and if you find it difficult to take a detached view, seek further opinions from people with a different but informed perspective—fellow publishers or booksellers, for instance. In the end, of course, you might decide that you like a book so much that you will publish it regardless of how many copies it sells. That's fine—but the important thing is to be realistic about your expectations.

Once you have produced your book's costings and start producing it, update your budgets to take into account any changes. If printing costs rise, for instance, examine how this will affect your margins, and consider what other costs you might reduce to maintain them. See the Print and Production chapter for more on predicting print runs and costs.

BOOK-KEEPING AND ACCOUNTING

Rigorous book-keeping is key to staying on top of your business. You can do it all yourself if you have the time and aptitude for the job, perhaps using a software system to help, or you can get an accountant to do it for you. Doing it yourself has the advantage of saving money and giving you a clear picture of how your business is doing, and even if you outsource it you will need to keep a close eye on things. Some publishers use an accountant to look after matters like tax, annual accounts and payroll, while doing the day-to-day book-keeping themselves.

However you do it, you should keep good records of all money coming in and going out of your business. In fact, it's the law, and companies are obliged to keep clear records and retain them for at least six years, in case they need to be inspected by HMRC. Make a record on your spreadsheet or cash book of all payments out, whether by cheque or electronic methods like BACS, and make a note of the type of expense for tax purposes. Keep track of petty cash for everyday expenses, and keep records of anything you buy for the business personally so you can reimburse yourself. Reconcile your cash book against your monthly bank statements, and check for any missing items.

If you use one, much of your sales income will be collected by your distributor, so make sure you have systems in place to get up-to-the-minute information fed into your own spreadsheet or database. If you handle sales yourself, keep a ledger of customers, totals invoices and payments. Maintaining this will help show which payments are outstanding and need to be chased at any given time. Try to update your cash book or ledgers daily or at least weekly. And remember the four Ss of accounting: Systems (so that you have practices to stick to); Security (so that errors or fraud can't affect your books); Separate (so that business and personal finances don't overlap); and Storage (so that your computerized records are backed up and your paper ones filed away safely).

For more detailed help with accounting and reporting, many publishers like to use off-the-shelf systems like Sage or Pegasus. These can manipulate the data you enter—or receive from your distributor—to automatically produce profit and loss accounts for your books and company as a whole, plus other reports and ratios. The data they compute would take a long time to compile manually, and some publishers find them essential when it comes to getting into the habit of analysing their performance. Software can also be invaluable when it comes to calculating royalties. For more on systems and the contact details of some recommended suppliers, see the Bibliographic and IT chapter. Many small publishers with basic book-keeping, though, find that Excel spreadsheets or other simple desktop packages are perfectly sufficient.

All limited companies or limited liability partnerships need to file annual financial accounts—usually made up of a balance sheet at the last day of your financial year and a profit and loss account for the previous year—with Companies House and HMRC. Guidelines for this are quite strict, and you will need to stay on top of the deadlines. Small businesses are entitled to various exemptions and may simply have to file a short balance sheet. Companies House and HMRC both have lots of resources, checklists and FAQs to help businesses meet all the legal requirements.

For more advice about book-keeping and accounting practices, see the Business Link website. It also has tools to help you make forecasts and measure the health of your business. The Institute of Chartered Accountants also has some useful guides to accounting methods and performance indicators.

MONITORING PERFORMANCE

Once your business is up and running, measure your performance against your forecasts at least every month and perhaps every week. New businesses need to stick as closely as they can to their projections, and if the reality is very different to the forecast, find out why as soon as you can. Was it because of poor forecasting or mistakes you made, or was it down to something out of your control? Adjust your forecasts if circumstances change and as you get a better feel for your market, but keep hold of your original totals so you can look back on them later. Once you have been trading for a year, you will also be able to start looking back on your performance in the corresponding month of the previous year.

When it comes to measuring performance, balance sheets—incorporating fixed and current assets and current and long-term liabilities—can be useful snapshots. But in these early days in particular, keeping a tight grip on cash flow is the secret to success. Using your sales and costs forecasts, draw up some cash flow projections on a spreadsheet, as tightly as you can and on a rolling basis for the year ahead, so you can see exactly how much money is going in and coming out of your business at any time. Business Link has a handy template spreadsheet that you can adapt with your own numbers, and accounting systems will do the job if you use them.

Check your progress relative to your forecasts frequently—once or even several times a week if you can—by updating your spreadsheet with all income that has or is due to come in, and all monies that have or are due to be paid. Looked at in relation to your bank balance, you should then be able to see well in advance if you have any cash flow problems and give yourself time to do something about it. Neglecting cash flow is a very common cause of businesses failing—even ones that are generally profitable. If you can see a time in the next few weeks when your cash is going to be reduced close to the limits imposed by the bank, you will have a better chance of solving the problem then than you will if it creeps up on you. See the section below for some tips on getting your cash flow in good shape.

Another thing to keep a close eye on is your gross profit margin—the difference between your net sales receipts and the basic costs of your books—production expenses and royalties. Try as hard as you can to keep this margin steady and on target, as it shows that your sales are running smoothly and your costs are under control. Stick to your margin like a limpet.

Above all, don't bury your head in the sand if your sales are lower than your forecasts, your costs higher or the margins on your books not as you hoped. This happens to just about all publishers at one time or another, so don't be disheartened. But do resolve to do something about it beyond hoping for the best.

TIPS FOR CASH FLOW

To help your cash flow along, always invoice for your sales promptly and set payment terms as tightly as you can. When money comes in, bank it immediately. Draw up some standard conditions for your invoices, including the right to charge interest on late payment (Business Link has some templates to help write these). Set strict credit limits on your customers unless you are totally confident you can trust them to pay. Invoicing and credit control is often done on publishers' behalf by distributors, but if you are doing the job yourself, chase late payment politely but vigorously, first by written reminder and then over the phone. If it is done by distributors, check every now and then that they are on top of it. If payment is more than a month overdue you might like to start charging interest, hire a debt collection agency or take legal advice, but first try to ascertain if there are genuine reasons for the delay, and be wary of antagonizing your customers. In general, the books business is fairly credit and trustworthy, but don't be afraid to apply pressure for payment, and run credit checks on any new customers you are not sure about, or existing ones if you think they are in trouble. It is particularly important to run credit checks or get rigorous references on overseas customers, since bad debt can be virtually impossible to recover in some territories. If you are in doubt about a new customer, ask for payment up front.

Other ways to stay on top of cash flow include paying as late as you can by using the full duration of terms on any bills you receive. As best as you can, schedule the movements of cash in and out so you always have some in reserve. If cash flow is looking very tight, talk to your suppliers and ask for a bit of extra leeway in paying bills. They will not always be able to oblige, but they may well be accommodating to valued customers, so long as you are upfront about matters.

Monitor your stock closely too. A lot of publishers' cash is tied up in book stock, and keeping it for too long—whether in a distributor's warehouse or elsewhere—can be expensive. If you have books that are not looking like shifting, you could free up some cash by selling it off at high discount, perhaps to a remainder dealer if necessary. Minimize returns by working with your customers to forecast sales accurately rather than optimistically (see the Sales chapter for more on this). Trim your list of any books that aren't selling, or switch them to print-on-demand only. Think afresh about your sales and marketing plans for the books that are left, and see if you can breathe a bit more life into them.

All good businesses need to be ruthlessly efficient when it comes to costs. Trim the costs of trading by doing as much as you can electronically (see the Bibliographic and IT chapter for ways of doing this). Keep your production expenses as low as you can without sacrificing quality, pushing printers hard for the best possible deal and reviewing all your suppliers regularly (see the Print and Production chapter for tips). Try to keep royalties and advances as low as you can whilst still being competitive. Advances in particular tie up money with no guarantee of a return, and many small publishers do not offer them. Monitor your day-to-day expenses like your office and travel prudently, though be wary of going too far and upsetting staff with strict economies.

Finally, talk to your bank. Press for the best possible terms on overdrafts, loans and charges. Ask for advice in managing your accounts in the most advantageous way. How much help and leeway banks can give will partly depend on the economic climate at the time, but they can sometimes be surprisingly accommodating with things like extended overdrafts or other short-term finance, and forthcoming with advice. Aim to establish a personal contact at the bank and stay in touch with him or her regularly, through good times and bad. Talk through any cash flow worries you may have, and outline what steps you are taking to alleviate them. Contrary to their reputations, many small companies consider their bank manager to be their best friend in business. If they are not helpful, threatening to take your business elsewhere tends to have a remarkable effect on the service you get.

TAX

Tax is no publisher's favourite topic. But don't shy away from it, and don't be afraid of paying it either. Some companies spend a lot of time and energy seeking tax avoidance measures when they should be thinking about their business. If you are having to pay a lot of tax, it means you are running a successful company.

The tax obligations on companies vary according to size and structure, and all new businesses need to investigate their obligations and options. HM Revenue & Customs, with whom all new companies need to register, has masses of advice on getting to grips with tax, on its website, through its advisers and via free regional seminars and workshops. Business Link has a useful online tool to help work out what taxes you will need to pay. And, of course, your accountant will be able to advise on everything you need to report or pay and when.

All limited companies in the UK must pay **corporation tax** on profits, at a rate—for small companies with profits of less than £300,000—of 21%, reducing to 20% in 2011. There are some exemptions for the likes of the self-employed, but this is a complicated area so check if you are in doubt. Once registered with HMRC, corporation tax can be self-assessed and paid via a company tax return and accounts, filed online or by post by statutory deadlines. These will be much easier to complete if you keep detailed, organized accounts as you go along (see above), but many companies prefer to get an accountant to do the job. He or she will also be able to advise on tax relief, deductible business expenses and capital allowances, which you should also research thoroughly yourself. And remember that corporation tax is ultimately your responsibility, so be sure your return and accounts have been correctly compiled.

If your business has a turnover above £70,000 a year, you will also need to register with HMRC for Value Added Tax (**VAT**). Printed books are, of course, zero rated for VAT, but e-books, audiobooks, CDs and some other publishing-related products are not.

If you are a director of your own company or employ others, you will need to pay **income tax** on your earnings and those of your staff. You can do this through the Pay As You Earn (PAYE) system, which can be organized online at HMRC's website. **National Insurance contributions** (NICs) will also have to be paid. Employers need to ensure they comply with guidelines relating to the minimum wage, statutory sick, maternity and paternity pay, and, because they are processing personal information about people, may have to register as a 'data controller' at the Information Commissioner's Office. Company directors and the registered self-employed will also have to complete an individual tax return about their income. HMRC has lots more advice about pay, PAYE and payroll issues.

If you buy or lease business premises or sell company shares, **stamp duty** may have to be applied. **Business rates** will have to be paid to local authorities—this requires separate registration—but check if you are eligible for small business discounts. And if and when you sell your business, you will probably need to pay **capital gains tax** on the proceeds.

HELP

Don't be afraid to ask for help when it comes to financial matters. There is plenty available. Possibly the best single source of advice will be an accountant. Some businesses manage all their book-keeping and tax affairs themselves, but money spent on a good accountant is usually a sound investment. Find a local one via directories or the Institute of Chartered Accountants, or ask other nearby businesses and fellow IPG members for recommendations. Try to find one with plenty of experience of working with small businesses and, even better, of working with small publishers, since the industry has quirks that not everyone will understand. A good solicitor will be very handy too; try the Law Society's directory for names. As your company grows, you may wish to consider appointing a full- or part-time financial director, whose job it is to look after the money side of the business while you or others get on with publishing books.

If you are not experienced in financial management, it might be useful to find a mentor. The IPG's mentoring scheme is a great way to get advice from experienced independent publishers. It could also be worth asking any financial experts that you know—either inside or outside of publishing—if they would consider joining your board of directors or advisers if you have one. Some active or retired publishers within the IPG already do this for other members. Local business networks or support groups might also be able to help suggest people in your area who are willing to become a mentor or board member.

Other common and recommended sources of support include Business Link, the government's massive database of resources and advice for UK businesses; specific departments like HMRC and BIS; the network of British Chambers of Commerce; and the Institute of Directors. For banking matters, the British Banking Association has some useful tips on business accounts.

For new small publishers, perhaps the best investment of all is a day spent learning more of the basics of financial management at the Publishing Training

Centre. The IPG organizes special courses for members at a discounted rate, and they are warmly recommended for giving a solid grounding in funding, planning, budgeting and accounting. Also available to members, free of charge, is the Croner Business Support Helpline, which can help with enquiries on countless aspects of business and regulations. Keep an eye on the IPG's e-bulletin and website for news of forthcoming training courses.

RESOURCES
THE ARTS COUNCIL

Arts Council England
The national development agency for English arts, funded by the government and the National Lottery. Supports the IPG and some independent publishers.
Web www.artscouncil.org.uk
Tel 0845 300 6200

Arts Council of Northern Ireland
Northern Ireland's version of the Arts Council.
Web www.artscouncil-ni.org
Tel 00 28 9038 5200

Arts Council of Wales
Wales' version.
Web www.artswales.org.uk
Tel 02920 376 500

Scottish Arts Council
Scotland's council.
Web www.scottisharts.org.uk
Tel 0131 226 6051

SOURCES OF FUNDING

British Council
Can help publishers establish overseas links, and has worked with the IPG on joint projects.
Web www.britishcouncil.org
Tel 0161 957 7755

Government Funding
A one-stop database of grants and awards available from various government departments and agencies.
Web www.governmentfunding.org.uk

National Federation of Enterprise Agencies
Umbrella group for enterprise agencies supporting small businesses, some of which might be able to help track down funding.
Web www.nfea.com
Tel 01234 831623

Paul Hamlyn Foundation
Charitable foundation established by the legendary publisher, promoting education and learning via various projects.
Web www.phf.org.uk
Tel 020 7227 3500

The Prince's Trust
Can offer support for people under 30 wanting to start their own business.
Web www.princes-trust.org.uk
Tel 020 7543 1374

Regional Development Agencies
Eight English regions each offering local advice about funding sources.
Web www.englandsrdas.com
Tel 020 7222 8180

UK Trade & Investment
Government agency to help companies export overseas. Can help publishers set up export links and identify opportunities for sales.
Web www.uktradeinvest.gov.uk
Tel 020 7215 8000

TOOLS TO HELP SEARCH FOR FUNDING

Business Link Grants and Support Directory
Very useful database of funding and other financial help, run by the Business Link portal and searchable by location and type of business.
Web http://www.businesslink.gov.uk/bdotg/action/gsd?r.li=1080758303&r.ll=1073858805&r.lc=en

FunderFinder
Offers software to help find grants and manage applications.
Web www.funderfinder.org.uk
Tel 0113 243 3008

GrantsNet
Free searchable database of grants for businesses and charities.
Web www.grantsnet.co.uk

GrantsOnline
Another searchable, subscription-based database of funding sources.
Web www.grantsonline.org.uk
Tel 01202 813452

ACCOUNTING AND TAX

Companies House
The national registrar of company accounts, with guidance on how to file.
Web www.companieshouse.gov.uk
Tel 0870 3333 636

HM Revenue and Customs
Lots of guidance on all forms of tax and employers' obligations and rights.
Regional offices also provide some useful workshops for new businesses and
employers.
Web www.hmrc.gov.uk
Tel 0845 010 9000

Information Commissioner's Office
Employers processing personal information for the payroll may have to register
here.
Web www.ico.gov.uk
Tel 08456 30 60 60 (Helpline)

Institute of Chartered Accountants
Directory of accountants across the country.
Web www.icaew.co.uk
Tel 020 7920 8100

TaxCafé

Impartial guide to UK taxation with various tools to help work through your obligations.

Web www.taxcafe.co.uk

Tel 01592 560081

Valuation Office Agency

The agency responsible for business rates in the UK, though these will be payable to your local authority.

Web www.voa.gov.uk

Tel 0845 602 1507

HELP

IPG Croner Helpline

Available free of charge to all IPG members to help with all your queries on business matters.

Tel 08445 618 133 and quote your members' scheme number

Better Payment Practice Group

Has some sound advice about ways to chase late payments.

Web www.payontime.co.uk

British Banking Association

Tips on making the most of your business bank account.

Web www.bba.org.uk

Tel 020 7216 8800

Business Link

Hugely helpful resource for all businesses, with masses of free online tips and a network of local offices.

Web www.businesslink.gov.uk

Tel 0845 600 9006

Chambers of Commerce

A countrywide network of businesses and support groups.

Web www.britishchambers.org.uk

Tel 020 7654 5800

Department for Business, Innovation and Skills
Government guidance on financial and regulatory matters.
Web www.bis.gov.uk
Tel 020 7215 5000

Financial Services Authority
Government guidance on understanding and sticking to financial regulations.
Web www.fsa.gov.uk
Tel 08456 061 234

Institute of Directors
Membership association for directors with some useful advice and networking opportunities.
Web www.iod.co.uk
Tel 020 7839 1233

TRAINING

Financial Management for Independent Publishers
Highly recommended day-long course, organized by the IPG with the Publishing Training Centre and tailored to the needs of small independents.
Web www.train4publishing.co.uk/guideto/ipg/finindep
Tel 020 8874 2718

BOOKS

Businesswise: Financial Planning for the Small and Medium-Sized Business by Peter Lyons (Tottel Publishing, £52, 9781845927219)

The Definitive Guide to Business Finance by Richard Stutely (Financial Times, £21.99, 9780273710950)

Directory of Grant-making Trusts by John Smyth and Dave Casson (Directory of Social Change, £99, 9781903991794). Regional guides are also available.

Financial Accounting and Reporting by Barry Elliott and Jamie Elliott (Financial Times, £43.99, 9780273712312)

Financial Management for the Small Business by Colin Barrow (Kogan Page, £15.99, 9780749445638)

Publishing for Profit: Successful Bottom-line Management for Book Publishers by Thomas Woll and Philip Kogan (Kogan Page, £19.95, 9780749429409)

Small Business Cash Flow by Denise O'Berry (John Wiley, £13.99, 9780470040973)

Start and Run Your Own Business by Alan le Marinel (How To Books, £12.99, 9781857039887)

Tax Planning for Family and Owner Managed Companies by Peter Rayney (Tottel Publishing, £98, 9781847661500)

Understanding Tax for Small Businesses by Sarah Deeks (Teach Yourself, £9.99, 9780340927410)

Writing Bids and Funding Applications by Jane Dorner (OUP, £7.99, 9780198606758)

13 PUBLISHING AND THE ENVIRONMENT

CONTENTS

Planning a green strategy / Paper and production / The supply chain /
The office / Resources

All human activity has some impact on the environment. Given its massive use of paper and complex supply chain involving lots of transportation and packaging, publishing contributes more to the problems of climate change and other eco impacts than many industries. It is far from the worst offender, of course, and it is also an industry that is becoming more and more ecologically aware. Publishers and booksellers are taking both small and large steps to cut down on their impacts, and no matter what its size, every company can do its bit to help out.

All businesses, especially small ones, have to find the right balance between being a sustainable business and being a profitable one. Going green can be expensive, but thankfully there are some financial as well as altruistic reasons to be more environmentally friendly. Reducing waste and energy can save you money, motivate your staff and impress your customers.

PLANNING A GREEN STRATEGY

Going green needs a dedicated strategy. All but the tiniest of companies should have a green or environmental policy—sometimes more grandly called an Environmental Management System—to help clarify their thinking and show staff, suppliers and customers that they are serious about this subject. It needn't be long—the shorter the better, in fact—but it does need to cover all your environmental aims and your plans for achieving them. For instance, it might include your targets for reducing your carbon footprint; your attitude to paper usage in your books; your plans for increasing recycling and reducing energy consumption in the office; and your policies for encouraging your suppliers to reach the same standards you set yourself. It needs to be understood and endorsed by everyone working for or with you, and should be integrated into your business plan.

Drafting a policy should begin with an honest and accurate assessment of your environmental impacts. You might like to measure your carbon footprint, and there are plenty of tools to help you do so, including free online calculators to do it yourself and agencies to do audits for you. Some, like The Carbon Trust, may have schemes to help small businesses assess their performance for free.

Once you've measured your footprint, identify the things that contribute most to it, and prioritize your actions accordingly. Use your footprint as a baseline for improvement, perhaps aiming for the target of reducing it by 10% by 2015 that was set to all publishing companies by the Environmental Action Group, a joint initiative of the Booksellers and Publishers Association. It might also help to set yourself some recognized national or international standards as a goal; there are plenty of these available, though some can be quite onerous for small companies. You might like to set yourself the target of becoming 'carbon neutral'—this is a popular buzz word in business and a great achievement to boast about, and various schemes exist to help you offset your carbon emissions and reach that goal. But it is also a misunderstood term, open to various interpretations and distortions. Perhaps a more realistic and honest target is to simply be a sustainable business—meaning you meet the needs of today without compromising the needs of tomorrow; by, for instance, making sure that enough trees are planted to replace the ones you have used for paper for your books. Put very simply, it means putting back at least as much as you take out.

However you approach it, think positive, and don't be daunted by the task ahead of you. Every small action helps in some way, and everyone has to start somewhere. Take a long-term view, but also identify some quick-win goals that can be achieved easily. Once you have set your policy, monitor your progress regularly. Quantify your improvements if you can—comparing your electricity bill from month to month is a simple way to start—and keep looking for ways to improve further. If you have a small number of staff, include your environmental targets in your regular meetings, set up a committee to oversee your strategy, or appoint an environmental champion to lead things.

PAPER AND PRODUCTION

Of all the environmental impacts delivered by publishers, use of paper is by some distance the most significant—by some estimates accounting for around three-quarters of the industry's carbon footprint. And making sure that the paper you use in your books is responsibly sourced and handled is probably the biggest thing you can do to reduce damage.

The most environmentally friendly papers are those that are either fully re-cycled or certified by the Forest Stewardship Council (FSC). Unhelpfully, there is no legal and agreed definition of recycled paper. Some manufacturers produce it from post-consumer waste (recycled newspapers, stationery, etc.), while some use pre-consumer waste (mill trimmings). As a rule, post-consumer waste can more truly be called 'recycled'. If you're keen to use recycled papers, always ask your printer or print buyer for an explanation of what it really means in each instance. Recycled paper also has distinct characteristics and might not be suit-able for all books. Its production involves plenty of energy consumption, so it's not necessarily a greener option by default.

Certification is an easier way of checking the source and history of your paper. To be accredited by the FSC, forests have to be managed in a sustainable way, acceptable to the environment and the nearby population, and paper has to be handled responsibly at every step of the manufacturing process. As a result, printers have to have a fully auditable process, and accreditation is not easily achieved, though many in the UK now have it. If you are concerned that your printer does not have it, ask; they may well be working towards full accreditation, and your pressure will help to speed up their efforts. You should also be wary of any supplier without FSC accreditation that makes other green claims about their products; these are usually hard to verify and often exaggerated for com-mercial gain. Ask also for proof of standard ISO 14001—the internationally recognized standard for environmental management systems.

The FSC's is not the only certification scheme—the Europe-wide Programme for the Endorsement of Forestry Certification (PEFC) initiative is another—but the former is probably the best known. You can use the FSC logo on books that are made up of fully certified paper, and as more and more people express concern about paper use, this could become something of a commercial advantage. Larger publishers might also consider joining the Publishers' Database for Responsible Environmental Paper Sourcing (PREPS)—a joint initiative to share information about the technical specifications and environmental credentials of various papers, allowing buyers to make more informed decisions. Members are so far mostly big, multinational publishers, though it is open to everyone.

Think too about the ink that your printer uses and the energy they use to run their machines. Vegetable-based inks generally have lower environmental impacts than others, and you might either ask your printer if they have a renew-able energy tariff or consider paying to offset emissions. Lastly, think about the impact that your printer's location has on your environmental impact. If you are printing in cheaper territories like China, shipping your books back home is obviously not ideal for the environment, though it is much better than flying them. With exceptions, printers in developing countries are generally much less likely to be environmentally responsible, and it can be difficult to verify any green claims they make. The greenest option of all would be to print all your books at the closest FSC-accredited printer to you—though you will obviously have to weigh up other considerations like price.

THE SUPPLY CHAIN

If you are serious about going green, it is as important to think about the environmental impacts of your suppliers and partners as it is to address your own. Look up and down your entire chain, and identify where you think environmental damage is being done. Ask everyone you work with in the chain for their environmental credentials. If you don't think they are doing enough, challenge them to do more and consider moving elsewhere. Pressure from their customers really does have an energizing effect on suppliers.

Distribution is likely to be a major area of energy use. Minimize the transportation of goods wherever you can. Think about the packaging materials used to dispatch your books, and ask your suppliers what they can do to reduce waste. Many carriers are now trying to switch from half-empty cardboard boxes to full and reusable totes, and pressure from publishers will force them to improve. Check that packaging materials are either recyclable or biodegradable, or at the very least recyclable—and if they're not, ask why not. If you are distributing your own books, try to consolidate your orders as much as possible, delivering in bunches rather than individually.

If you are bringing back books from printers overseas or shipping them abroad, always use sea freight instead of air unless it's absolutely essential to fly things. Make sure your freight carrier is filling containers to the brim rather than sending them half-empty. More and more of them are consolidating consignments to ensure this.

One of the best ways to cut waste in the chain is to keep returns to a minimum—though that's easier said than done. In some sectors, you could choose to offer firm sale only, and while it's likely to meet with opposition from retailers, openness to the idea is increasing, especially on backlist books. If you do agree on sale or return, try to encourage retailers to order sensibly, and work with them to forecast the demand for a book as best you can. It is in no one's interests to order too many or too few copies. Don't be too ambitious in your sales estimates, since returns are bad news financially as well as environmentally.

There are several cross-trade initiatives in the supply chain that are attempting to increase efficiencies and reduce waste. The Industry Returns Initiative tries to make returns between publishers and booksellers much more straightforward, and is also cutting costs. The e4books initiative and Batch system both promote electronic commerce, so reducing the amount of paper flowing through the system. It is also worth trying to follow the guidelines laid out by the Booksellers and Publishers Associations for the life cycle of a book.

THE OFFICE

Although the carbon footprint of your office is likely to be small compared with that of your production and distribution, going green starts at home. Review your entire office arrangements to make sure you are producing as little waste as possible, try to prioritize improvements, and make sure all staff are committed to them and have the chance to contribute their own ideas.

Use recycled or properly sourced paper in your stationery, marketing and publicity and catalogues. Print on both sides of computer paper, and don't print at all if you can help it. Keep recycling bins for all office paper waste, and set targets to increase the percentage of materials recycled. Remove desk-side bins to encourage greater recycling. If you use plastics in your direct mailing, ask about using biodegradable ones. Market electronically if you can—sending material by email is less wasteful, not to mention cheaper.

Turn computers off when they are not being used. Use energy saving light bulbs and switch them off on bright days and overnight. Think about using renewable energy suppliers. Source your office products from green suppliers, and buy fair trade tea and coffee. Recycle office equipment like old computers, toner cartridges, CDs and batteries. Consider ethical banks like the Co-operative or Triodos.

If you have to travel far from your office, use public transport wherever possible, and think about rewarding staff for taking the bus or train or cycling to work. Loans for public transport season tickets are a good idea, as are initiatives for cycling to work like Cyclescheme. Always consider if your overseas travel is essential, or if you could talk to contacts by phone, Skype, tele or video conferencing instead. Think about paying a little to offset any flights or long car journeys you take. If you visit the Frankfurt Book Fair, do as more and more publishers do and take the train. It's more comfortable and interesting as well as more environmentally friendly.

RESOURCES
TRADE ASSOCIATIONS

Environmental Action Group
Joint initiative of the Publishers and Booksellers Association to raise awareness of eco issues in the industry.
Web www.green4books.org.uk

IPG
See our website for more expert tips on becoming more environmentally friendly.
Web www.ipg.uk.com (click on 'Member Info' and then 'Publishers and the Environment')

PRELIMS (Publishers Resolution for Ethical International Manufacturing Standards)
Umbrella group for better and greener standards of book production, with advice on working with manufacturers and suppliers.
Web www.prelims.org

Publishers Green Network
Forum for discussion of green issues in publishing with quarterly meetings—free to join and open to everyone in UK publishing.
Web www.green4books.org.uk

SUPPORT FOR BUSINESS

Act on CO2
Government campaign to spread advice on energy saving.
Web www.actonco2.direct.gov.uk
Tel 0800 512012

Business Link
Lots of advice and resources to assess and reduce your environmental impact.
Web www.businesslink.gov.uk
Tel 0845 600 9006

The Carbon Trust
Offers lots of practical support as part of its mission to reduce carbon emissions in business.
Web www.carbontrust.org
Tel 0800 085 2005

Centre for Sustainable Energy
Advice to help you improve your sustainable energy policy.
Web www.cse.org.uk
Tel 0117 934 1400

Cyclescheme
A government initiative to provide tax-free bikes for employees wanting to cycle to work.
Web www.cyclescheme.co.uk
Tel 01225 448933

EnviroWise
Useful government programme with advice on writing an environmental policy as well as lots of tips for a sustainable business.
Web www.envirowise.gov.uk
Tel 0800 585794 (free advice line)

Incpen (The Industry Council for Packaging and the Environment)
Research into more environmentally friendly packaging, production and distribution.
Web www.incpen.org
Tel 0118 925 5991

Institute of Environmental Management and Assessment
Useful portal for businesses wanting to be greener.
Web www.iema.net
Tel 01522 540069

NetRegs
Free guidance to the myriad of environmental regulations required of businesses.
Web www.netregs.gov.uk

Recycle Now
Everything you could ever need to know about recycling.
Web www.recyclenow.com

Wrap (Waste and Resources Action Programme)
Useful advice for businesses on making better use of resources and packaging material in particular.
Web www.wrap.org.uk
Tel 0808 100 2040

ENVIRONMENTAL STANDARDS AND OFFSETTING

British Safety Council
Has a 'Five Star Environmental Audit' to benchmark your green efforts.
Web www.britishsafetycouncil.co.uk
Tel 020 8741 1231

British Standards
The national agency for standards, including several environmental targets.
Web www.bsi-global.com
Tel 020 8996 9000

The Carbon Neutral Company
Offers consultancy on climate change as well as offsetting schemes.
Web www.carbonneutral.com
Tel 020 7833 6000

Climate Care
Has calculators to work out your carbon footprint and advice for reducing it.
Web www.climatecare.org
Tel 01865 207 000

Eco Management and Audit Scheme
Cross-Europe voluntary initiative to improve companies' environmental performance.
Web www.iema.net

International Organization for Standardization
Has standards for environmental policies in business.
Web www.iso.org
Tel 00 41 22 749 01 11

PAPER AND PRODUCTION

Forest Stewardship Council
Runs certification schemes for paper that has been properly and sustainably sourced.
Web www.fsc-uk.org
Tel 01686 413916

Lovely as a Tree
Co-operative site to help graphic designers be greener in day-to-day work.
Web www.lovelyasatree.com

Paper Profile
Voluntary Europe-wide environmental declaration scheme to help paper buyers make ethical choices.
Web www.paperprofile.com

PREPS (Publishers' Database for Responsible Environmental Paper Sourcing)
Joint initiative from publishers to share information about the environmental impacts of various papers.
Web www.preps-uk.com

Programme for the Endorsement of Forestry Certification
Cross-Europe scheme to promote ethically sourced paper.
Web www.pefc.org
Tel 00 41 22 799 45 40

SUPPLY CHAIN INITIATIVES

Batch
For electronic invoicing and payments.
Web www.batch.co.uk
Tel 020 7802 0847

e4Books
Promotes the use of e-commerce and the reduction of paper waste.
Web www.bic.org.uk/e4books
Tel 020 7607 0021

Industry Returns Initiative
Cross-industry project to reduce returns.
Web www.bic.org.uk
Tel 020 7607 0021

Life Cycle of a Book
Guidelines for how new books should be distributed, sold and returned in order to maximize efficiencies.
Web http://www.booksellers.org.uk/industry/display_report.asp?id=2406

BACKGROUND INFORMATION

BBC Climate Change
Useful backgrounder on climate issues.
Web www.bbc.co.uk/climate

Guardian Environment
Practical tips for greener living as well as information on environmental damage.
Web www.guardian.co.uk/environment

BOOKS

101 Ways to Turn Your Business Green by Rich Mintzer (Entrepreneur Press, £11.99, 9781599182636)

The Business Guide to Sustainability by Darcy Hitchcock and Marsha Willard (Earthscan, £29.95, 9781844073207)

Cradle to Cradle: Rethinking the Way We Make Things by William McDonough and Michael Braungart (Rodale Press, £17.99, 9780865475878)

Good Green Guide for Small Businesses (A&C Black, £12.99, 9780713689327)

Green Business Practices for Dummies by Lisa Swallow (Wiley, £14.99, 9780470393390)

The Green Guide for Business by Roger East (Green Profile, £9.99, 9781846688744)

The Green Marketing Manifesto by John Grant (John Wiley, £14.99, 9780470723241)

Green to Gold: How Smart Companies Use Environmental Strategy to Innovate, Create Value and Build a Competitive Advantage by Daniel Esty and Andrew Winston (Yale University Press, £14.50, 9780300119978)

Positively Responsible: How Business Can Save the Planet by Erik Bichard and Cary Cooper (Butterworth-Heinemann, £15.99, 9780750684750)

The Sustainability Handbook by William Blackburn (Earthscan, £49.95, 9781844074952)

14 SELLING UP

CONTENTS

Planning a sale / Working with brokers or advisers / Identifying a buyer /
Valuing your business / Grooming a business for sale / Securing a buyer /
Completing the sale / Confidentiality and staff / After a sale /
Other exit options / Resources

For the majority of independent publishers, selling a business will be something that is done only once in a lifetime. For that reason, it is not an undertaking for which many can draw on previous experience, and it can be a stressful, laborious process. But done with thorough preparation and attention to detail, it can be the successful culmination of many years of hard work—and hopefully a good reward for it too. For a small handful of IPG members, it has also been the prompt to do it all over again and start another publishing company.

PLANNING A SALE

Plan your strategy for a sale as far in advance as you can. As far as possible, work to a timetable that suits you. Always try to be aware of your motivations for running your own business and your long-term ambitions, and be crystal clear about your reasons for exiting the business—whether they are to make money, to reduce your workload or to try something new.

Set some objectives, including the date by which you want to sell or the level of turnover and profitability at which you might sell; the price you would like to get; and how you would like the business to be run after you cut your involvement. You may wish to sell the business outright, but if you want to stay with it in some way, it is best for everyone if you are very clear about your desired level of involvement. Whatever your intentions, planning as far ahead as possible will give you the best chance of getting the right outcome. It can take several years to plan and prepare for an exit, and remember to factor into your schedules the time it takes to go through the legal and administrative processes of actually selling a business—typically not less than six months and frequently longer.

It is not uncommon for publishers to receive unsolicited approaches from potential purchasers or intermediaries before they are ready to sell. Unless you consider an offer is too good to refuse, or there are compelling reasons to sell at short notice, don't let these offers distract you from your own strategies and timetables. Given that independent publishers do not have to answer to share holders, a polite no is usually enough to fend off unwanted advances. But don't put anyone off entirely, and if you think you might be more receptive to an offer in a few years' time, say so and suggest you talk again then. Be friendly to all your colleagues and competitors. You never know when you might see or need them again.

If you don't already have them, get a good solicitor and accountant on board to help you plan and execute the sale. The first will be invaluable when it comes to jumping through the endless legal hoops that lie ahead, while the second can provide advice from the outset about making a sale as tax efficient as possible. Solicitors in particular need to have experience of dealing with mergers and acquisitions, so don't be afraid to call in extra help if your current lawyer doesn't have this. Competition among solicitors can be quite high, so invite several to pitch for the work if you like. The Law Society and the Institute of Chartered Accountants are good places to find qualified specialists.

WORKING WITH BROKERS OR ADVISERS

Because most people who sell a business will be doing so for the first and only time, it is important to get help with the process. And unless your business is very small indeed, it is likely that you will want to sell it through a broker. In publishing, the two leading specialists, both highly recommended by IPG members who have used them, are Quayle Munro and Bertoli Mitchell. Both are very experienced in all sectors of publishing, and can provide assistance and advice at all stages of the process of selling a company.

There are plenty of other acquisition brokers, but most will provide a general service and will not have the specialist knowledge of publishing that can be very valuable in the sales process. When choosing one to work with, ask around in the IPG on as confidential a basis as you can for recommendations. Look for evidence of experience and good contacts, and request testimonials. Ask brokers how they think they could help you, and get to know people before you hire them. Compare quotes—you may be surprised at how much they vary. Be confident that you will be able to work effectively with your broker—you will be going through a lot together, and trust is absolutely essential on both sides.

Brokers are usually happy to provide informal advice if you are considering a sale at some time in the future, and it is worth contacting them as early as possible. Even if a sale is merely a possibility several years down the line, initial contact can help to sharpen your strategy and work towards preparing your business for sale. Brokers generally welcome all contact from publishers, even if enquiries are tentative, and work on a totally confidential basis. Some brokers will have a minimum transaction price below which they may not wish to work, so they will not be able to help very small publishers—but they are often still happy to provide brief advice at first contact.

One advantage of working with a broker is that they are more likely than you to know companies who are seeking acquisitions. They have an expert understanding of the market, and will probably have been alerted by prospective buyers to keep an eye out for suitable acquisitions. Brokers can help you to get the best price for your business and may be able to raise bids substantially if there are several interested parties. They will present your business to buyers as professionally as possible, leaving you with more time to actually run the operation while they sell it. By advising on legal and regulatory matters and putting you in touch with their networks of experts, they should also make the process of selling up a lot less laborious and stressful.

The main downside of working with brokers is that they will charge a fee for their services, typically ranging from 1% to 5% of the purchase price, though this will vary according to size. But in the vast majority of cases, the increased price that a broker can secure for your business compensates for this charge many times over. Agree a clear fee structure before you start working with anyone, and decide whether you would prefer to pay on a fixed-rate or contingency fee basis.

IDENTIFYING A BUYER

In the close-knit world of publishing, it is likely that you will know your buyer already—or at least know *of* them. They could be competitors in the same field that might be seeking to grow their business through acquisition. They could be publishing in a similar or related field and have a gap in their publishing into which your business might fit. They could be a much larger publishing company that is looking for acquisitions in several niches, or a new entrant seeking bolt-ons to grow fast. They may be an outsider investment or private equity group. Or they could be a 'long shot' company—one that you had not been aware was even seeking to acquire businesses, or one that you have not even heard of.

Following publishing developments in the trade press can alert you to companies that might be looking to buy other businesses, and you could even consider placing an advertisement here if you want to flush out interest. Keep an eye out too for overseas companies wishing to establish themselves in the UK. Brokers will have databases of companies to approach about a sale and will probably have a better idea than you about overseas targets. Book fairs can be good places to identify and court potential buyers from overseas.

VALUING YOUR BUSINESS

Valuing publishing businesses is tricky. Like all businesses, they have assets that can be valued like buildings, equipment and stock, but far more important to buyers—and more difficult to value—is the intellectual property they own. Put simply, your business is worth whatever someone is willing to pay for it. Any structured valuations will depend on many factors, including some—like confidence in the wider publishing or economic climate—that are out of your control. Despite all the tools used by both buyers and sellers, valuations are still more of an art than a science.

Whether you get the best price for your business will depend on whether you pick the right time to sell. Broadly speaking, this is when the market for your books is buoyant and profits and sales are both increasing. Buyers will not want to pick up a business that has reached its peak, because the only way from there is down. Take seasonal cycles into consideration—if you are a trade publisher, for instance, your business may look healthier just after the Christmas rush than it would when returns have come back in March. It is usually wiser to sell when the economy is strong rather than weak, but remember that publishers are as a rule more immune to recessions than most industries.

It is quite common for small companies to sell too early and regret that they had not built their business up more before securing a better price. At the same time, it is important to be realistic and to avoid over-valuing your business. Since its value will be determined by other people's interest, always bear in mind what it is about your business that others will like, and be focused on increasing its value.

As a rule, acquiring publishers look for high quality lists and top-line growth. Quality counts for a lot in publishing, and purchasers need to know that your books are well planned, produced to the highest standards and valued by their readers. They need to see that there is a long-term future for your products and that they meet a clear need. Growth in sales is more appealing than growth in profits because acquiring publishers will consider themselves able to improve margins once they have integrated the business. But they need to be reassured that top-line sales are increasing and will continue to do so. Bear in mind your competition, and ask whether the performance of your rivals might affect your own valuation. Your value will be higher if you are the leader—or indeed the only publisher—in your niche.

Prospective buyers will also be interested in intangible things like your company's brand, people and relationships with the buyers of your books.

Demonstrating that your business has a close, professional relationship with customers is crucial. Don't underestimate the value of what is commonly called goodwill—given that publishing is a people-driven business, a strong, hardworking and professional staff can often be highly prized by buyers. A publisher's brand is sometimes worthless, but if you have evidence that yours has particular resonance in the market, then factor this into your valuation. Also remember to include the value of any publishing licences.

There are plenty of benchmarks available to help you put a broad value on your business, and the best provider of these are brokers (see above). Publishing specialists like Quayle Munro and Bertoli Mitchell have benchmarks that are tailored to the quirks of publishing, and they can also base a valuation on their long list of previous transactions and other research. Most brokers will provide a broad valuation on a no-obligation basis. And even if you are not considering an imminent sale, regular valuations of your business can be very useful, benchmarking your performance, identifying possible areas of improvement and measuring growth.

It may be worth asking around trusted contacts in publishing to try to establish a value for your business. Following news of recent transactions in the trade press can also give you an indication of the state of the market and may help you towards a rough estimate. Rules of thumb in publishing have traditionally valued trade companies at about one to one and a half times annual turnover; educational, academic, professional and STM companies at two to four times turnover; and journals companies at anything upwards of three times turnover. Although these valuations can fluctuate rapidly depending on the conditions of the market and particular businesses, it generally holds true that academic, professional and STM publishers command a higher value than their trade or educational equivalents because they are more profitable and exercise greater control over their intellectual property.

There are plenty of other valuation techniques, including price to earnings ratios and entry cost calculations, which work out what it would cost a competitor to build a similar business from scratch rather than buying it. Useful guides and calculators for valuations are provided by Business Link and the Institute of Directors among others.

GROOMING A BUSINESS FOR SALE

Brokers will help you groom your business to ensure it is presented to potential buyers in the best possible light. But there is plenty that you can do on your own to maximize its appeal too. As with most things in selling up, the further ahead you can plan for this, the better. Start thinking about getting your company in shape a year to 18 months before you actually plan to sell it.

Changes need to be operational as well as cosmetic. Make sure your financial records are up to date and neatly presented. Try to prove the financial stability of your business, making the most of your working capital position. Get your credit and stock control in good order, so that bad debts and unnecessary overheads do not reduce your valuation. Sell off any unnecessary equipment to reduce debts, and get valuations for what you have left. And make sure all the figures in your accounts and forecasts are accurate and realistic. All data will be pored over in fine detail, so errors or exaggerations will be found out at some point down the line, potentially leading to mistrust.

Get all your contracts with authors, distributors, printers, landlords and other partners straight, and take a legal audit of them if you can to check they are all watertight. Try to formalize into contracts any casual relationships that you have. Make sure you are meeting all employment, tax and health and safety legislation, and that your management and financial systems are in good order. Buyers will want to access data and information at short notice, and you should be able to answer queries promptly. They will want to know about your customers, so present sales breakdown clearly; and they will want to see how they can cut costs, so compartmentalize these as neatly as you can.

Tidy up your backlist of books, killing off the ones that aren't making you any money and injecting new life into the ones that are. Get your forward publishing programme in order so that buyers can project what their future income from the business might be. Sort out your own sales forecasts and growth strategies, and make it as easy as possible for buyers to see how they will be able to make money out of your business. Get the company structure right so you can illustrate the strength of its people.

Most company transactions start with a sales memorandum, information memorandum or prospectus—the document that presents your business to prospective buyers. Brokers and solicitors will be able to help you with this, but much of the text will be best coming from you. It is the opportunity to market your business and persuade buyers that they would like to know more. Make your company sound as attractive as possible, but be honest and back up your arguments with hard evidence. Point out the future opportunities for the business and try to illustrate that you have a broad customer base, not reliant on a small number of buyers. Outline your publishing programme and demonstrate the market and distribution channels for it. A memorandum can include key financials like sales, profit, assets, debts and cash flow plus details of staff, but the amount of detailed, confidential information about the business that you include is at your discretion. You may wish to present much of it to seriously interested parties only, and use a memorandum merely to flush out initial interest.

As you prepare your business for a sale, try to prepare yourself, too. It can be a very tough process, taking its toll emotionally and physically. Talk to members in the IPG who have sold their businesses to get an idea of what sellers go through. Most of the IPG's Patrons have experience of going through the process and will be happy to share advice in confidence where they can.

SECURING A BUYER

Whether or not you are working with a broker, try to draw up a shortlist of prospective buyers. Break this down into favoured parties who you think have a serious interest, and back-up options to pursue if need be. If you have one, a broker will make the initial approaches to potential purchasers, and very rarely is it better for publishers to do so themselves. Brokers can help to keep your business confidential until they are sure a buyer is serious, and will also ensure discretion as discussions progress. If confidentiality is a particular concern or you are worried about sharing sensitive data, ask all interested parties to sign a non-disclosure agreement. Control the flow of information out to bidders.

Following circulation of a sales memorandum or approaches from brokers, serious buyers should soon become clear. Whittle down non-serious enquiries, and try to ascertain as quickly as you can whether those that remain are truly able to pay. Some bidders may be spurious, so ask for proof of financial backing if necessary—if you have any doubts, it is best to do this early on rather than leaving it until negotiations are advanced. Draw your shortlist of buyers closer to your business, providing more information on request and introducing them to other staff if you are involving them in the sale.

Once indicative offers begin to be made, don't be afraid to ask for improved ones and to hold out for the price you want. Play bidders off against each other, and call their bluffs. Serious buyers will rarely walk away from the table for good. Try not to pursue a single buyer too enthusiastically, or they will quickly realize they have no competition and are in the driving seat when it comes to negotiations. In terms of negotiations and psychology, selling a business is much like selling a house.

Pay very close attention to the terms of all offers you are made. Bidders may offer options like deferred payments, earn-outs that are linked to future sales or share options, but insist on the form of payment that suits you, especially if that involves a large proportion of cash upfront. Consider the tax implications of the timing of payments—as well as overall capital gains tax liabilities and entrepreneurs' relief—or ask your accountant to do so. Seek advice from your broker or a specialist solicitor if you don't understand anything, especially when it comes to the warranties and indemnities that buyers attach to their bids. Contracts are usually loaded with these, asking sellers to meet responsibilities for things like debts, tax and wages for an agreed time, but scrutinize all the terms very carefully.

Try to assess offers in their entirety rather than being distracted by the simple value of the bid. Look at the timelines suggested by bidders and make sure they suit you. Avoid long delays in completion as they will disrupt your business. Set the terms for your future involvement—many buyers will want you to carry on with the business for at least a handover period, but others may want to have a free rein. If you want to work elsewhere in publishing after selling, do not sign any agreements that restrict your activities.

COMPLETING THE SALE

Once you have chosen a buyer, the aim is to complete a deal as quickly as possible, though this often takes much longer than expected. Try to agree heads of terms or heads of agreement for a sale quickly, outlining things like price, regulatory matters, confidentiality and restrictive arrangements. Don't try to change the basic terms after this, since trust will be eroded. Don't let your buyer try to do so either, and be particularly wary of this practice if you are dealing with private equity buyers. After signing heads of terms, it is customary to end talks with other parties. Tell your other bidders that a deal has been agreed, but try to maintain friendly contact with one or two of them in case the deal does fall through.

Depending on the size of your business, due diligence can take as little as a few weeks or as much as several months. It can be a laborious and challenging procedure, requiring a fine toothcomb to be run through the business by your buyer or their advisers, but try to stay patient and helpful. Detailed accounts may need to be prepared and inspected, and buyers may wish to independently verify many of the things you have told them, so try to have everything at your fingertips. Visits to your offices may be necessary, but try to do as much as you can elsewhere to avoid disruption. Purchasers may try to bargain down the price because of things they claim to have uncovered during due diligence, but hold as firm as you can and do not be intimidated by brinkmanship. If a company seriously wants to buy yours, it is unlikely to walk away from the purchase.

Once due diligence is completed, a final sales agreement can be drawn up, outlining all the terms you have already agreed and adding more detail. Even if you have been checking things carefully throughout the sales process, take time to inspect every line of the agreement, and ask for clarification if anything looks odd. Some negotiation will probably be required to agree the final draft, but hold firm on the terms you want and do not be pushed into changing significant details at the last minute.

Once sold, all businesses need to inform Companies House and HM Revenue & Customs about the changes in their circumstances.

CONFIDENTIALITY AND STAFF

Keeping the sale of a business confidential can be very difficult. Publishing is well known for its rumours and leaks, and preserving total secrecy is a challenge. But for the sake of securing the best price for your business, it is best to keep details as closely under wraps as you can. Rumours about a sale can make relationships with your suppliers, authors and staff very awkward.

In a small, close-knit business, where employers usually keep staff informed about all company developments on a regular basis, it can be very hard for managers to keep things secret. Staff may well later resent not being told of a sale, and you risk losing them as a result. You may choose to take particularly long-serving, senior or close staff—or indeed all of them—into your confidence. If you do, try to keep them updated with all progress in the sale and stress the importance of confidentiality at all times. If you don't, try to explain your reasons for secrecy as honestly as you can as soon as you are able. You may also wish to consider sharing some of the proceeds of a sale among staff.

AFTER A SALE

Many IPG members who have sold their businesses report that while the months after a sale provide the chance for a welcome break, dealing with life outside of publishing can be a challenge. It can be particularly hard to watch a business to which you have devoted so much time and energy be changed by its new owners in ways you don't like.

Many independent publishers wish to ensure that the name, staff and premises of their company are protected and respected by the purchaser after the sale is completed. If this is important to you, it is worth stipulating from the outset of any sale negotiations so that potential purchasers understand your wishes. It is not always possible to secure guarantees, and almost impossible to make them legally binding for any length of time, so you will have to take any promises made on trust. Purchasers may often agree to maintain staff numbers and premises for a limited time—perhaps for one to two years—and if they want to acquire your company strongly enough, they may well agree to abide by your wishes. Their basic obligation will be to maintain staff's terms and conditions after the sale—check the Transfer of Undertakings (Protection of Employment) regulations (known as TUPE) from the government—though this is not the same as guaranteeing a long-term job, and you may wish to insist on more than that. But it is usually naïve to assume that your publishing name will remain intact forever, or that your former colleagues will be able to carry on working exactly as they did before.

OTHER EXIT OPTIONS

Selling up is not the only way to exit a business. If you do not wish to sell—or are unable to find a buyer—you will need to consider other options, and it is again important to plan well in advance. A popular way is for the founder to take on a non-executive role—perhaps as chairman—while delegating day-to-day responsibility for running the business to others. In this scenario, identifying future leaders of your business is crucial. This should be an ongoing process, and you will need to make sure that your key staff are adequately trained and mentored if they are to increase their responsibilities. If you have the right staff and are looking after them properly, you should almost make your role in the company redundant—or at least be able to concentrate on the parts of the business that you want to. See the Staff chapter for more on training and grooming your staff.

Succession strategies will depend on the particular circumstances of a company. If you are the sole owner, you will be able to dictate the pace and terms of succession. It becomes more complicated if a business is co-owned and one partner wishes to step back. If you wish to continue in the business, you will have to find a way of taking money out without selling—options here include equity funders or, if the amount required is relatively small, mortgaging or remortgaging assets to secure capital. It may be worth securing the help of a solicitor or broker to ensure that these processes are conducted professionally and to mutual satisfaction.

Family successions are common in all small businesses and often work well, but it is worth carefully considering potential pitfalls. If you have more than one possible family successor, try to identify the best person for the job as early as possible, and be open and honest with all candidates. If there is only one, be sure that his or her skills and experience are up to the job. If they are not—or if they decide they do not want to be involved in the family business—don't be afraid to consider other succession options and make contingency plans. Be wary of splitting responsibilities for the business equally between two or more family members, since this may just store up disagreements and difficulties for the future. Set clear boundaries between work and home so that personal relationships are not jeopardized. Seek some impartial advice if you can—opinions from outside of the family can be much clearer and honest than those from within it. And get your accountant's advice on the tax implications of family succession.

Mergers in publishing are not common but not unheard of either. They can be a good idea for two companies working in similar but not overlapping fields, offering some economies of scale through greater buying and selling power. But be wary of equal mergers where each party is the same size, since these can lead to tensions over who is responsible for making decisions at the new business if both parties want to remain involved. Someone has to be in charge.

If it is large enough to have one, selling the business to some or all of its management team is another option. In many cases, they might not offer the best price for the business, but they do have the advantage of preserving more of the company as it stands. Floating a business on either the London Stock Exchange or—more likely—the Alternative Investment or PLUS markets is very occasionally done by independent publishers, though this is usually more of a capital-raising strategy than an exit. New shareholders will probably want the previous management to continue to be involved in the company, at least for some time, and exiting the business immediately after selling shares in it will not instil confidence. Bear in mind that while a flotation can bring in useful new money, it is also a very expensive process and may take overall control of the business out of your hands since you will be accountable to new shareholders.

Liquidation is a fairly common exit strategy in small businesses, and while it is usually associated with failed companies it does not necessarily have to be the result of a crisis in your company. It simply means selling the assets you have left and stopping trading.

If your business is no longer able to pay debts and you cannot arrange a period of administration to try to recover it, then you need to propose a Creditors' Voluntary Liquidation (CVL), whereby a meeting of creditors is called and a liquidator appointed to wind up the business and pay creditors as much of what they are owed as possible. The Insolvency Service and Companies House both provide advice on liquidation and employers' responsibilities.

RESOURCES
BROKERS
Bertoli Mitchell
With Quayle Munro, one of publishing's two leading acquisition and merger broker specialists.
Web www.bertolimitchell.co.uk
Tel 020 7812 6416

Quayle Munro
Adviser to publishers seeking to sell or buy in all sectors.
Web www.quaylemunro.com
Tel 020 7907 4200

ADVICE AND SUPPORT

Business Link
Government agency for small businesses with lots of useful and free advice on selling up, including valuation guides and a tool to guide you through the tax implications.
Web www.businesslink.gov.uk
Tel 0845 600 9006

Companies House
The national centre for business registrations with advice on what you need to do after a sale and how to liquidate your company.
Web www.companieshouse.gov.uk
Tel 0870 3333 636

Department for Business, Innovation and Skills
Government advice on your legal obligations to staff and others in a sale.
www.bis.gov.uk
Tel 020 7215 5000

HM Revenue & Customs
Plenty of online tools to help you work out the tax implications of a sale.
Web www.hmrc.gov.uk
Tel 08457 143 143

Institute of Directors
Association with advice for members about all aspects of selling a business, including tools to value it.
Web www.iod.com
Tel 020 7766 8666

ACCOUNTANTS AND SOLICITORS

Institute of Chartered Accountants
Database of accountants should you need help from one before and during a sale.
Web www.icaew.co.uk
Tel 020 7920 8100

The Law Society
Directory of solicitors across the country.
Web www.lawsociety.org.uk/choosingandusing/findasolicitor.law
Tel 020 7242 1222

FLOTATION

London Stock Exchange and Alternative Investment Market
Tips on floating your company on either exchange and deciding if it's the right move to make.
Web www.londonstockexchange.com
Tel 020 7797 1000

PLUS Market
The alternative stock exchange for small- and medium-sized businesses.
Web www.plusmarketsgroup.com
Tel 020 7553 2000

LIQUIDATION

The Insolvency Service
Government agency offering guidance for companies wishing to wind up.
Web www.insolvency.gov.uk
Tel 0845 602 9848

BOOKS

Beswick and Wine: Buying and Selling Private Companies and Businesses edited by Susan Singleton (Tottel Publishing, £85, 9781847660961)

Buying and Selling a Business by Hugh Williams (Lawpack Publishing, £12.99, 9781905261222)

Buying and Selling a Business: An Entrepreneur's Guide by Jo Haigh (Piatkus, £12.99, 9780749928391)

Company Acquisitions Handbook (Tottel Publishing, £68, 9781845924577)

How to Value and Sell Your Business by Andrew Heslop (Kogan Page, £30, 9780749451172)

Selling Your Business by Lee Hadnum (Taxcafé, £24.95, 9781904608721)

GLOSSARY

The IPG's guide to some of the most common abbreviations and terms in the publishing industry. See the Index for references to many of the terms, and the Publishing Directory for the contact details of many of the organizations.

AAA Association of Authors' Agents

AAP Association of American Publishers

AAs Author's Alterations. Corrections to proofs made by authors

A format A standard size for mass market paperbacks: 178 mm by 110 mm

Abridged An audiobook that has been condensed from its print version

ACE Arts Council England

Add-on Something added to a book to enhance its value (e.g. CD, web link, sampler)

Advance Money paid to an author to secure a book or books, and deductible from future royalty earnings. Usually paid in three parts: on agreeing the contract, delivering the book and publication

Advance copy A book, usually not yet fully edited or corrected, that is supplied to retailers or reviewers ahead of publication

Aggregator A company, usually web-based, which bundles together content from several publishers to sell on

AI Advance Information sheet. Includes all the information about a book that a bookseller or media contact might need, such as ISBN, publication date, synopsis, author biography, cover, etc.

Airport edition The paperback export edition of a book that is sold at airport bookshops ahead or instead of other editions

ALCS Authors' Licensing and Collecting Society

ALPSP Association of Learned and Professional Society Publishers

AoI Association of Illustrators

APA Audiobook Publishing Association

Appendix Supplementary material at the end of a book

ARC Advance Reading Copy or Advance Review Copy. See Advance copy

Auction Process whereby an agent invites bids from publishers for a book to secure the best deal for it

BA The Booksellers Association

Back flap The part of the dust jacket that folds inside the back cover, usually containing information about the author

Backlist Publishers' books that have been published for some time (usually taken to mean at least a year ago) and are still in print

Bar codes Machine readable graphic on a book's jacket, based on its ISBN and used by various people in the supply chain to scan information about it

BCA Book Club Associates. Britain's biggest mail order bookseller

BECTA British Educational Communications and Technology Agency

BESA British Educational Suppliers Association

B format A paperback format larger than the typical mass market size: 198 mm by 129 mm

BIC Book Industry Communication. An independent organization promoting standards for e-commerce and supply chain efficiency

Binding The process of fixing pages together in a book, using glue or stitches

Bio Biography. Short paragraph about the author

BIS Department for Business, Innovation and Skills

Blad Book Layout And Design. A printed sample of a book that helps to show its format and content, often used to sell it in advance

Bleed The part of an image or text that runs over the borders of a page

Block or **book block** Bound sections of a book

Blog Weblog, an online diary

Blurb Short promotional copy on the front or back of a book that describes its content and helps to sell it to readers

BML Book Marketing Limited

Boilerplate A standard template of a contract between author and publisher that can be usually altered to suit specific agreements

Bound proofs See proofs

BPIF British Printing Industries Federation

Break even In publishing, the sales of a book you need to achieve before you cover all your costs and start making money

BTBS The Book Trade Benevolent Society

Bulk The thickness of either a book or the paper on which it is printed

© Copyright symbol

Cased Hardback book

CD Rom Compact Disc with Read Only Memory. Popular form of electronic publishing before the dawn of the internet

C format Large paperback format measuring 216 mm by 135 mm

Chromalin Proofing stage to check the colours in a book have been correctly reproduced

Chunking Dividing up content for sale by part rather than offering an entire book for sale; increasingly popular in educational publishing

CIF Cost, Insurance and Freight

CILIP Chartered Institute of Library and Information Professionals

CIP Cataloguing-in-Publication. The British Library's programme to catalogue new and forthcoming books for listing on the British National Bibliography

CLA Copyright Licensing Agency

CLE Cumann Leabharfhoilsitheorin Eireann, the Irish publishers' association

Closed market A market for a publisher's books that has been solely and exclusively granted to one agent to sell into

CMS Content Management System, used to manage the progress of material through its various stages to publication

Co-edition A book bought with or sold to a third party for publication, either in the UK or an overseas market

Colophon The logo of a publisher used on a book. Originally used to describe the publisher's information, presented at the back of a book

Consignment sales Books that are paid for by retailers or overseas distributors only as they are sold. Unsold stock can be returned to the publisher

Consolidation Bundling a number of small consignments for transport into one, larger dispatch

Contract Legal binding agreement between publisher and author or publisher and publisher, covering rights, responsibilities and payment

Contract publishing Producing a book on behalf of a client, perhaps a company, institution or a fellow publisher

Co-publication Joint publishing arrangement between two or more companies

Copy-editing The process of turning an author's material into a book ready for publication, correcting errors and making style consistent

Copyright Legal protection of the ownership of a book for authors and publishers. In publishing, copyright endures 70 years from the end of the year in which an author dies

Copyright page The page of a book outlining its copyright ownership, usually placed overleaf from the title page

Counterpack Presentation box or stand to display books by a retailer's till

CRC Camera Ready Copy. The text supplied to a printer ready to print

CRM Customer Relationship Management

Crossover A book that appeals to two markets, for instance, children's and adults

Crown octavo Book format measuring 189 mm by 123 mm

Crown quarto Book format measuring 246 mm by 189 mm

CSR Corporate Social Responsibility

CTP Computer to Plate, a printing term to describe the way pages are taken from a digital file and got ready to print

DACS The Design and Artists Copyright Society

DAD Digital Asset Distributor. An intermediary selling publishers' digital content in return for commission or a flat fee

DCF Digital Content Forum

DCMS Department for Culture, Media and Sport

DfE Department for Education

Demy octavo Book format measuring 216 mm by 138 mm, commonly used for hardbacks

Dewey Decimal The classification system by which books are usually arranged in libraries

Discount The cut in the advertised price that publishers offer to retailers or wholesalers to buy their books

Distributor Company storing publishers' books and supplying them to retailers. Some are independent while others are owned by large publishers, though most now work on behalf of many different publishers

DOI Digital Object Identifier. A code by which digital content like chapters or tables can be tagged and protected from misuse

DPA Data Publishers Association

DRM Digital Rights Management. Term covering both rights issues around electronic content, and the tool used to manage or restrict use of publishers' material in digital forms

DTP Desktop Publishing

Dues Book orders that a publisher collects in advance of publication; or the money that is payable on orders

Dummy A mocked-up version of a book, often used to sell it to booksellers or other publishers in advance of publication

Dumpbin Presentation stand holding several dozen copies of a book, used to promote it to browsers in shops

Dust jacket Cover wrapped around a hardback book, originally to prevent it from gathering dust

e4books Cross-industry initiative to promote e-commerce and reduce the amount of transactions done on paper

EAN European Article Number. The bar code standard used on books

Earn out Selling enough copies of a book to earn in royalties all the money advanced to an author

E-book Catch-all term for book content published in electronic form, distributed via a website or standalone reading device

EDI Electronic Data Interchange. The transfer of data in transactions between publishers, booksellers and others in the supply chain

EDItEUR International standards organization for the book trade, co-ordinating the development of e-commerce in particular

Edition The whole printing of a book. A second edition is the second printing, for instance

EFL or **ELT** English as a Foreign Language and English Language Teaching, important sectors of educational publishing

Embargo The restriction placed by a publisher on a book to prevent it either being sold or covered in the media before its official publication date

EMEA Europe, the Middle East and Africa, a commonly identified region in publishing

End matter Material at the end of a book like end-notes, appendices, acknow-ledgements, bibliography and index

EPOS Electronic Point of Sale. Means by which retailers use tills to collect data on books sold

Epub Industry standard file extension of an XML format for books

Erratum Correction of mistakes in a book, sometimes inserted into finished copies via a slip of paper

E-tail Internet-based retail business

Extent The length of a book, usually measured in pages

Fair dealing The exemption to copyright that allows publishers to reproduce material in the context of criticism or review

FEP Federation of European Publishers

Firm sale Books that cannot be returned by retailers if they do not sell

First edition The first printing of a book

Flap copy The text about a book and its author on the front and back flaps of a dust jacket

Folio An individual page in a book or its number

Fore edge The right hand edge of a book

Foreign rights The rights sold by a publisher or agent to publish a book in overseas markets

Format The shape and size of a book

Freight forwarder An agent who arranges the transport of books on behalf of a shipper, importer or exporter

Front flap The part of the dust jacket that folds around the front of a book's cover, usually containing information about the content

Frontispiece Illustrated page facing the title page of a book

Frontlist Publishers' new books that have either been recently published (usually taken to mean within a year) or are just about to be

Front matter The preliminary first few pages of a book, including the title page, copyright notices, contents, acknowledgement, preface and foreword

FSC Forest Stewardship Council

Furnish The pulp and chemical constituents of paper

Galleys See proofs. This is a term little used in the UK now, though still in use in the US

GLN Global Location Number. A unique 13-digit code, recognized internationally for identifying the location of booksellers, distributors and others in the supply chain

GSM Grams per Square Metre. The scale by which the weight of a paper is measured. Most papers used in book printing are between 70 and 130 gsm

Gutter The margin between facing pages of a book

HMRC Her Majesty's Revenue & Customs

House style The rules of style and formatting that a publisher follows when editing a book

HTML Hyper Text Markup Language. The most commonly used language for making up web pages

IDPF International Digital Publishing Forum, formerly the Open eBook Forum

Imprint The name or brand of a publishing company, or the list of books within it, usually with its own distinctive subject or style

Industry Returns Initiative Ongoing project to streamline the returns system and reduce the costs involved, co-ordinated by BIC

Inspection copy A book sent to those in education who might recommend it for use on a particular course

IP or **IPR** Intellectual Property or Intellectual Property Rights. The content or books that a publisher owns

IPA International Publishers Association

iPad Tablet computer developed by Apple as a platform for audio and visual media, including books

IPG Independent Publishers Guild

IPO Intellectual Property Office

IRI Industry Returns Initiative

ISBN International Standard Book Number. A 13-digit code used to uniquely identify a book and its publisher

ISSN International Standard Serial Number. An 8-digit code used to uniquely identify a journal or magazine

ISTC International Standard Text Code. An identifier of a textual work independent of a published manifestation

JISC Joint Information Systems Committee. An agency supporting the use of ICT in education

Kindle The handheld reading device sold by Amazon

Lamination The coating applied to book jackets to provide a glossy finish

Large Crown Octavo Book format measuring 198 mm by 129 mm

Lead time The time between the start of the process of producing a book and the publication date

Leading The spacing between lines of text in a book

Leaf A spread of two facing pages in a book

Legal deposit The system by which publishers supply copies of all their books to six nationally designated library archives

Licence Agreement giving publishers or others the right to publish and sell a book, either on an exclusive or non-exclusive basis

List Collective books published by a company

List price The price of a book printed on its jacket

Litho Abbreviation of offset lithography, a well-established method of printing using plates and rollers

Long tail A phrase coined to describe the books that individually do not sell in large numbers but that collectively are worth more than the handful of top sellers

Manuscript The text of a book, usually referring to the author's original version of it

MARC MAchine Readable Cataloguing. A language for communicating bibliographic records in the library market

Marketing mix The four Ps of marketing: product, place, promotion and price

Mass market paperback See A format

Metadata Data about data. In publishing, this refers to the tagging of text, enabling it to be identified and searched online

Midlist Referring to books or authors that sell respectably but not enough to become bestsellers

Monochrome Black and white printing

Monograph A scholarly work on a single subject, usually based on an author's academic research

Moral rights Extra rights given to writers in addition to copyright, including the right to be identified as the author of a work

MS Manuscript

MSS Multiple manuscripts

NBA Net Book Agreement. The mechanism by which booksellers sold all books at their full recommended retail prices until its abolition in 1995. Also sometimes used now to abbreviate New Book Announcement

Net receipts Money received by a publisher for its books after its discount to the trade has been deducted

NSR Net Sales Revenue. See net receipts

NYP Not Yet Published

OA See Open Access

OEBF Open Ebook Format

Offset Abbreviation of offset lithography, a well-established method of printing using plates and rollers

Offset fee Money paid by one publisher for the right to print and publish another's book, usually in a new format

ONIX ONline Information eXchange. The international standard for structuring and communicating information about a book in the electronic environment

OP Out of Print

Opacity The extent to which a book's paper is transparent. If a book has low opacity it will be possible to see the text on the reverse side of a page

Open access Model of publishing, especially in journals, that makes any work available to view for free

Open content Means of publishing that allows far freer use and copying of material than traditional copyright

Option The rights bought by a film or TV production company that give it the exclusive opportunity to buy fuller rights to turn a book into a film

Orphan works Published material for which no copyright holder can be found

OS Out of Stock

Ozalid Process of printing pages from a film. Ozalids are pages produced as a result, used as a final check before printing

P&A Price and Availability

PA Publishers Association

Packager A company supplying ready-made books to publishers for sale under their own imprints

Pallet Wooden platforms on which books are transferred

Paternity rights The moral right of an author to be identified as the creator of his or her work

Pay per view Mechanism by which people using the web pay to get access to individual articles, pages or chapters of a book. An increasingly popular way of publishing academic, professional and educational material

PDA Personal Digital Assistant

PDF Portable Document Format. A file format commonly used to display pages of a book electronically and ready for print

Perfect binding Method of gluing and holding together the pages of a book

Permissions Process of granting rights from one publisher to another to use copyright material in a book

Pick and pack The process of retrieving and dispatching books from the warehouse of a distributor or wholesaler for onward delivery

Plate section A group of pages, usually colour, that are bound within a book

PLR Public Lending Right

PLS Publishers Licensing Society

POD Print-on-Demand. The method of digitally printing quantities of books, usually small, to order

Podcast Audio file for use on iPods or other MP3 players. Used by publishers to distribute spoken word material like an extract from a book or a promotion for it

Point Type size

POS Point of Sale. The place where a book is purchased, usually a till in a shop. POS material is tools used to advertise and promote a book where it is being sold like dumpbins or posters

PP Publisher Price

PPA Periodical Publishers Association

PPC Publishers Publicity Circle

PPI Pages Per Inch, a scale for measuring thickness of paper

PR Public Relations or Price Received

Pre empt Pre emptive offer made for a book by a publisher to an agent to prevent other publishers bidding for it

Pre flight check A series of tests done by a printer to ensure that a book is correctly prepared for press

Prelim or **prelims** The first few pages of a book; see Front matter

PREPS Publishers' Database for Responsible Environmental Paper Sourcing

Presenter A file, paper or electronic, used by publishers to outline their books and the plans they have for them to prospective retail or rights buyers

Price point The standard marks at which books are priced. Paperback fiction, for instance, usually has a price point of £6.99 or £7.99

Print run The number of copies of a book ordered by a publisher from a printer

Pro forma invoice An invoice requiring payment to be made before goods are dispatched, perhaps because the two parties are trading together for the first time

Proof or **proofs** Pages of a prepared and typeset book that are closely read for errors before being sent for printing

Proof marks The set of notes and symbols produced by the British Standards Institution that are commonly used to mark proofs

Proofreading The process of carefully checking a book's manuscript for errors and consistency

Proposal Document prepared by an author to describe a book and its sales potential in the hope of a publisher taking it on

Pub date Publication date for a book

Puff The enthusiastic text on the front or back of a book promoting it to readers

Pulping The destruction of unsold or unwanted stock

QCA Qualifications and Curriculum Authority

RAN Returns Authorization Number

Reader A handheld reading device manufactured by Sony

Recto A right-hand page in a book (verso is the left-hand page)

Reissue A new print of a book that has been updated or changed in some way

Remainders Publishers' leftover stock that is sold off cheaply, often through bargain bookshops

Rep Sales representative; the publisher's member of staff or freelance agent who sells books into shops

Reprint A new print run of a book with no changes. A revised reprint is a new print with very minor changes

Reprint rights Rights granted by one publisher to another to publish a book in another format—for instance, a paperback after it has already been published in hardback

Repro Reproduction of illustrations. A repro house is a company specializing in this

Returns Books that are sent back unsold by booksellers to publishers

Reversion The point at which any rights are returned to their original holder. When a publisher sells sub rights to another, they agree a date for those rights to revert back to the seller

RFID Radio Frequency IDentification. A 'smart' bar code sometimes used by booksellers or libraries to scan books and identify where they are at any time

RFO Regularly Funded Organization

Royal octavo Book format measuring 234 mm by 156 mm, commonly used for hardbacks

Royalties The percentage of revenue from a book paid by the publisher to the author

RP Reprint or reprinting

RPUC Reprint Under Consideration

RRP Recommended Retail Price. The price at which a publisher suggests a book should be sold, printed on the jacket

Run Print run; the number of copies of a book to be printed

Running head The heading of each page of a book, usually the book or chapter title

Run on Additional copies printed beyond the specified run, sometimes to be sold cheaply

Saddle stitching Simple binding technique to staple pages folded together. Usually used for booklets or brochures rather than books

Safe sales See Consignment sales

SAN Standard Address Number. A unique seven-digit code identifying the location of booksellers, distributors and others in the supply chain

Scale out The process of distributing books across a chain of bookshops to individual branches

Scout or **literary scout** An individual who identifies and sources authors or books for a publisher in return for a fee. Many literary scouts work on behalf of publishers around the world, seeking UK books they might be interested in

Section A group of folded pages in a book, usually 32

Self-publishing Practice of an author arranging the production and publishing of his or her own book

Sell through The books that are sold by a retailer and not returned to a publisher, often expressed as a percentage. Can also refer to the process of earning out royalties; see Earn out

SfEP Society for Editors and Proofreaders

Slice and dice The model of selling content on a piecemeal basis—by chapter or page, for instance—rather than offering all or nothing. An increasingly popular technique in educational publishing in particular

Slipcase Cardboard box into which one or several books can be inserted

Slotted binding Method of binding involving gluing of sections rather than pages

Slush pile The heap of unsolicited manuscripts sent to publishers by authors or agents

SME Small and Medium Enterprises

SoA Society of Authors

SOR Sale Or Return. The means by which most books are sold into retailers, who are then able to return unsold copies with authorization

Spec Specification. A briefing document drawn up to outline the style and format of a book or series, perhaps for use by a designer or printer

Spine The side or backbone of a book

Spinner Rotating stand used to present multiple books, perhaps all titles within a series, in a shop

Spread Two facing pages in a book

STM Scientific, Technical and Medical

Stock The books held by a publisher or bookseller; or the type of paper used to print a book

Stocklist A publisher's list of all available books, usually accompanied by an order form. A basic version of a catalogue

Sub agent An individual or company selling rights for a publisher on their behalf

Sub or **subscription sales** Sales made in advance of publication

Sub or **subsidiary rights** The rights in a book beyond the basic rights to publish a book in the UK, like serial, translation or audio rights

SYP Society of Young Publishers

TeleOrdering The clearing house for booksellers that directs their multiple orders to the appropriate publisher or distributor

Terms The discount given to booksellers by publishers

TI Title Information sheet, containing key bibliographic, content and other information about a book. See AI

Ti-hi Term used in distribution to indicate how many books can be fitted in a layer on a pallet (Ti) and how high they can be stacked (Hi)

Title page Front page in a book displaying title, author and publisher

Title verso Early page in a book, usually directly after the title page, displaying the book's bibliographic details including ISBN and printing history

Topping rights Opportunity granted to a publisher by an agent to match or exceed the sum already bid for a book by another publisher

TOS Temporarily Out of Stock

Tote Plastic container used to transport books

Trade Shorthand for the book trade, usually referring to booksellers and wholesalers catering for the general public

Trade paperback See B format paperback

Trim The dimensions of a book after a printer has cut pages to size

Typeface Font or design of characters in a book

Typescript Author's original version of text for a book

Typesetting The process of turning copy-edited text into a neatly laid out book ready to be printed

Typo Typographical error in a book from keying of text

UKTI UK Trade and Investment

Unabridged An audiobook that is read or dramatized from its print version in its entirety

USP Unique Sales Proposition or Point. In publishing, the quality that sets a book apart from its competition

Vanity publishing Producing and publishing a book for an author in return for a fee

Verso A left-hand page in a book (recto is the right-hand page)

Viral marketing Promoting a book using the internet, email and social networks

VLE Virtual Learning Environment, for which educational publishers now produce material

Wasting See Pulping

WATCH Writers, Artists and Their Copyright Holders

Web 2.0 Loose term for the improved functionality of the internet, in particular covering its increased interactivity and creativity

Wholesaler Company buying books from publishers in bulk and selling them on to retailers in smaller numbers

Widget or **web widget** Portable code that can be embedded onto websites or emails—often graphics, photos or videos that can be used by publishers for promotional purposes

WiP Women in Publishing

WIP Work In Progress

WIPO World Intellectual Property Organization

WOM Word Of Mouth. The practice of readers telling others about a book

XML eXtensible Markup Language. A language for structuring and tagging material to prepare it for various electronic formats and help it flow onto screens to be read

PUBLISHING DIRECTORY

Listed below are the key associations, societies, groups and charities that independent publishers might find useful, plus some recommended blogs to follow and a diary of major events in the publishing calendar. For many more groups relevant to particular fields and disciplines of publishing, see the Resources sections of relevant chapters. The IPG also has clickable links at www.ipg.uk.com/links.

MAIN TRADE ASSOCIATIONS

Independent Publishers Guild
The essential association for independent publishers of all shapes and sizes!
Web www.ipg.uk.com
Tel 01437 563335

Book Industry Communication
Promotes standards and communication across the UK book business. Part funded by the Publishers Association, Booksellers Association, Chartered Institute of Library and Information Professionals and the British Library.
Web www.bic.org.uk
Tel 020 7607 0021

Booksellers Association
Represents bookshops of all sizes in the UK and Ireland.
Web www.booksellers.org.uk
Tel 020 7421 4640

Chartered Institute of Library and Information Professionals
Professional body for librarians and related trades.
Web www.cilip.org.uk
Tel 020 7255 0500

Publishers Association
Trade association for publishers. Works closely with the IPG and other bodies in the industry.
Web www.publishers.org.uk
Tel 0207 691 9191

Publishing Scotland
Formerly known as the Scottish Publishers Association, representing about 70 publishers in Scotland. Aims to promote Scottish books as well as the interests of members.
Web www.publishingscotland.org
Tel 0131 228 3220

Welsh Books Council / Cyngor Llyfrau Cymru
Supports publishing in Wales and promotes books from the country, especially Welsh-language titles.
Web www.cllc.org.uk
Tel 01970 624151

SPECIALIST TRADE ASSOCIATIONS

Association of Learned and Professional Society Publishers
Looks after the interests of not-for-profit professional publishers, with a range of events and resources.
Web www.alpsp.org
Tel 01275 856444

Audiobook Publishing Association
Helps to promote audiobooks in the UK. Formerly known as the Spoken Word Publishing Association.
Web www.theapa.net

British Educational Suppliers Association
Trade group for companies supplying materials to schools and higher education.
Web www.besanet.org.uk
Tel 020 7537 4997

British Printing Industries Federation
Main body for book printers in the UK and a useful source of information about printing in general.
Web www.britishprint.com
Tel 020 7405 4085

Data Publishers Association
Represents data, directory and search publishers.
Web www.dpa.org.uk
Tel 020 7405 0836

Digital Content Forum
Represents publishers' interests while helping to shape government policy on the use of digital material.
Web www.dcf.org.uk
Tel 020 7665 8440

National Union of Journalists
Trade union with a book branch for publishers, and editorial workers in particular.
Web www.nujbook.org
Tel 020 7278 7916

Periodical Publishers Association
The UK body for publishers of consumer and business media, including magazines and journals.
Web www.ppa.co.uk
Tel 020 7404 4166

PUBLISHING SOCIETIES, CLUBS AND GROUPS

Book Marketing Society
Represents marketing professionals in publishing and offers events and resources.
Web www.bookmarketingsociety.co.uk

British Printing Society
Society for printers, related trades and enthusiasts.
Web www.bpsnet.org.uk

Diversity in Publishing Network
Forum promoting the status of new and existing publishing professionals from diverse ethnic groups.
Web www.diversityinpublishing.com

Environmental Action Group
Joint initiative of the Publishers and Booksellers Association to raise awareness of eco issues in the industry.
Web www.green4books.org.uk

The Galley Club
A social society for anyone involved in publishing or book production, organizing speaker events through the year.
Web www.galleyclub.co.uk

Inpress
A web-based umbrella group offering sales, marketing and distribution to small, independent publishers in the UK, backed by Arts Council England.
Web www.inpressbooks.co.uk
Tel 020 8832 7464

Oxford Publishing Society
Group for publishers in the industry's second city with several dozen members.
Web www.opusnet.co.uk

Publishers Green Network
Forum for discussion of green issues in publishing with quarterly meetings—free to join and open to everyone in UK publishing.
Web www.green4books.org.uk

Publishers Publicity Circle
A professional and social group for book publicists, with regular speaker events and an awards programme.
Web www.publisherspublicitycircle.co.uk

Society for Editors and Proofreaders
Promotes the work of its members and campaigns for high editorial standards.
Web www.sfep.org.uk
Tel 020 8785 5617

Society for the History of Authorship, Reading and Publishing
Friendly society for anyone with an interest in the history of books or the books business.
Web www.sharpweb.org

Society of Indexers
The UK professional body for indexing, providing training and resources and promoting the value of a good index.
Web www.indexers.org.uk
Tel 0114 244 9561

Society of Young Publishers
Long established society for people wanting to break into publishing or work their way up the ladder.
Web www.thesyp.org.uk

Women in Publishing
Represents women in publishing and related trades and promotes their status there. Organizes monthly meetings, regular training programmes and awards.
Web www.wipub.org.uk

ASSOCIATIONS FOR AUTHORS AND AGENTS

The Association of Authors' Agents
Represents literary agents in the UK.
Web www.agentsassoc.co.uk

Society of Authors
Main association for UK writers, promoting their interests and answering their queries on aspects of publishing and contracts.
Web www.societyofauthors.org
Tel 020 7373 6642

The Writers' Guild of Great Britain
Trade union representing authors in books as well as TV, film and other sectors.
Web www.writersguild.org.uk
Tel 020 7833 0777

INTERNATIONAL ASSOCIATIONS

Association of American Publishers
The leading trade group in the US.
Web www.publishers.org
Tel 00 1 212 255 0200

CLÉ
Cumann Leabharfhoilsitheorin Eireann—the Irish book publishers' association.
Web www.publishingireland.com
Tel 00 353 1 6394868

Federation of European Publishers
Umbrella group for publishers' associations around the continent.
Web www.fep-fee.be
Tel 00 32 2 770 1110

International Digital Publishing Forum
Umbrella organization for worldwide thinking on digital publishing content and standards.
Web www.idpf.org
Tel 00 1 905 235 4373

International PEN
Worldwide association for authors.
Web www.internationalpen.org.uk

International Publishers Association
The global federation of publishers' associations.
Web www.internationalpublishers.org
Tel 00 41 22 346 3018

TRADE PRESS AND BOOK NEWS

Book2Book
Rounds up coverage of books and publishers in the media each morning via a web and email service.
Web www.booktrade.info

BookBrunch
Website and daily e-bulletins on news around publishing, produced by former editors of *The Bookseller* and the now defunct *Publishing News*.
www.bookbrunch.co.uk
Tel 020 7242 9972

The Bookseller
Weekly magazine bringing news and views from across the industry each Friday. The website is constantly updated with the latest developments.
Web www.thebookseller.com
Tel 020 7420 6000

Books for Keeps
Monthly magazine about children's books for schools and libraries, with reviews of new titles, news and features.
Web www.booksforkeeps.co.uk
Tel 020 8852 4953

CILIP Update
Monthly magazine of the Chartered Institute of Library and Information Professionals—the best source of news on libraries.
Web www.cilip.org.uk/update
Tel 020 7255 0580

Information World Review
Monthly newspaper about information and content management.
Web www.iwr.co.uk
Tel 020 7316 9245

Independent Publisher
'The voice of the Independent Publishing Industry' in the US
Web www.independentpublisher.com

Learned Publishing
Journal of the Association of Learned and Professional Society Publishers
Web www.alpsp.org
Tel 01767 604954 (subscriptions for non-members)

Logos
Worldwide journal for publishers of all disciplines.
Web www.logos-journal.org
Tel 01628 483371

NewBooks
Monthly magazine for readers and reading groups.
Web www.newbooksmag.com

Newspapers
The online books pages of the *Guardian*, the *Independent*, *Daily Telegraph* and *The Times* are useful sources of news about books and publishing.
Web www.booksunlimited.co.uk
www.independent.co.uk/books
www.telegraph.co.uk/books
www.timesonline.co.uk/books

Print Week
Trade press covering news and views in the printing industry.
www.print-week.com
Tel 020 8267 4397

Publishers Weekly
The leading source of news from the US book industry.
Web www.publishersweekly.com
Tel 00 1 646 746 6758

BOOK CHARITIES

Book Aid International
A charity promoting better lives through books, especially in developing countries.
Web www.bookaid.org
Tel 020 7733 3577

BookPower
Charity making textbooks available to young people in poorer countries.
Web www.bookpower.org
Tel 020 7843 1938

The Book Trade Charity
The UK's book trade charity, looking after the welfare of former workers and organizing fundraising events through the year.
Web www.booktradecharity.wordpress.com
Tel 01923 263128

Booktrust
An independent educational charity promoting the value and pleasure of books and reading in England.
Web www.booktrust.org.uk
Tel 020 8516 2977

National Literacy Trust
Campaigns for better standards of literacy in the UK and promotes the joys of reading.
Web www.literacytrust.org.uk
Tel 020 7587 1842

Paul Hamlyn Foundation
Charitable foundation established by the legendary publisher, promoting education and learning via various projects.
Web www.phf.org.uk
Tel 020 7227 3500

Scottish Booktrust
Scotland's version of the English Booktrust.
Web www.scottishbooktrust.com
Tel 0131 524 0160

World Book Day
Annual spring celebration of books and reading, organized as a co-operative event by publishers and booksellers.
Web www.worldbookday.com
Tel 01634 729810

MAJOR BOOK AND PUBLISHING PRIZES

IPG Awards
The Oscars of independent publishing, presented at the IPG's annual conference in March. Nominations close the preceding December.
Web www.ipg.uk.com/awards

British Book Awards and British Book Industry Awards
Separate prizes for the best books and publishing companies of the year, presented in April and May respectively.
Web www.britishbookawards.com

Costa Book Awards
Prizes in several categories as well as an overall winner, presented in January.
Web www.costabookawards.com

Man Booker Prize for Fiction
The big literary prize of the year, presented in October.
Web www.themanbookerprize.com

Orange Broadband Prize for Fiction
Open to female novelists only and a major influence on book sales.
Web www.orangeprize.co.uk

Booktrust
Useful directory of other book prizes in the UK.
Web www.booktrust.org.uk
Tel 020 8516 2977

RECOMMENDED BLOGS

Atlantic Books
Day-to-day life at a London-based independent publisher.
Web www.atlantic-books.co.uk/blog

The Bedside Crow
Entertaining observations of a south London independent bookseller.
Web www.booksellercrow.typepad.com

Bloggerel
Publishing blog from Alma Books and Oneworld Classics.
Web www.bloggerel.com

The Book Depository
Daily thoughts from the editor of the online books retailer.
www.bookdepository.co.uk/weblog

Booksellers Association
Interesting views on the 'Brave New World' of digital content and technologies.
Web www.bookseller-association.blogspot.com

Crockatt and Powell
Life in the independent bookselling business.
Web www.crockattandpowell.blogspot.com

Dovegrey Reader
Thoughts from a self-confessed book addict.
Web www.dovergreyreader.typedpad.com

Eoin Purcell
Musings on the book business from an Irish publisher.
Web www.eoinpurcellsblog.com

Fidra Books
Edinburgh-based firm on life as an independent.
Web www.fidrabooks.co.uk/blog

Guardian Books
Daily blogs from various writers on the worlds of publishing and writing.
Web www.blogs.guardian.co.uk/books

Hesperus Press
Views from the desk of the classic and translation specialist.
Web www.hesperuspress.wordpress.com

Inpress
Regularly updated thoughts from the independent publishers' umbrella site.
Web www.inpressbooks.co.uk/blog.aspx

Mostly Books
News and views from the Abingdon bookshop. Bills itself as 'The pleasures (and perils) of running an independent bookshop'.
Web www.mostly-books.blogspot.com

Publishing Talk
Musings on books and new media.
Web www.publishingtalk.eu/blog

Salt Publishing
News and views from the office of IPG member and poetry and short story specialist Salt Publishing.
Web www.saltpublishing.com/blogs

Snowbooks
Directors Emma Barnes and Rob Jones blog daily about publishing matters and anything else that crops up.
Web www.snowbooks.com/weblog

Tonto Books
A Newcastle based independent publisher blogs about its books and business.
Web www.tontobooks.blogspot.com

DIARY OF KEY PUBLISHING EVENTS, CONFERENCES AND FAIRS

JANUARY

CIANA
Fair specializing in remainder sales.
Web www.ciana.co.uk
Tel 020 8682 1969

MARCH

IPG Annual Conference
Three days of essential presentations and discussions, plus the Independent Publishing Awards Gala Dinner and great networking opportunities.
Web www.ipg.uk.com
Tel 01437 563335

Academic, Professional and Specialist Booksellers Group Conference
Annual gathering of specialist retailers, organized by the Booksellers Association and attended by many publishers in their fields.
Web www.booksellers.org.uk
Tel 020 7802 0802

Bologna Book Fair
The main annual event for children's publishers, held each March or April.
Web www.bookfair.bolognafiere.it
Tel 00 39 051 282361

Salon du Livre
France's book fair.
Web www.salondulivreparis.com
Tel 00 33 1 44 41 40 50

World Book Day
March celebration of the written word, with accompanying promotions by booksellers and publishers.
Web www.worldbookday.com
Tel 01634 729810

APRIL

The London Book Fair
The book world's main spring fair at Earls Court. The IPG offers members space on a collective stand here.
Web www.londonbookfair.co.uk
Tel 020 8910 7910

MAY

BookExpo America
America's most important book fair, held in a different city each year.
Web www.bookexpoamerica.com
Tel 00 1 203 840 5890

Booksellers Association Annual Conference and AGM
Annual gathering of booksellers across the UK, attended by some publishers.
Web www.booksellers.org.uk
Tel 020 7802 0802

The Guardian Hay Festival
Major gathering of writers and publishers on the English–Welsh border.
Web www.hayfestival.com
Tel 0870 787 2848

JUNE

Independent Booksellers Week
Annual initiative to celebrate independent retailers—a good opportunity to put on events and promotions with them.
Web www.loveyourlocalbookshop.co.uk

Library and Information Show
Major annual gathering of the library profession at the NEC in Birmingham.
Web www.lishow.co.uk
Tel 020 7316 9532

AUGUST

Edinburgh International Book Festival
Runs for two weeks as part of the city's wider arts festival.
Web www.edbookfest.co.uk
Tel 0131 718 5666

SEPTEMBER

Association of Learned and Professional Society Publishers International Conference
Annual gathering of the association.
Web www.alpsp.org.uk
Tel 01275 856444

Beijing International Book Fair
Asia's biggest book fair and a useful way to break into the China market.
Web www.bibf.net
Tel 00 86 10 6586 6995

CIANA
Fair specializing in remainder sales.
Web www.ciana.co.uk
Tel 020 8682 1969

OCTOBER

The Frankfurt Book Fair
The autumn gathering of publishers, and the largest book fair in the world. The IPG offers space on a collective stand here.
Web www.book-fair.com
Tel 00 49 69 21020

DECEMBER

Online Information

Annual London fair dedicated to electronic publishing.
Web www.online-information.co.uk
Tel 020 7316 9572

INDEX

This index cites references in the main text of each chapter. It does not include references in each chapter's Resources section, in which extra information about particular subjects and organisations can be found. Please also refer to the Glossary, which has definitions of several hundred publishing terms.

IPG
Exclusive Offer
2014

...am Content Group is delighted to offer IPG members two exclusive opportunities to help you sell more books around the world using ...tning Source Print-on-Demand (POD) technology and Ingram's Global Sales & Distribution Channels.

...er One

- IPG members receive free market access fee, enabling publishers to place and sell titles through our global distribution network.
- Free set-up for any titles supplied in digital format.
- No market access fee payable for the first year and free thereafter, when titles sell 100 copies or more per year.*
- To maximise the sales potential of these titles, they must be made available in all global channels served by Lightning Source*

...the first year, if a title sells fewer than 100 copies per year, IPG members can remove the title or leave the title in Ingram's global distribution network and pay ...nual market access fee, currently £7 per title.

...al channels served by Lightning Source, include the US, UK, Australia, Canada and the European Union and, through our Global Connect channels in Brazil, Russia ...ermany.

...r Two

- IPG members also have access to free set-up of hardback versions of books that are currently available only in paperback formats with Lightning Source.
- The market access fee is waived here too & this particular offer is limited to 100 titles per publisher, per year for those titles that are currently selling more than 25 copies per year via Lightning Source's selling network.

...Chief Executive Bridget Shine:

"We know from talking to our members that many are seeking to grow their international sales and take advantage of print on demand. We ...ope these offers will be a great way for them to achieve both goals. We are pleased to have been able to work with Ingram to offer members ...nother valuable benefit of belonging to the IPG."

...d Taylor, Group Managing Director at Lightning Source UK and
...r Vice President, Content Acquisition International at Ingram Content Group:

"We know how important export sales are to many IPG members; we also know that it can be expensive and risky given traditional ways ...accessing overseas markets. Our offers help remove upfront costs around file set up and market access fees for members who want to ...ke full advantage of our growing global distribution network."

...IPG members wishing to take advantage of the exclusive offers
...d email contactalison@ingramcontent.com in the first instance.

9 780956 6878